MANAGEMENT OF CLASSROOMS

Management of Classrooms

Michael Medland
Humboldt State University

Michael Vitale
Dallas Independent School District

Holt, Rinehart and Winston

New York   Chicago   San Francisco   Philadelphia
Montreal   Toronto   London   Sydney
Tokyo   Mexico City   Rio de Janeiro   Madrid

Library of Congress Cataloging in Publication Data

Medland, Michael.
 Management of classrooms.

 Includes bibliographies and index.
 1. Classroom management. I. Vitale, Michael
II. Title.
LB3013.M39   1984   371.1'02   83-12588

ISBN 0-03-063694-9

CBS COLLEGE PUBLISHING
Holt, Rinehart and Winston
The Dryden Press
Saunders College Publishing

To all the teachers who made it possible
—MM

To my mother, Emilie Vitale Borovy
—MV

PREFACE

Management of Classrooms provides a systematic solution to a major educational problem: effective classroom management. Through the application of principles of behavior, a set of interrelated tools and procedures are presented which can solve the difficult classroom management problems today's teacher faces. These tools and procedures, often thought of as skills, represent a technology in the broadest sense. There are three components of this technology.

The first component provides the analysis tools and procedures required for determining what behaviors are to be managed. The teacher must build an elusive substance—human behavior. Not only is human behavior fleeting and short-lived; it is also often difficult to determine what behaviors are the foundation of a larger, more complex repertoire. Therefore, the analysis skills are critical for successful classroom management. Chapters 2 and 7 are devoted to the analysis of human behavior, as are portions of Chapters 1, 9, and 12.

The second component is the basic tools and procedures required to build the behaviors identified. For the teacher, these are for the most part verbal—the teacher's statements to students determine how they will behave. Chapters 3, 4, 5, 6, and 8 present these verbal tools and procedures in isolation; Chapters 9, 10, and 11 bring them together to provide a system of classroom management.

The third component provides procedures to solve complex management problems that require more than the basic tools and procedures. For the teacher, this means that some inappropriate and appropriate behaviors cannot be eliminated or constructed as easily as others. Thus, a set of procedures is required to adapt or construct tools and procedures to solve these problems. Chapter 12 and parts of Chapters 1, 9, and 10 are devoted to problem solving.

Without the components of a technology, teaching, like art, medicine, engineering, and the other professions, would not produce what is desired and needed by our culture. Thus, the text approaches technology as a positive force in our lives, one which helps to identify the products of interest (behaviors) through the tools and procedures of analysis, to delineate tools and procedures to construct the products of interest, and to supply higher level procedures to adapt and solve difficult problems.

But technology is not the entire story. A fourth component is included. The quality of teaching—like the quality of art, medicine, and engineering—is also dependent on such human factors as curiosity, creativity, and the desire to work for the good of humanity. Yet for the teacher and other professionals, a thorough knowledge and an almost automatic application of technology will facilitate the expression of these qualities, thus providing the foundation for the next steps in the evolution of the profession and the culture. For the teacher, this fourth component consists of teaching skills to students which have survival value.

Management of Classrooms is designed to function effectively as a primary or supplementary text in a wide range of settings. It is effective as a primary text in undergraduate and graduate education courses dealing with teacher preparation in general and classroom methods in particular, and in public school in-service and continuing education programs. As a supplementary text, it functions effectively in psychology and educational psychology undergraduate and graduate courses covering applied behavior analysis, behavior modification, and educational psychology; in education graduate courses covering school administrative practices and the supervision of instruction; and in business courses dealing with the basic tools and procedures of human management.

ACKNOWLEDGMENTS

For the philosophical and theoretical foundations which guided the authors, acknowledgment must go to B.F. Skinner. His work for the last fifty years has expanded our culture's knowledge of behavior. We are also in debt to all of Skinner's contemporaries, whose work set the context for the tone and focus of this text.

Acknowledgment also must be given to all the teachers who, for over twenty years, have provided us with the experiences necessary for such a text to be written. Special thanks go to Harriet Belzer, Renita Ferguson, Sally Harris, and Katherine McClure, who happily implemented many of the tools and procedures as they are presented here.

Betty Arwine must be thanked for guiding the preparation of the manuscript. We appreciate her assistance in coordinating all of the drafts, a seemingly impossible task she accomplished with an amazing ease and calm.

M.M.
M.V.

NOTE TO INSTRUCTORS

Instructors using *Management of Classrooms* will discover an unusual blend of structure and flexibility. The structure of the text follows from the behavioral science principles that underlie effective management of the classroom, the authors' arrangement of classroom management skills provided in the text, and the procedures teachers must follow to learn and apply these skills to be effective classroom managers. In each chapter, students first learn basic terms and procedures through analytic discussions of examples, followed by procedural summaries of the major steps required for application. In addition, each chapter includes practice activities that establish generalizability of the skills through an interplay of classroom observation, simulated rehearsal, verbal discussion, and direct application in the classroom. Based upon the authors' experience, the text was designed to build upon the adult's standard verbal repertoire and to guide the development of teachers' key verbal delivery procedures, so that virtually all teachers can master the skills required for successful classroom management. As with any mastery learning setting, the time and effort required will vary. However, as teachers read and complete the activities for a given chapter, the skills they learn will be immediately applicable within the school classroom.

Instructors have extensive flexibility in using the text across a variety of learning settings. Although the chapters are designed to be effective sequentially, they are also designed to be used independently as instructors choose, depending upon specific instructional objectives or the entry skills of students. For example, some may prefer to branch to Chapter 11 after completing Chapter 4; others may choose to begin teaching from Chapters 4 through 6 and Chapter 7 concurrently immediately upon completion of Chapter 2. In making such adaptations, instructors will find that the structured subtopic headings within the table of contents serve as a detailed index for topic selection.

Interpretation of the procedures in the text in terms of underlying theory and research is another important area in which instructors are afforded maximal flexibility. The vocabulary and procedures used to present the technology will support many different theoretical conceptions and preferences. To allow for this flexibility, footnote references within the text have been omitted (end-of-the-chapter references have been provided). The authors' opinion is that the choice of theory underlying this text is important in regard to possible future extensions of the technology presented rather than in the learning and application of the technology to classroom settings. Thus, the intent of the text is to provide a self-contained technology of classroom management based upon well-known and widely accepted behavioral principles, not to convince the student through scholarly argument that these techniques work. The latter task is best undertaken directly by instructors.

NOTE TO STUDENTS

The technology presented in *Management of Classrooms* offers a systematic solution to the practical problem of classroom management. In this regard, students using the book are encouraged to read both the "Preface" and the "Note to Instructors" on the preceding pages. As a guide for students, the detailed chapter subheadings in the table of contents serve as a structured index of topics. To master the management skills in the text, several distinct learning audiences will need to use the text differently.

First, to obtain maximum benefit, individuals who are engaged in preservice teacher education training and have no prior classroom experience are advised to complete the practice activities within each chapter requiring classroom implementation as they work through the text. Failure to do so may make the initial implementation of the complete system far too difficult for a beginning teaching assignment. Should this happen, new teachers should review the skills in order of introduction and then simply phase in their use, cumulatively adopting the management system across time.

Such a phase-in procedure is also recommended for a second type of student, regular classroom teachers who are learning to use the system on their own or as part of a school-based in-service program. In addition, these teachers should make a special effort to have their delivery procedures critiqued by colleagues or supervisors, as appropriate.

For a third type of student, who has prior classroom experience but is not engaged in teaching while working through the text (e.g., summer workshops, full-time graduate students), rigorous practice on and mastery of activities in simulations may substitute for the majority of the application activities within regular classrooms. However, such students must make special efforts through a regular rehearsal program to maintain these skills for any planned future classroom use. Even then, a modified phase-in of the skills required to implement the system may be required.

The fourth group of learners includes those involved in the training and supervision of teachers' classroom performance. The authors believe this text will serve these readers as an invaluable resource, particularly the building routines and skill checklists serving as chapter summaries. Of course, the extent to which individuals engaged in such activities must master the skills before undertaking supervision or training is greatly dependent upon specific circumstances and individual professional judgment. It is recognized that a technology of teacher supervision and training can certainly be considered independent from a technology of classroom management.

CONTENTS

9 THE EVOLUTION OF BEHAVIOR 180

10 ESTABLISHING COMPATIBLE CONTINGENCIES 209

11 THE CLASSROOM MANAGEMENT SYSTEM 233

MANAGEMENT OF CLASSROOMS

CHAPTER ONE

INTRODUCTION TO CLASSROOM MANAGEMENT

Generally, "management" refers to the prudent use of means to accomplish ends. For teachers, means comprise procedures for interacting with students and ends, the student attainment of educational objectives. This chapter depicts the role of teacher means, student ends, and their relationships within effective classroom management. In presenting this picture, the chapter simplifies not only the teacher skills introduced but the classroom's natural complexity as well. The following chapters expand these key introductory skills into the comprehensive procedures required for effective management in the regular classroom.

INSTRUCTIONAL MANAGEMENT VERSUS CLASSROOM MANAGEMENT

This text focuses upon teacher skills for classroom management as opposed to instructional management. It defines "classroom management" as encompassing all activities undertaken by teachers to ensure that academic materials are presented under maximally effective conditions for learning. Classroom management, therefore, first ensures that students' social behavior is compatible with whatever academic program teachers present and, second, motivates students to progress in academic achievement. Thus, classroom management is a necessary condition for effective student learning. In comparison, instructional management involves the processes of structuring and presenting academic materials, including how examples are presented, how materials are sequenced, and how often materials are presented and reviewed. When they are consistent with principles of human behavior, instructional and classroom management work together to establish sufficient conditions for student learning.

ELEMENTS IN CLASSROOM MANAGEMENT

The elements of management represent the means teachers use and the educational ends students obtain. Settings, conditions, and consequences comprise the means; student social and academic behavior, the ends. Together, these elements serve as a foundation for teachers' thinking about classroom management problems and procedures.

Settings The setting is the physical background or location in which instruction occurs, typically the classroom with its tables, chairs, desks, and blackboards. The various arrangements of these components contribute to the achievement of educational goals. Accordingly, Chapter 4 delineates some general rules of classroom structure. However, the remarkable consistency in the size and physical arrangement of classrooms in the United States makes the setting the least important source of classroom management problems.

Conditions Conditions include all events arranged by teachers that guide and prepare students for learning. Under effective conditions, students perform the behaviors necessary for attending to instruction. Within the regular school classroom, the most powerful conditions are provided by teachers' statements and by procedures for structuring classroom activities. Teachers may establish conditions by stating classroom rules, giving directions, and dividing classes into different instructional activities. Chapters 4 and 5 deal directly with the analysis, construction, and use of conditions within the classroom. Their use is expanded in Chapters 8 and 10, and 11 to include advanced management systems applications.

Consequences Consequences include all events that follow from student behavior. The arrangement of consequences by teachers is a crucial factor in influencing future student behaviors. Thus, behavior consequences are used to increase the frequency or duration of appropriate student social and academic behaviors, while decreasing inappropriate behaviors. The most powerful consequences available are what the teacher says when appropriate and inappropriate student behaviors occur. Also, the specific information communicated to students determines whether a verbal consequence will be effective or ineffective in changing behavior in the manner teachers intend. Accordingly, Chapters 3 and 6 present the analysis, construction, and use of social consequences in classroom management. These procedures are subsequently refined and expanded in Chapters 8, 9, 10, and 11.

Behaviors Behavior includes all that a student says and does, including thinking and feeling. From the standpoint of classroom management, student academic and social behaviors are always either appropriate or inappropriate in classroom settings and conditions. The arrangement of conditions and consequences in accordance with established behavior principles leads to appropriate classroom behaviors. The identification of desired student behaviors by teachers before and during classroom activities, so that conditions and consequences can be effectively presented, is a key to effective classroom management. Chapters 2, 4, and 7 provide procedures for the definition and classification of behaviors which are drawn upon by all the chapters. By observing patterns of student behavior across time, teachers can take the first step toward influencing complex student academic and social behaviors. Consideration of student behavior is always involved when settings, conditions, and consequences are addressed.

THE CONCEPT OF CONTINGENCIES IN CLASSROOM MANAGEMENT

As discussed, a major function of teacher management skills is the arrangement of conditions and consequences in the classroom setting to change student behavior. Figure 1.1 presents a framework for representing the interrelationships among these elements. The arrows in Figure 1.1 indicate that student behavior is directly influenced by conditions and consequences established by the teacher. In practice, the conditions and consequences that surround behavior determine whether it will be changed or maintained.

These teacher arrangements of conditions and consequences (means) in relation to desired or anticipated student behavior (ends) are called "contingencies." All contingencies have four elements: (1) conditions, (2) behaviors, (3) consequences, and (4) the relationships among conditions, behaviors, and consequences (e.g., when, where, and how they are presented). Although Figure 1.1 indicates that teachers establish conditions and consequences to influence student behavior, the relationships between these elements require critical consideration. Otherwise, the

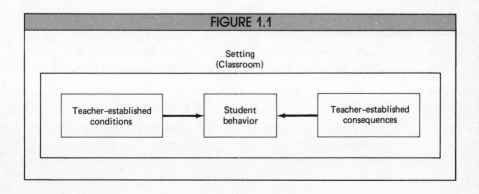

FIGURE 1.1

Setting
(Classroom)

Teacher-established conditions → Student behavior ← Teacher-established consequences wrong conditions and consequences may be related to desired behavior, and an ineffective management practice may result.

A teacher's arrangement of a single, isolated classroom contingency is a relatively simple task. However, in the regular classroom—with numerous students and many different contingencies—an extensive set of management skills is required to obtain desired student outcomes. Although the effective classroom manager plans only as many contingencies as necessary to ensure the successful implementation of an instructional program, the existing complex of unplanned contingencies typically remains the major cause of classroom management problems.

The following sections identify critical contingency elements and relationships which form a basis for teacher management skills. Once teachers master advanced forms of these and other supporting skills, virtually all classroom management problems become solvable. Each series of examples is accompanied by questions to illustrate what classroom teachers must ask themselves when planning or implementing a classroom management procedure.

Distinguishing Appropriate and Inappropriate Student Behaviors Student behaviors are "appropriate" when they match established classroom conditions. Since classroom conditions determine the student behaviors required for learning, "inappropriate" student behavior prevents educational goals from being met. The following condition-behavior matches and nonmatches encompass typical academic and social behaviors of students and are designed to help teachers learn the processes underlying them. In these simplified examples, a range of verbal instructions by a teacher is paired with subsequent individual or group student behavior. The reader should begin by studying the examples that provide answers and then go on to the examples that direct the reader to provide answers. (The answers for the latter examples in this and the following sections are shown before the "Practice Activities" at the end of this chapter.)

1. Condition   **Behavior**

Teacher says, "John,   John sits in his seat.
please sit in your seat."

Is there a condition-behavior match or nonmatch? _Match._
So, is the behavior appropriate or inappropriate? _Appropriate._

2. Condition   **Behavior**

Teacher shows a picture of   All students respond, "an
an elephant to everyone   elephant."
and asks, "What is this?"

Is there a condition-behavior match or nonmatch? *Match.*
So, is the behavior appropriate or inappropriate? *Appropriate.*

3. Condition   **Behavior**

Teacher shows a picture of   Zelda responds, "A horse."
an elephant and asks, "What   All other students say, "An
is this, everyone?"   elephant."

Is there a condition-behavior match or nonmatch? *Nonmatch.*
So, is the behavior appropriate or inappropriate? *Inappropriate.*

4. Condition   **Behavior**

The class rule during group   As students read, they all
reading is, "Point to every   point to every word.
word as it is read."

Is there a condition-behavior match or nonmatch? *Match.*
So, is the behavior appropriate or inappropriate? *Appropriate.*

5. Condition   **Behavior**

Teacher says, "John, I want   John gets up from his seat
you to sit in your seat during   several times during
spelling."   spelling.

(Write your answers on a sheet of paper.)
Is there a condition-behavior match or nonmatch?
So, is the behavior appropriate or inappropriate?

6. Condition   **Behavior**

One class rule for social   Zelda returns her finished
studies is, "Return completed   worksheet to box.
worksheets to the "'finished
box.'"

Is there a condition-behavior match or nonmatch?
So, is the behavior appropriate or inappropriate?

7. Condition   **Behavior**

Teacher says, "Everyone put   John puts his book away.
your book away before we   Bill does not put his book
start math."   away.

Is there a condition-behavior match or nonmatch?
So, is the behavior appropriate or inappropriate?

8. Condition   **Behavior**

Teacher says, "Bring your   All pupils bring their
homework to class   homework to class the
tomorrow."   next day.

Is there a condition-behavior match or nonmatch?
So, is the behavior appropriate or inappropriate?

The preceding examples introduce an important classroom management discrimination skill, which is repeatedly practiced and refined throughout the text. Within a classroom setting, this skill is part of a sequence in which teachers first identify the behaviors of students in relation to specified conditions; second, decide whether the behaviors match the condition; third, select a consequence; and fourth, deliver the consequence for the behaviors observed. These examples illustrate that identifying appropriate or inappropriate student behavior implies a teacher decision regarding a condition-behavior match.

At this point, the reader should review all the examples in the sequence, considering first each behavior and then each condition accompanying it. In determining each condition-behavior pair, the reader should ask and answer two questions: (1) *Does the behavior match the condition?* (2) *Is the behavior appropriate or inappropriate?* The reader should notice that sometimes the behavior focuses on groups and sometimes on individuals. This feature makes the identification of condition-behavior matches and nonmatches difficult within the classroom setting. In addition, some examples illustrate student social behaviors, and others illustrate student academic behaviors (see Chapter 2). Typically, the teacher is faced with all these categories of behavior simultaneously. For example, ten students may be working diligently on a worksheet, while one or two others may be doing anything from passing notes to fighting. In these situations, the task of the teacher is to maintain appropriate student behaviors while changing inappropriate behaviors. A major goal of subsequent chapters is to prepare teachers to accomplish this task in the most effective and affectively positive manner possible.

Targeting Inappropriate Student Behaviors for Change   The identification of inappropriate student behaviors is a first step in determining the changes required to make student behaviors appropriate. The second step in the management sequence requires teachers to specify what student behaviors would match stated classroom conditions. The next series of short practice examples illustrates this process.

1. Condition   **Behavior**

Teacher says, "Martha,   Martha blurts out her
please raise your hand   answer without raising
before answering."   her hand.

Is this behavior appropriate or inappropriate? *Inappropriate.*
Why? *Because the behavior does not match the condition.*
If inappropriate, what behavior would be appropriate for
conditions? *Martha raises her hand before answering.*

2. Condition   **Behavior**

Teacher points to a picture   All students but one
of an "a" and says,   respond with the sound
"Everybody, what sound?"   "aaaaaa."

Is this behavior appropriate or inappropriate? *Inappropriate.*
Why? *Because the behavior does not match the condition.*
If inappropriate, what behavior would be appropriate for
conditions? *All students respond with the sound "aaaaaa."*

3. Condition   **Behavior**

Teacher asks all students,   All students read the
"Read the word 'carrot,' on   word correctly on signal.
the board when I point to
it."

Is this behavior appropriate or inappropriate? *Appropriate.*
Why? *Because the behavior matches the condition.*
If inappropriate, what behavior would be appropriate for
conditions? *Behavior is appropriate.*

4. Condition   **Behavior**

The class rule is that   Bill leaves his name off
students must write their   his spelling test.
name on all work.

(*Write your answers on a sheet of paper.*) Is this behavior
appropriate or inappropriate?
Why?
If inappropriate, what behavior would be appropriate for
conditions?

5. Condition   **Behavior**

The class rule is, "Raise   Sally breaks her pencil
your hand for permission   and walks to the
to leave your seat."   sharpener.

Is this behavior appropriate or inappropriate?
Why?
If inappropriate, what behavior would be appropriate for
conditions?

6. *Condition*   *Behavior*

Teacher presents Art with a   Art waits a few seconds,
difficult word problem and   then answers correctly.
says, "Please think before
you answer."

Is this behavior appropriate or inappropriate?
Why?
If inappropriate, what behavior would be appropriate for
conditions?

7. *Condition*   *Behavior*

Teacher says, "Please clear   Bill and Martha keep
your desks before recess."   coloring their pictures.

Is this behavior appropriate or inappropriate?
Why?
If inappropriate, what behavior would be appropriate for
conditions?

8. *Condition*   *Behavior*

Teacher says, "Remember to   All but three students forget
correct your spelling errors   their assignment.
by tomorrow."

Is this behavior appropriate or inappropriate?
Why?
If inappropriate, what behavior would be appropriate for
conditions?

These exercises introduce the idea that when teachers observe behavior in relation to conditions, they must identify what behavior would
match the conditions as an implicit part of the process of determining a
behavior-condition match. As subsequent chapters will show, conditions
serve as teacher-established behavior standards that are either met or
not met by the student. By making classroom discriminations about appropriate or inappropriate student behavior in terms of behaviors required for matching conditions, teachers are better able to reach the degree of consistency necessary to maintain or increase appropriate student
behavior while decreasing the level of inappropriate student behavior.

At this point, the reader should review answers to the exercises before continuing. As part of the review process, the reader should first
consider the behaviors and conditions, and then ask the following sequence of three questions: (1) *Is there a condition-behavior match?* (2) *Is
the behavior appropriate?* (3) *If the behavior is inappropriate, what behav-*

ior would be appropriate? These questions represent part of a teacher management process that must occur before and during instruction. Expansion activities at the end of this chapter and in subsequent chapters provide additional practice on this important management skill.

Determining Consequences to Present to Students Once teachers have learned to distinguish appropriate from inappropriate student behaviors, the next key skill is deciding what type of consequences to present contingent upon student behavior. In keeping with behavior principles, the type and timing of consequences that teachers present are of crucial importance because they are a major determiner of future student behavior. Thus, teacher-presented social consequences are a primary classroom management tool.

Within this text, two broad categories of consequences are stressed: *Reward consequences increase the future occurrence of appropriate student behavior. Correction consequences decrease the future occurrence of inappropriate behavior.* A reward consequence follows a condition-behavior match; a correction consequence follows a nonmatch.

The following examples are designed to provide practice on the discrimination skills required to determine whether a reward or correction contingency should be used and to predict the resulting change in behavior.

1. | *Condition* | *Behavior* | *Consequence* |
|---|---|---|
| Teacher says, "John, please sit in your seat." | John sits down. | ? |

Is there a condition-behavior match or nonmatch? *Match.*
So, should a reward or correction consequence be presented? *Reward.*
Is the desired management outcome to increase or decrease future occurrences of the behavior? *Increase.*

2. | *Condition* | *Behavior* | *Consequence* |
|---|---|---|
| Teacher shows a picture of an elephant and asks, "What is this?" | All students respond, "An elephant." | ? |

Is there a condition-behavior match or nonmatch? *Match.*
Should a reward or correction consequence be presented? *Reward.*
Is the desired management outcome to increase or decrease future occurrences of the behavior? *Increase.*

3. *Condition*   *Behavior*   *Consequence*

Teacher shows a picture of an elephant and asks, "What is this, everyone?"	Zelda responds, "A horse." All others say, "An elephant."	?

Is there a condition-behavior match or nonmatch? *Nonmatch.*
Should a reward or correction consequence be presented?
Correction.
Is the desired management outcome to increase or decrease future occurrences of the behavior? *Decrease.*

4. *Condition*   *Behavior*   *Consequence*

The class rule during group reading is, "Point to every word as it is read."	As they read, all students point to every word.	?

(*Write your answers on a sheet of paper.*)
Is there a condition-behavior match or nonmatch?
Should a reward or correction consequence be presented?
Is the desired management outcome to increase or decrease future occurrences of the behavior?

5. *Condition*   *Behavior*   *Consequence*

Teacher says, "Bring your books to class tomorrow."	All pupils bring their books the next day.	?

Is there a condition-behavior match or nonmatch?
Should a reward or correction consequence be presented?
Is the desired management outcome to increase or decrease future occurrences of the behavior?

6. *Condition*   *Behavior*   *Consequence*

Teacher says, "Everyone, please put your book away before we start math."	John puts his book away; others don't.	?

Is there a condition-behavior match or nonmatch?
Should a reward or correction consequence be presented?

Is the desired management outcome to increase or decrease future occurrences of the behavior?

7. *Condition*	*Behavior*	*Consequence*
Teacher says, "Sally, I want you to keep working on your seatwork."	Sally gets up from her seat several times before finishing.	?

Is there a condition-behavior match or nonmatch?
Should a reward or correction consequence be presented?
Is the desired management outcome to increase or decrease future occurrences of the behavior?

These examples illustrate, in simplified fashion, how teachers use the following general rule to determine whether a reward or correction consequence should be presented to students:

If behavior is appropriate for the conditions, then present a reward consequence to increase future occurrences; if the behavior is inappropriate for the conditions, then present a correction consequence to decrease future occurrences.

Consistency in following this rule is necessary for effective management. The first step toward consistency is gaining the skill to see if the behavior is appropriate or inappropriate, and the second is to construct and present appropriate reward or correction statements. This text is designed to build these teacher skills. Finally, as Chapter 6 will show, correction consequences should not be confused with punishment techniques. All of the procedures presented in this text are nonaversive. At this point, readers should check their answers and review the examples.

Identifying Reward Consequences The presentation of reward consequences when appropriate behavior occurs increases the future probability of the behavior. In implementing this rule, the presentation of the reward is said to be "contingent" upon the behavior. That is, when appropriate behavior (a condition-behavior match) occurs, then and only then is a reward consequence presented. This is a necessary procedure for teachers to follow for two reasons. First, if teachers present reward consequences when inappropriate behavior occurs, then students will tend to behave inappropriately more often. Second, if teachers never present reward consequences for appropriate behavior, students will behave in an appropriate manner less often. These two "reward errors" occur in many classrooms and are a major cause of many classroom management problems.

The initial step in constructing and presenting reward consequences is to distinguish forms of rewards that are effective. As a teacher verbalizes statements, a reward consequence (1) reflects or references a condition-behavior match and (2) indicates teacher approval of the appropriate behavior. The following examples are designed as an informal introduction to verbal reward statements.

1. Condition	Behavior	Consequence
Teacher says, "John, please sit in your seat."	John sits down.	Teacher says, "Thank you, John. I appreciate your following directions to sit down."

Does the consequence reference the condition-behavior match? *Yes*.
Does the consequence show approval for the match? *Yes*.
Therefore, does the consequence illustrate a verbal reward statement for the match? *Yes*.
Will the consequence help the condition-behavior match to occur more often? *Yes*.

2. Condition	Behavior	Consequence
Teacher says, "John, please keep working until you finish your work."	John works until finished.	Teacher says, "I like the way you worked until you finished today, John."

Does the consequence reference the condition-behavior match? *Yes*.
Does the consequence show approval for the match? *Yes*.
Therefore, does the consequence illustrate a verbal reward statement for the match? *Yes*.
Will the consequence help the condition-behavior match to occur more often? *Yes*.

3. Condition	Behavior	Consequence
Teacher says, "John, please keep working until you finish your work."	John works until finished.	Teacher says, "I hope you work better tomorrow."

Does the consequence reflect the condition-behavior match? *No.*
Does the consequence show approval for the match? *No.*
Therefore, does the consequence illustrate a verbal reward statement for the match? *No.*
Will the consequence help the condition-behavior match to occur more often? *No.*

4. Condition

Teacher shows picture of an elephant and asks, "Everyone, what is this?"

Behavior

All students respond, "An elephant."

Consequence

Teacher says, "That's right, everyone. This picture is an elephant."

Does the consequence reference the condition-behavior match and show approval of the match? *Yes.*
Does the consequence illustrate a verbal reward statement for the match? *Yes.*
Will the consequence help the condition-behavior match to occur more often? *Yes.*

5. Condition

The class rule during group reading is, "Point to every word as it is read."

Behavior

All students point to each word.

Consequence

Teacher says, "OK, put away your books and get ready for math."

(*Write your answers on a sheet of paper.*)
Does the consequence reference the condition-behavior match and show approval of the match?
Does the consequence illustrate a verbal reward statement for the match?
Will the consequence help the condition-behavior match to occur more often?

6. Condition

The class rule during group reading is, "Point to every word as it is read."

Behavior

All students point to each word.

Consequence

Teacher says, "All of you are pointing to your words correctly. Good work!"

Does the consequence reference the condition-behavior match and show approval of the match?
Does the consequence illustrate a verbal reward statement for the match?

Will the consequence help the condition-behavior match to occur more often?

7. Condition	Behavior	Consequence
The class rule for social studies is, "Return completed work to the 'finished' box."	Zelda returns her finished worksheet to the box.	Teacher says, "Zelda, you got six of eight problems correct on your math yesterday."

Does the consequence reference the condition-behavior match and show approval of the match?
Does the consequence illustrate a verbal reward statement for the match?
Will the consequence help the condition-behavior match to occur more often?

The presentation of verbal consequences is an important skill that teachers must use in establishing classroom management practices. In addition, identifying the elements of verbal reward consequences is a key troubleshooting skill in solving management problems. (Chapters 3 and 8 will help teachers construct basic and advanced forms of reward statements.)

At this point, the reader should review the examples to make sure that he or she can identify the relationship among the condition, behavior, and reward statements in each.

Identifying Correction Consequences Reward consequences are presented to increase future occurrences of appropriate behavior; correction consequences are presented to reduce future occurrences of inappropriate behavior. Thus, correction consequences are presented because there is a condition-behavior nonmatch. Rather than being punitive, their primary function is to set the stage for future appropriate behavior by identifying and directing student attention toward it. As a teacher verbal statement, a correction consequence (1) reflects or references an existing condition-behavior nonmatch and (2) describes the appropriate (matching) behavior. The following exercises introduce examples and nonexamples of verbal correction statements. (Note that we use the term "nonexamples" to indicate samples of inappropriate teacher behavior or statements.)

1. Condition	Behavior	Consequence
The classroom rule is to try hard.	Mark hits his neighbor with a spitball.	Teacher says, "The rule is to try hard, not throw spitballs."

Does the consequence reference the condition-behavior nonmatch and/or target the desired behavior? *Yes.*
Therefore, does the consequence illustrate a verbal correction statement for the nonmatch? *Yes.*
Will the consequence help the condition-behavior nonmatch to occur less often? *Yes.*

2. | **Condition** | **Behavior** | **Consequence** |
| --- | --- | --- |
| Teacher says, "Will you all take out your math books." | John does not take out his math book. | Teacher says, "Thank you all for taking out your math books." |

Does the consequence reference the condition-behavior nonmatch and/or target the desired behavior? *No.*
Does the consequence illustrate a verbal correction statement? *No.*
Will the consequence help the condition-behavior nonmatch to occur less often? *No.*

3. | **Condition** | **Behavior** | **Consequence** |
| --- | --- | --- |
| The class rule is, "Students can break not more than one rule per lesson without being warned." | Mildred talks out of turn twice. | Teacher says, "Mildred, that is the second time you have talked out. This is a warning. Please follow the rules." |

Does the consequence reference the condition-behavior nonmatch and/or target the desired behavior? *Yes.*
Does the consequence illustrate a verbal correction statement? *Yes.*
Will the consequence help the condition-behavior nonmatch to occur less often? *Yes.*

4. | **Condition** | **Behavior** | **Consequence** |
| --- | --- | --- |
| The class rule is that no student may put another in danger. | James throws a book across the room. | Teacher says, "James, throwing a book puts others in danger. Please go sit in the back of the room until I can talk with you." |

(*Write your answers on a sheet of paper.*)
Does the consequence reference the condition-behavior
nonmatch and/or target the desired behavior?
Does the consequence illustrate a verbal correction statement?
Will the consequence help the condition-behavior nonmatch to
occur less often?

5. *Condition*	*Behavior*	*Consequence*
The teacher says, "John, what is the answer to the fifth question?"	John does not pay attention to the teacher.	Teacher says, "Mary, would you please answer the question correctly. John was not listening."

Does the consequence reference the condition-behavior
nonmatch and/or target the desired behavior?
Does the consequence illustrate a verbal correction statement?
Will the consequence help the condition-behavior nonmatch to
occur less often?

6. *Condition*	*Behavior*	*Consequence*
The teacher holds up a picture of an elephant and asks, "What is this?"	Someone says, "A cow."	Teacher says, "This is an elephant, not a cow."

Does the consequence reference the condition-behavior
nonmatch and/or target the desired behavior?
Does the consequence illustrate a verbal correction statement?
Will the consequence help the condition-behavior nonmatch to
occur less often?

As in the case of reward consequences, the identification of correction
consequences and the conditions under which they should be used is a
necessary troubleshooting skill for teachers. The examples presented are
illustrations that subsequent chapters will develop into advanced forms
of statements for use by teachers.

At this point, the reader should review the examples, making sure to
identify the relationships among the condition, behavior, and consequence statement in each.

Using Conditions in Classroom Management All the preceding examples have been simplified by limiting conditions to statements describing desired student behavior. However, the condition statements in subsequent chapters are far more complex and serve as important management tools. The following examples illustrate how condition statements can be expanded to include classroom reward and correction procedures that specify student behaviors. The examples also illustrate how reward and corrective verbal consequences can be altered to reflect both the observed condition-behavior match and the procedures that are part of the classroom contingencies.

1. *Condition*	*Behavior*	*Consequence*
The established classroom procedure is to award achievement points for correct answers. The teacher shows a picture of an elephant and asks, "What is this picture?"	All students answer, "An elephant."	Teacher says, "Correct, this is an elephant. Everyone earns a point."

Was there a condition-behavior match or nonmatch? *Match.*
Therefore, was the contingent consequence reward or correction? *Reward.*
Did the contingent consequence reference both the condition-behavior match and the condition procedure? *Yes.*
Would this contingency increase or decrease the student behavior illustrated? *Increase.*

2. *Condition*	*Behavior*	*Consequence*
The established classroom procedure is to warn students when they break a rule more than once. The class rule is to pay attention and try hard.	Marvin is writing notes for the second time.	Teacher says, "Marvin, this is a warning. The rule is to pay attention. Writing notes is not considered to be following the rules."

Was there a condition-behavior match or nonmatch? *Nonmatch.*
Therefore, was the contingent consequence reward or
correction? *Correction.*
Did the contingent consequence reference both the condition-
behavior match and the contingent condition procedure? *Yes.*
Would this contingency increase or decrease the student
behavior illustrated. *Decrease.*

3. | **Condition** | **Behavior** | **Consequence** |
|---|---|---|
| The established classroom procedure is to predict the future success of students when they perform well. The teacher says, "John, try and get at least five of seven items correct on your math assignment." | John gets six of seven test items correct. | Teacher says, "Six out of seven correct. John, I knew you could do it. Keep it up and you will make an A in mathematics." |

(*Write your answers on a sheet of paper.*)
Was there a condition-behavior match or nonmatch?
Therefore, was the contingent consequence reward or
correction?
Did the contingent consequence reference both the condition-
behavior match/nonmatch and the condition procedure?
Would this contingency increase or decrease the student
behavior illustrated?

4. | **Condition** | **Behavior** | **Consequence** |
|---|---|---|
| The established classroom procedure is that students who work quietly at their desks get to go to recess early. | Everyone has worked quietly and finished the assigned work. | Teacher says, "You all have followed the 'work quietly' rule today and finished your work. Therefore, let's start recess three minutes early." |

Was there a condition-behavior match or nonmatch?
Therefore, was the contingent consequence reward or
correction?
Did the contingent consequence reference both the condition-
behavior match/nonmatch and the condition procedure?
Would this contingency increase or decrease the student
behavior illustrated?

5. *Condition*	*Behavior*	*Consequence*
The established classroom procedure is to remove students from the classroom if they endanger another student. The class rule is that students must be considerate of others.	Bill throws a book across the room at Sally.	Teacher says, "Bill, throwing that book could have hurt Sally. The rule is to be considerate of others. Move to the rear of the classroom until I can take you to the principal's office."

Was there a condition-behavior match or nonmatch?
Therefore, was the contingent consequence reward or
correction?
Did the contingent consequence reference both the condition-
behavior match/nonmatch and the condition procedure?
Would this contingency increase or decrease the student
behavior illustrated?

Subsequent chapters emphasize teacher skills in constructing condition statements and procedures to solve classroom management problems. In reviewing the preceding examples, the reader should make certain how the components of the reward and corrective consequences relate to both the condition-behavior match/nonmatch and to the procedures specified in the conditions. Chapters 4, 5, and 10 show how these relationships serve as the basis for well-managed classrooms.

Identifying Contingency Errors This final introductory section presents examples of another key teacher management skill: discriminating and eliminating errors in using reward and correction contingencies. Two rules are applied in order to identify contingency errors:

1. The delivery of a reward consequence (a) requires a condition-behavior match and (b) references this match.

2. The delivery of a corrective consequence (a) requires a condition-behavior nonmatch and (b) reflects both the non-match and the desired match.

Because they result in future decreases in appropriate behaviors or increases in inappropriate behaviors, contingency errors are a common cause of management problems. For this reason, error identification is an important teacher skill. Again, simplified examples provide an informal introduction.

1. Condition	*Behavior*	*Consequence*
The classroom rule is, "Cooperate with others."	Bill helps Glenda pick up the books she dropped.	Teacher says, "John, thank you for helping Glenda."

Was there a condition-behavior match or nonmatch? *Match.*
Should the consequence be reward or corrective? *Reward.*
Does the consequence reflect the condition-behavior match/nonmatch? *Yes.*
Therefore, was there a contingency error? *No.*
Will the contingency illustrated tend to increase appropriate behavior or decrease inappropriate behavior? *Yes.*

2. Condition	*Behavior*	*Consequence*
The classroom rules state, "Cooperate with others."	John refuses to help with art cleanup.	Teacher says, "John, sit in your seat."

Was there a condition-behavior match or nonmatch? *Nonmatch.*
Should the consequence be reward or corrective? *Corrective.*
Does the consequence reflect the condition-behavior match/nonmatch? *No.*
Therefore, was there a contingency error? *Yes.*
Will the contingency illustrated tend to increase appropriate behavior or decrease inappropriate behavior? *No.*

3. Condition	*Behavior*	*Consequence*
The teacher says, "Please get out your maps and rulers."	Kathy gets out her map and ruler.	Teacher says, "Now find the distance between the places listed on the board."

Was there a condition-behavior match or nonmatch? *Match.*
Should the consequence be reward or corrective? *Reward.*
Does the consequence reflect the condition-behavior
match/nonmatch? *No.*
Therefore, was there a contingency error? *Yes.*
Will the contingency illustrated tend to increase appropriate
behavior or decrease inappropriate behavior? *No.*

4. *Condition*	*Behavior*	*Consequence*
The teacher says, "Please get out your map and ruler."	Kathy gets out her map and ruler.	Teacher says, "Kathy, sit up straight before we start."

Was there a condition-behavior match or nonmatch? *Match.*
Should the consequence be reward or corrective? *Reward.*
Does the consequence reflect the condition-behavior
match/nonmatch? *No.*
Therefore, was there a contingency error? *Yes.*
Will the contingency illustrated tend to increase appropriate
behavior or decrease inappropriate behavior? *No.*

5. *Condition*	*Behavior*	*Consequence*
The class rule during reading is, "Point to every word as it is read."	As students read, they all point to every word.	Teacher says, "Everyone must point. Let's read it again until everyone points correctly."

(*Write your answers on a sheet of paper.*)
Was there a condition-behavior match or nonmatch?
Should the consequence be reward or corrective?
Does the consequence reflect the condition-behavior
match/nonmatch?
Therefore, was there a contingency error?
Will the contingency illustrated tend to increase appropriate
behavior or decrease inappropriate behavior?

6. *Condition*	*Behavior*	*Consequence*
Teacher shows a picture of an elephant and asks, "What is this?"	Zelda responds, "A horse"; all others say, "An elephant."	Teacher says, "That is right, everyone, an elephant."

Was there a condition-behavior match or nonmatch?
Should the consequence be reward or corrective?
Does the consequence reflect the condition-behavior
match/nonmatch?
Was there a contingency error?
Will the contingency illustrated increase appropriate behavior
or decrease inappropriate behavior?

7. *Condition*	*Behavior*	*Consequence*
Teacher says, "Everyone pay attention while I work this problem."	Martha looks out the window and daydreams.	Teacher says, "Martha, please pay attention."

Was there a condition-behavior match or nonmatch?
Should the consequence be reward or corrective?
Does the consequence reflect the condition-behavior
match/nonmatch?
Was there a contingency error?
Will the contingency illustrated increase appropriate behavior
or decrease inappropriate behavior?

8. *Condition*	*Behavior*	*Consequence*
One class rule for social studies is, "Return completed worksheets to the 'finished box.'"	James returns finished worksheet to box.	Teacher says, "Thank you, James, for returning your worksheet. That helps me get my job done."

Was there a condition-behavior match or nonmatch?
Should the consequence be reward or corrective?
Does the consequence reflect the condition-behavior
match/nonmatch?
Was there a contingency error?
Will the contingency illustrated increase appropriate behavior
or decrease inappropriate behavior?

Contingency errors are the nonexamples of effective management. Their identification represents the extent to which teachers know the limits of what encompasses effective classroom contingencies. This knowledge is especially helpful during the learning process because teachers, like everyone else, will make errors. If they can identify these, they can correct and improve their skills. Once proficiency is achieved, contingency error identification will help maintain the skills learned.

In summary, the basis for teacher management skills are concerned with establishing effective contingencies. To achieve this end, teachers must, as a first step, identify critical contingency elements and relationships. There are three elements. The first is the conditions that precede student behavior. These involve not only verbal statements by the teacher but also classroom procedures and rules. The second element, student behavior, includes the identification of both appropriate and inappropriate behavior. The consequences which follow student behavior are the third element and includes identifying both rewards and corrections.

Two relationships require identification. The first relates the condition and the student behavior elements. If the behavior matches or mirrors the conditions, it is appropriate; if not, it is inappropriate and there exists a condition-behavior nonmatch. The second relationship involves student behavior and the consequences that follow it. The relationship rule is the following: If there is a condition-behavior match, present a reward consequence; if there is a nonmatch, present a corrective consequence. Only when the first relationship can be reliably identified can the second relationship be reliably identified. Thus, identification of the second relationship is dependent on identification of the first.

These identifications are the foundation of management's decision-making component. When classroom procedures and the problem-solving components also reach proficiency, teachers will be effective classroom managers.

TOWARD THE DEVELOPMENT OF CLASSROOM MANAGEMENT SKILLS

Classroom management is a system of skills that teachers learn in order to work effectively with students. While some of the subtle features of effective management are an art, credible preparation of the teacher as an artist requires mastery of the existing technology of the discipline. This technology involves more than just the application of classroom procedures; it includes decision-making and problem-solving skills as well. Every classroom has its own unique set of conditions, students, and problems which requires adaptations of the classroom procedures. Without the decision-making and problems-solving skill components, effective management could never be achieved because classroom procedures would be erroneously applied. Because the technology is founded on validated principles of human behavior, teachers will find that the skills learned are effective.

This text presents the technology of classroom management by interrelating, distinguishing, and building important skill categories. Management skills are developed sequentially in a cumulative and expanding fashion so that they have increasing value for classroom practice. In this general sequence, teachers first learn to observe and classify student behaviors, use reward statements with consistency, establish classroom rules, and use correction statements. Once these procedures are learned and applied successfully, they are expanded and combined with more general classroom management skills. Some of these subsequent skills include procedures for changing student behavior across time, establishing compatible contingencies, building a complete management system, and diagnosing classroom problems. Throughout the text, both prerequisites for complex skills and supporting classroom activities are provided to facilitate transfer and application of the skills learned. Designed to be used with professional supervision or independently, these transfer activities are a key element of the text.

ANSWERS TO EXERCISES IN THE TEXT

Distinguishing Appropriate and Inappropriate Student Behaviors
- **#5** *Nonmatch, inappropriate*
- **#6** *Match, appropriate*
- **#7** *Nonmatch, inappropriate*
- **#8** *Match, appropriate*

Targeting Inappropriate Student Behaviors for Change
- **#4** *Inappropriate, because the behavior does not match the condition. Bill writing his name on his spelling test.*
- **#5** *Inappropriate, because the behavior does not match the conditions. Sally raising her hand for permission to leave her seat.*
- **#6** *Appropriate, because the behavior matches the conditions.*
- **#7** *Inappropriate, because the behavior does not match the conditions. Bill and Martha clearing their desks.*
- **#8** *Inappropriate, because the behavior does not match the conditions. All students in the class completing their assignment.*

Determining Consequences to Present to Students
- **#4** *Match, reward, increase.*
- **#5** *Match, reward, increase.*
- **#6** *Nonmatch, correction, decrease.*
- **#7** *Nonmatch, correction, decrease.*

Identifying Reward Consequences
- **#5** *No, no, no.*
- **#6** *Yes, yes, yes.*
- **#7** *No, no, no.*

Identifying Correction Consequences
- **#4** *Yes, yes, yes.*
- **#5** *No, no, no.*
- **#6** *Yes, yes, yes.*

Using Conditions in Classroom Management
- **#3** *Match, reward, yes, increase.*
- **#4** *Match, reward, yes, increase.*
- **#5** *Nonmatch, correction, yes, decrease.*

Identifying Contingency Errors
- **#5** *Match, reward, no, error, no.*
- **#6** *Nonmatch, corrective, no, error, no.*
- **#7** *Nonmatch, corrective, yes, no error, yes.*
- **#8** *Match, reward, yes, no error, yes.*

P R A C T I C E   A C T I V I T I E S

1. Settings and behavior (pp. 2, 4)
   1.1 Generate examples for group discussion: What settings and behaviors would you expect to observe in schools?
      a. List five examples of different classroom or school settings.
      b. List an example of appropriate student behavior for each setting.
      c. List an example of an inappropriate behavior for each setting.
   1.2 Visit a school classroom. For items 1.1a–c, describe your observations for group discussion: What settings and behaviors did you see?

2. Conditions (pp. 2, 17)
   2.1 Generate examples for group discussion: What conditions would you expect to observe in schools?
      a. List five examples of conditions within a typical setting. Specify two parts of each condition:
         (1) Verbal statement of a rule.
         (2) The procedure the teacher follows when the rule is or is not met.
      b. List an example of an appropriate behavior matching each condition. (p. 4)
      c. List an example of an inappropriate behavior not matching each condition. (p. 6)
   2.2 Visit a school classroom. For items 2.1a–c, describe your observations for group discussion: What conditions and examples of behavior-condition matches and nonmatches did you see?

3. Targeting inappropriate student behaviors for change (p. 6)
   3.1 Generate examples for group discussion: What change in behavior and resulting appropriate behavior would eliminate the nonmatch?
      a. List five examples of inappropriate student behavior. Specify the setting and conditions for each.
      b. For each example, list a change in student behavior that would result in appropriate student behavior (i.e., an appropriate behavior that would eliminate the nonmatch).
   3.2 Visit a school classroom. For items 3.1a and b, describe your observations for group discussion.

4. Determining consequences to present (pp. 2, 9)
   4.1 Generate examples for group discussion: For each of the examples listed in 3.1, state:
      a. Whether the occurrence of the behavior specified for each setting and condition should be increased or decreased.
      b. Whether a reward or correction consequence would be used to accomplish this outcome.
   4.2 Visit a school classroom. For each of the items in 4.1, describe your observations for group discussion. (Combine these observations with those for item 3.2.)

5. Verbal reward consequences (p. 11)

  5.1 Generate examples for group discussion: List five reward consequences, along with the associated behavior, condition, and setting. Specify the following two parts of each reward consequence:

    a. The behavior-condition match.

    b. Teacher approval.

  5.2 Visit a school classroom. Describe your observations for group discussion:

    a. List five examples of a reward consequence, along with the associated behavior, condition, and setting.

    b. For each example, note whether the reward consequence included both parts (a condition-behavior match description, approval) and which parts were missing. Generate an example to supply any missing parts observed.

    c. Choose one appropriate behavior from the above list. Note how often teachers present reward consequences when the behavior occurs. Do this by observing either an individual student or a group of students for 5–10 minutes.

6. Verbal correction consequences (p. 14)

  6.1 Generate examples for group discussion: List five examples of a correction consequence, along with the associated behavior, condition, and setting. Specify the following two parts of each correction consequence:

    a. Teacher description of the condition-behavior nonmatch.

    b. Specification of the appropriate behavior.

  6.2 Visit a school classroom. For each item below, describe your observations for group discussion.

    a. List five examples of a correction consequence, along with the associated behavior, condition, and setting.

    b. For each example, note whether the correction consequence included both parts (a condition-behavior nonmatch description, appropriate behavior) and which parts were missing. Generate an example to illustrate any missing parts.

    c. Choose one inappropriate behavior from the above list. Note how often teachers present correction consequences when the inappropriate behavior occurs. Do this by observing an individual student or group of students for 5–10 minutes.

7. Identifying contingency errors (p. 19)

  7.1 Generate examples for group discussion.

    a. List five examples specifying a setting, a condition-behavior match, and a reward consequence. Specify the two components of the reward consequence.

    b. For each example above, illustrate a possible reward-contingency error. Explain the implications of the reward error upon future occurrences of the appropriate behavior if the reward error is repeated frequently.

    c. List five examples specifying a setting, a condition-behavior nonmatch, and a correction consequence. Specify the two components of the correction consequence.

    d. For each example above, illustrate a possible correction contingency error. Explain the implications of frequent repetition of the contingency error upon future occurrences of the inappropriate behavior.

7.2 Visit a school classroom. For each item below, describe your observations for group discussion.

    a. List five examples of a reward error and a correction error. Specify the setting, conditions, behavior, and consequence for each.

    b. Select an appropriate and an inappropriate student behavior for observation. For each, count the number of consequences presented and the number of contingency errors. Do this by observing an individual student or a group of students for 5–10 minutes.

REFERENCES

For many, the terms "discipline" and "classroom management" are synonymous. Although the authors see discipline as an element of classroom management, they agree that discipline has been the major problem in the public schools over the last two decades. As T. R. McDaniel pointed out, in ten of the eleven Gallup polls taken between 1969 and 1980, the public selected discipline as the number one public school problem. J. G. Taylor and R. H. Usher surveyed the educational response to this public outcry and discovered thirteen approaches to discipline or classroom management. Although the contents and procedures of this chapter were developed independently, they satisfy a great many of the stated requirements of the thirteen approaches. Also, the text's procedures are consistent with the pioneering work by J. S. Kounin on the description of teacher discipline and group management skills.

Kouin, J. S. *Discipline and Group Management in Classrooms.* New York: Holt, Rinehart and Winston, 1970.

McDaniel, T. R. Exploring alternatives to punishment: The keys to effective discipline. *Phi Delta Kappan,* 1980, *61,* 455–458.

Usher, R. H., & Taylor, J. G. *A Baker's Dozen for Classroom Discipline.* Louisville: Kentucky Education Association, 1981.

The theoretical and procedural directives for the content and construction of classroom management skills were derived from the work of B. F. Skinner, who not only has provided the theoretical foundation in the form of the analysis of the contingencies of reinforcement but also has clearly related them to classroom management.

Skinner, B. F. Teaching science in high school—what is wrong? *Science,* 1968, *159,* 704–710.

Skinner, B. F. *The Technology of Teaching.* New York: Appleton-Century-Crofts, 1968.

Skinner, B. F. *Contingencies of Reinforcement: A Theoretical Analysis.* New York: Appleton-Century-Crofts, 1969.

Skinner, B. F. Contingency management in the classroom. *Education,* 1970, *90,* 93–100.

Skinner, B. F. The free and happy student. *Phi Delta Kappan,* 1973, *55,* 13–16.

The terms "setting" and "condition-behavior match" also have historical antecedents. Sidney Bijou and Donald Baer explicated the importance and use of setting events, and the condition-behavior match is equivalent to the behavior analysis training paradigm of "matching to sample." Fester and Culbertson as well as Millenson and Leslie detail the paradigm's use in behavior analysis research.

Bijou, S. W., & Baer, D. *Child Development,* Vol. 1. New York: Appleton-Century-Crofts, 1961.

Ferster, C. B., & Culbertson, S. *Behavior Principles,* 3rd ed. Englewood Cliffs, N. J.: Prentice-Hall, 1982.

Millenson, J. R., & Leslie, J. C. *Principles of Behavioral Analysis,* 2nd ed. New York: Macmillan, 1979.

CHAPTER TWO

ANALYZING BEHAVIOR: PART I

B uilding a classroom management system requires, as a first step, the analysis of desired behavioral ends. An analysis defines student behaviors so that teachers can accurately observe their occurrence and change over time. Definition and observation are necessary requirements for the design and subsequent implementation of classroom management procedures. When definition or observation skills are missing or weak, teachers cannot act on critical condition-behavior matches and non-matches. The resulting contingency errors will produce an ineffective management system in which inappropriate student behavior predominates. Thus, analysis skills are crucial in both planning and implementing an effective classroom management system.

FOUNDATIONS OF BEHAVIOR ANALYSIS

For the process of analysis, the teacher needs two basic ingredients: a language to talk about behavior and procedures to define the behavior being discussed. A behavioral language constructs a "picture" or representation of behavior and its change. Such a picture includes the following components: (1) the "units" of behavior, (2) the "relationships" among behavioral units, (3) the "evolution" of behavior, and (4) the "patterns" of behavioral evolution.

The first two components give the teacher a "static" or "structural" picture of behavior. The units are the desired student behaviors, and the relationships are the dependence or independence between these behaviors. The second two components provide a "dynamic" picture of the process of behavior change across time. The evolution of behavior entails the "emergence" and "alteration" of the units of behavior. The pattern of evolution explicates the "form" or "flow" of behavior change. Once mastered, a behavioral language allows teachers to talk about what behaviors are, what interactions are involved in behaviors, and how behavior evolves across time.

Talking about the nature of behavior is just a first step. The second is to define the behaviors of interest so that the talk has content. This requires procedures that help (1) define units of behavior, and (2) determine relationships among behavioral units. Once the definitions and relationships are established, the teacher can implement the text's management procedures to obtain the desired behaviors through acceptable patterns of change. With implementation, the teacher moves from the analysis to the synthesis of behavior.

This chapter provides a behavioral language and the procedures to define behavioral units. These tools must be mastered if the classroom management procedures presented throughout this text are to be used with maximal effectiveness.

THE UNITS OF BEHAVIOR

The language and underlying considerations required for defining the units of behavior include the following: (1) observable versus unobservable behavior (2) behavior instances and classes, and (3) class attributes. Each plays a critical part in helping teachers gain a picture or perspective of what behavior is and the requirements for definitions that allow for the effective implementation of classroom management procedures. Behavior relationships are presented in Chapter 7, along with procedures to define the relationships. Chapter 9 outlines procedures to facilitate the evolution of behavior and the patterns of change.

Instances and Classes of Behavior   There are two types of behavioral units. The first, a unit of observation or anaylsis, represents individual occurrences of behavior. These individual occurrences are "instances" whose future occurrence is increased or decreased (see Chapter 1). The second, a unit of definition, represents sets of similar behavioral instances. A set of related instances is called a "class" or "class of behavior." Examples of behavior classes are thinking, loving, demanding, driving to work, wrecking cars, reading books. The definition of the class represents the similarity among instances.

A class and its instances are analogous to the terms "set" and "member" in mathematics. An instance is a class representative or member that occurs at a specific time and place. For example, a specific somersault performed at 8:33 A.M. yesterday is an instance of the somersault class. While a somersault instance occurs only once, a "somersault" class, via its definition, represents specific instances that have occurred or could occur. The following list illustrates some classes and instances:

Class	*Instances*
1. Talking to others	Talking with Mary at 7:45 P.M. Talking to the family at 9:21 A.M. Talking to her brother at 12:34 P.M.
2. Writing complete sentences	The complete sentence written in Mrs. Hayes's class. The complete sentence written in a letter to Maria. The complete sentence written while riding in the car.
3. Reading	Reading a book on September 14. Reading a poem yesterday. Reading an advertisement in the paper the day before yesterday.

Through the analysis of instances, the attributes of a class definition are identified. In turn, a class is well defined when its specific instances are accurately and reliably observed. Teachers who can observe specific behavioral instances and interpret them as being representative of behavior classes have achieved the first step toward implementing an effective management system.

Defining Behavioral Classes in Observable Terms The first and most general characteristic of classes requires that they be defined in observable terms. If they are not, teachers will be unable to accurately and reliably see their occurrence and, thus, be unable to deliver effectively the conditions and consequences required by a management system.

When classes are defined in observable or unambiguous terms, teachers can reliably agree upon the occurrences of instances. When this cannot be done, the definition contains one or more unobservable terms. In most cases, when a behavioral definition results in nonagreement, the problem comes from the term or terms having ambiguous behavioral referents. Consider the objective of having students "appreciate music." To what does it refer? What are its observable referents? The strategy is to translate the unobservable term into as many observable terms as possible. The question to ask is, "What do I see the students doing when they are _____?" In this case, the teacher asks, "What do I see the students doing when they are appreciating music?" For example, appreciating music might be considered an unobservable behavior, or at least one not defined clearly. However, translating "music appreciation" into a series of observable behaviors might begin by identifying the following student behaviors:

1. *Listening to music* at least one hour per day.
2. *Buying music records* at least once each month.
3. *Attending free musical performances* once each week.
4. *Verbally encouraging other students* who write, perform, or study music.
5. *Assisting in fund-raising efforts* to support musical performance and study.
6. *Participating in a "music club,"* in which members share musical experiences.

Each of the six behaviors is far more observable and could singularly or in combination define what the teacher means by "appreciating music." Whether everyone agrees with the definitions listed is not important in and of itself. Others are free to define the activity in terms clearly referencing other observable behaviors. But once a definition is selected, all should agree on the occurrence and nonoccurrence of class instances using the definition.

Often when eliminating unobservability, the translation procedure has to be reapplied. For example, consider the definition of "understanding math." What are some of the observable referents? What are the students doing when they are understanding math? Some possibilities follow:

1. Solving computation problems.
2. Solving word or story problems.
3. Applying mathematical operations to solve real life problems.

"Solving," "applying," "computation," and "story problems" are far less ambiguous than "understanding"; but these definitions' level of observability still makes the teacher's reliable application of conditions and consequences doubtful. In each of the three definitions, the strategy must be reapplied. For example, in the first, computation problems could involve addition, subtraction, multiplication, and/or others. Also, one could ask how the "solving" is to be performed: with or without pencil and paper? Further specification reduces the ambiguity of what the student is doing and the teacher observing.

The following is a list of some of the terms that have ambiguous referents and some related terms that reduce the ambiguity. Notice that several of the less ambiguous terms are in several of the unobservable classes. Such is the way of ambiguity.

1. To value: to choose
   to rate
   to select
2. To know: to define
   to memorize
   to repeat
   to list
3. To perceive: to define
   to identify
   to recognize

4. To grasp: to describe
   to explain
   to identify
5. To internalize: to memorize
   to repeat
   to recall
   to follow
6. To believe: to compare
   to apply
   to state

In using the analysis strategy for defining behavior, which is presented later in this chapter, the teacher will see that all elements of a behavioral objective contribute to reducing the ambiguity for behaviors of interest.

Qualitative and Quantitative Attributes of Behavioral Classes   The descriptive elements of a class definition are its qualitative and quantitative attributes or characteristics. *Quality* pertains to what the behavior is; what it is one expects to see. Identifying qualities of a general class such as reading, writing, experimenting, or high jumping increases the accuracy and reliability of the observation. *Quantity* pertains to the rate, speed, or amount of the qualities involved in the class definition. When all of the qualitative and quantitative terms and phrases are put together, a highly accurate and reliable observable definition of behavior emerges. "Appreciating music" represents an ambiguous or general class that was further clarified by six qualitative terms or phrases: listening to music, buying records, attending free musical performances, verbally encouraging other students, assisting in fund raising, and participating in a music club. The quantitative attributes were one hour per day, once each month, and once each week.

Describing "high jumping" would lead to clarifications involving (1) clearing the bar, (2) landing safely, and (3) using a "western" technique. The most relevant quality for high jumping is the height at which the bar is cleared. It could be 3'6'' or 7'0'', depending on the learner. As a rule, a general behavioral class can be clarified in two ways: (1) by the addition of detailed qualitative attributes and (2) by the addition of quantitative attributes.

The attributes or characteristics of behavior classes serve as "membership rules" for deciding whether a given instance of behavior is a member of a behavioral class. As the above examples suggest, quantitative and qualitative attributes of behavior provide as such rules. Within the high jump example, a specific jump (i.e., instance) would have to clear the bar at a height of 5'7'' and land safely before it could be classified as a "successful jump." Or if a jumper, on a specific attempt, exhibited the behavior sequence of approaching, jumping, and landing smoothly, then the "appropriate technique" class would have been exhibited. Thus, the behavioral attributes act as rules for interpreting whether instances are members of a class.

Social and Academic Behavior   As defined in Chapter 1, academic behavior is any class of behavior that results directly from instruction, while social behavior is any class of behavior required for the occurrence of planned instruction. With these two attributes serving as membership rules, most social behaviors in a classroom are easily distinguished from academic behaviors. For example, consider the following list of behaviors:

1. Solving a math problem.
2. Sitting quietly.
3. Raising a hand to answer a math question.
4. Answering questions on a social studies worksheet.
5. Turning in a social studies worksheet.
6. Reading a textbook assignment.

The academic behaviors are items 1, 4, and 6; the social behaviors are items 2, 3, and 5. In considering the class attributes, if hand raising were eliminated from item 3, the behavior of answering would be academic. Also, item 4 (working on a social studies worksheet) is an academic behavior, but item 5 (turning in a worksheet) is a social behavior dealing with the general procedures of the classroom.

Specifying the social behaviors necessary for academic instruction to occur is dependent upon the actual instructional conditions. For example, if a student is completing mathematics problems on an independent worksheet, the teacher knows that the student is performing the following social behaviors:

1. Sitting in one's seat.
2. Looking at one's paper.
3. Letting classmates work.
4. Following teacher instructions.

On the other hand, during a teacher presentation of science material to a class, appropriate student social behavior might include the following:

1. Sitting quietly in one's seat.
2. Looking at the teacher.
3. Answering questions when asked.
4. Letting others answer questions.
5. Raising one's hand for permission to speak.

Thus, for these two sets of examples, additional attributes of social behavior might be considered: one defining appropriate student behavior when "working independently," and a second defining appropriate student social behavior during "teacher lecture." (Procedures for analyzing student social behavior are discussed further in Chapter 4.)

PROCEDURES FOR BEHAVIORAL ANALYSIS AND CLASSIFICATION

Chapter 1 identified two tasks for classroom management: (1) establishing conditions and consequences for ensuring the presence of necessary social behaviors, and (2) providing conditions that "focus" students on the elements of the instructional activities and consequences that help increase the academic behaviors learned. In this regard, teachers must clearly define academic behavior so that contingent conditions and consequences can be delivered.

The procedures for defining social and academic behaviors within some broad domain, such as cooperation or reading, are extensive. Thus, for individual teachers to define relevant behaviors from "scratch" would be a formidable, if not an impossible, task. Fortunately, teachers can determine the behaviors related to classroom management using an existing curriculum as an aid. This section details procedures for defining academic behavior by analyzing the behavioral objectives (or similar specifications) of the curriculum. (Procedures for defining social behaviors are presented in Chapter 4.)

Analyzing Academic Behavioral Objectives Within curriculum programs, behavioral objectives come in many forms. But in all cases, unambiguously written objectives have three elements teachers need for classroom management. These elements are conditions, behavior, and standards. In order for objectives to be clearly written, all three components must be specified as follows:

Behavior. The behavior specified in an objective is ideally stated as a class in observable terms. The greater the ambiguity, the more teachers will have to interpret or clarify the behavior so that it can be easily observed in their classrooms. If clarity is not present, the teacher must objectively define and example the class. The examples of observable behavior in preceding sections provide relevant examples for this project. A few more examples follow:

1. Discriminate between similes and metaphors.
2. Compare two nonfiction selections.
3. Read a passage.
4. Write instructions.
5. Identify facts that support a conclusion.
6. Run the 100-yard dash.

But even these definitions of behavior classes are not sufficient to observe behavior to the degree required. The more complete picture is provided by conditions and standards that represent further quantitative and qualitative attributes of the behavior class.

Conditions. The conditions of an objective provide the context in which the behavior takes place: the time or place the behavior is to occur, and the type of equipment, or aid, to be used or *not* used. Some examples of conditions follow:

1. Given a list of references . . .
2. Without using any references . . .
3. With only pencil and paper . . .
4. Given a story problem of the following form . . .
5. Without the use of a calculator . . .
6. On a standard sized (25′ × 25′) practice mat . . .
7. Without the aid of a light meter or range finder . . .
8. At night on roads without streetlights . . .

Linking the above behaviors with conditions makes it easy to discern the extent to which conditions clarify behavior. The conditions in the following examples are in italics.

1. *Given a list of similes and metaphors,* the student will discriminate between them.
2. *In class and without reference aids,* the student will compare two *short (300 words or less)* nonfiction selections.
3. *Given a passage containing words with the same phonetic makeup as those taught in class,* the student will read the passage.
4. *Given a household product,* the student will write instructions for its use.
5. *Given an argument with an underlined conclusion,* the student will identify the facts that support the conclusion.
6. *Given a student without previous track experience,* the student will run the hundred-yard dash.

These partial objectives are written primarily in a "standard form" with the conditions specified first. Example 2 deviates from this form by inserting the length limit of the selection or passage in the middle of the behavior, but clarity is not lost. The fourth example clarifies the behavior a little by adding "for its use." The phrase could be linked to the conditions, but it would be awkward. Lastly, the sixth example sets conditions by specifying what the learner cannot have—"previous track experience." The reason for this type of condition will become clear in the section on standards.

Not only do conditions clarify behavior, but changes in conditions alter the complexity of behavior. In example 2, the "comparing" behavior becomes less "independent" if the student performs the comparison with "reference aids in the library," or more complex if the "short" passage is exchanged for a "book." In example 5 the lack of an "underlined conclusion" would require the student to do things differently. And, in example 6, a very different outcome would be expected if the runner had "two or more years of high school track experience."

Standards. The standards of an objective specify the criteria by which any behavioral instance is judged adequate or acceptable. The qualities and quantities specified in the preceding sections on behavior classes readily apply to objectives. The following standards illustrate quantitative and/or qualitative attributes of behavior:

1. With three or less errors.
2. To the criteria specified in the department training manual (see pages 34 and 35 of the manual).
3. Within plus or minus two-tenths of an inch.
4. So that another student can perform the task as specified by the manufacturer.
5. Within two minutes and in the sequence outlined in the class text.
6. Nine out of ten completed so they can be interchangeable with any standard model.
7. So that no injury results.

Even without indicating the behavior, the above standards specify meaningful attributes. Example 1 is quantitative. Example 2 could be either quantitative or qualitative depending on the criteria specified in the manual. Example 3 concerns the quantity of accuracy. Example 4 has a standard with possible quantitative and qualitative attributes (depending on the manufacturer's criteria). Example 5 provides two quantitative attributes. Example 6 has the qualitative attribute "interchangeable" and the quantitative attribute "Nine out of ten." Example 7 has the qualitative attribute "injury," and the quantitative attribute "no."

Adding standards to the partial objectives presented earlier shows how standards clarify behavior. The standards are underlined:

1. Given a list of similes and metaphors, the student will discriminate between them <u>in nine out of ten cases</u>.
2. In class and without reference aids, the student will compare two short (300 words or less) nonfiction selections <u>using the five comparative criteria listed in the course text</u>.
3. Given a 200-word passage containing words with the phonetic makeup of those taught in class, the student will read the passage <u>in one minute and thirty seconds with less than five errors</u>.
4. Given a household product, the student will write instructions for its use <u>so that an individual unfamiliar with that class of product can use it with the results specified possible by the manufacturer</u>.
5. Given an argument with an underlined conclusion, the student will identify the facts that support the conclusion <u>with 90 percent of the facts being identified eight out of ten times</u>.
6. Given a student without previous track experience, the student will run the hundred-yard dash <u>with a 20-percent decrease in time by the end of the semester</u>.

A small amount of ambiguity remains in each objective. However, enough clarity exists so that students' behavior can be accurately and reliably rewarded or corrected.

Like conditions, changes in standards modify the complexity of behavior. In example 2 of the completed objectives, expanding the five criteria to ten would greatly complicate the behavior. In example 3, lowering the time to one minute and the errors to two would require the student to decode the passage with greater quickness. Thus, reading behavior would appear much "smoother," at which point qualitative differences begin to enter into a description of the behavior. In example 6, a change to 30-percent improvement could require the use of some different running techniques, with rewards or corrections being delivered only if such techniques were or were not exhibited.

When analyzing a set of behavioral objectives specified for subject area and grade, teachers must look for all three components of objectives to obtain a clear specification of what the behavior is and what it will look like in the context of the classroom. If ambiguity exists, the teacher must clarify. Only then can observation take place and the appropriate consequences be delivered without error.

THE OBSERVATION OF BEHAVIOR

Once behavior has been analyzed and defined by the teacher, the next step is to build conditions and consequences which surround, support, and reward the behavior. The following chapters show how this is done. But the teacher also needs to see the behaviors of interest in the classroom, not just on paper. The surprising thing is that once the teacher spends time analyzing academic behaviors, the skill of seeing behavior in the classroom requires only continuously scanning the classroom and listening to what is going on as instruction is being delivered. There is no need for timers or any other type of signaling device. One helpful skill for teachers is to practice the scanning without the students, while going through teaching activities as if the students were there. This activity is introduced in the practice exercises that follow.

AN ANALYSIS ROUTINE
FOR ACADEMIC BEHAVIOR

The purpose of an analysis routine is to assist the teacher in defining the academic behaviors to which the management procedures throughout this text are applied. The steps of the routine follow:

1. *Identify the major classes of behavior in the curriculum* (e.g., reading, chemistry, mathematics).
2. *Within the curriculum class, identify the grade level at which teaching is to occur.* This makes the number of objectives manageable.
3. *Identify for each objective in the curriculum:*
   a. *The behavior*—remember to define it in unambiguous terms if necessary.
   b. *The conditions under which the behavior occurs*—it should provide further qualitative and/or quantitative attributes.
   c. *The standard of acceptable performance*—this should also provide further qualitative and quantitative attributes.
4. *Rate the observability of the objective by asking, Can the behavior defined this way be reliably and easily observed?* If the answer is yes, then the objective is unambiguous and appropriate to the teacher's management needs.

Once teachers have defined a large portion of the objectives of interest, the condition and consequence procedures specified in Chapters 3 through 6 can be learned and implemented with success. The practice activities will provide help in clarifying objectives that may exist in a curriculum.

PRACTICE ACTIVITIES

1. Seeing behavior (pp. 30, 31)
   1.1 Generate examples for discussion.
   List five instances of classroom behavior. Ask "How would I describe the behavior I see if I were taking a picture of it?" Specify the setting for each behavior instance.
   1.2 Visit a school classroom. Describe your observations for group discussion.
   List five instances of behavior as they occur. Describe each in terms of what someone would see if they were looking at a picture of it. Specify the setting for each.

2. Behavior attributes (p. 33)
   2.1 Generate examples for group discussion: Think of behavior attributes as characteristics that could stay the same or change. For quantity attributes, ask "How could behavior change in terms of amount, frequency, probability, rate, or duration?" For quality attributes, ask "How could behavior characteristics change in ways that could have been seen across a series of pictures?"
   a. For the five examples of behavior in 1.1, list a quantity attribute for each. Ask "In what way could the behavior change in terms of frequency?"
   b. For each example, specify the setting, then illustrate the quantity attribute of the behavior changing across time.
   c. For each example, list a quality attribute of behavior, Ask "In what way could the behavior change in terms of characteristics that could be seen in a series of pictures."
   d. For each example, specify the setting, then illustrate the quality attribute of the behavior changing across time.
   2.2 Visit a school classroom. In the items below, describe your observations for group discussion.
   a. List five student behaviors, specifying the setting for each. Then, for each behavior, describe a quantity and quality attribute.
   b. Select one of the examples above. Observe the behavior across a period of time. Describe how the behavior fluctuates naturally across time regarding quantity and quality attributes.
   c. List five inappropriate student behaviors in the setting. Describe in terms of quantity or quality attributes how the behavior must change to become appropriate.

3. Behavior classes: observable versus unobservable behaviors (pp. 30, 31)
   3.1 Generate examples for group discussion. List an example of a poorly defined or ambiguous behavior (e.g., music appreciation, being careful, being thoughtful, being happy), then follow the procedure below to clarify it as an observable behavior:
   a. List a variety of typical settings in which the behavior would occur. Ask "Where would I have to go to see this behavior occur?"

    b. For each setting, list a specific instance of any observable behavior that would show the ambiguous behavior was occurring. Ask "What would I see to tell me the behavior is occurring?"

    c. For each setting, list a specific instance of any observable behavior that would show the ambiguous behavior was not occurring. Ask, "What would I see to tell me the behavior was not occurring?"

    d. Add any important specific behaviors and/or settings that have been left out.

    e. Test each specific behavior listed as follows: Ask "Would the presence of this observable behavior tell me that the ambiguous behavior occurs, and will the absence of this observable behavior tell me that the ambiguous behavior did not occur?"

3.2 Visit a school classroom. For each item below, describe your observations for group discussion.

    a. Name an ambiguous behavior (e.g., cooperation) that would occur repeatedly in a classroom setting across a group of students. Then list all specific occurrences of the behavior in the setting for a specified time.

    b. Specify a student behavior that would occur repeatedly in different classroom settings for similar students. Then list specific occurrences of the behavior across settings.

4. Defining classes and instances (pp. 30, 31, 33)

4.1 Generate examples for group discussion.

    a. Specify the name of a behavior class. List a series of specific instances representative of the behavior class. Try to make the instances as different as possible.

    b. Specify a description of the behavior class that does the following: tells other individuals what attributes of behavior they should pay attention to in order to decide whether an instance is or is not a member of the class. Use quantity and/or quality attributes as needed.

    c. List a series of specific noninstances (i.e., inappropriate instances) that are as close as possible to the behavior class. Make sure the attributes in the behavior class description can distinguish instances from noninstances.

    d. Try out your class definition by seeing if another person can use it to distinguish positive instances from noninstances. Then see if the other person can generate five instances of the behavior class by following your definition.

4.2 Visit a school classroom. In the items below, describe your observations for group discussion.

    a. Observe instances of a behavior class in a regular school classroom. Construct a definition of the behavior class in terms of quantity and quality attributes, as appropriate.

    b. State your definition to another observer. See to what extent you agree that instances of the behavior class occur when you both observe the same classroom behavior.

5. Distinguishing social and academic behaviors (p. 34)
   5.1 Generate examples for group discussion.
       a. List five examples of student academic behavior classes. Specify the setting for each.
       b. For each example, list two student social behaviors required for the academic behavior to occur.
       c. For the series of five examples, list two student social behaviors that would be required for *all* of the academic examples.
   5.2 Visit a school classroom.
       a. Within a given classroom setting, list one or more student academic behaviors.
       b. For the academic behaviors considered together, list all major student social behaviors that are required.
       c. Construct a behavior class definition for each of the social behaviors, using quantity and quality attributes of behavior.

6. Analyzing academic behavioral objectives (p. 35)
   6.1 Generate examples for group discussion.
       a. Obtain a curriculum manual or teacher guide to instructional materials in five different curriculum areas. Select an informally stated behavioral goal in each area.
       b. Specify a formal behavioral objective for each "goal," including observable behavior, conditions, and standards. The behavior specification can emphasize quantity and quality attributes, as appropriate.
   6.2 Visit a school classroom. Describe your observations for group discussion.
       a. Identify a behavioral goal that is the intended achievement outcome for instruction within a given classroom setting.
       b. Specify a formal behavioral objective for the goal, including behavior, conditions, and standards.
       c. Observe student performance and informally estimate the percentage of students who have mastered the objective.

REFERENCES

The historical antecedents for this chapter rest on two distinct sets of research. The first set provides the foundation for analysis of behavior via the terms "classes" and "instances." Although B. F. Skinner first defined these terms in the early 1930s, the references put them in the context of research and classroom management.

Ferster, C. B., & Culbertson, S. *Behavior Principles,* 3rd. ed. Englewood Cliffs, N. J.: Prentice-Hall, 1982.

Millenson, J. R., & Leslie, J. C. *Principles of Behavioral Analysis,* 2nd ed. New York: Macmillan, 1979.

Skinner, B. F. *The Technology of Teaching*. New York: Appleton-Century-Crofts, 1968.

White, O. R., & Haring, N. G. *Exceptional Teaching*. Columbus, Ohio: Merrill, 1976.

Robert Mager contributed the founding effort to the chapter's second major historical antecedent, the behavioral objective. In the early 1960s, he identified, modeled, and showed the educational community the importance of behavioral objectives. These objectives' place in education has continually expanded, as an examination of the following references will indicate.

Barker, R. L., & Schutz, R. E. *Instructional Product Development*. New York: Van Nostrand, 1971.

Davis, R. H., Alexander, L. T., & Yelon, S. L. *Learning Systems Design*. New York: McGraw-Hill, 1974.

Gagné, R. M. *The Conditions of Learning,* 3rd ed. New York: Holt, Rinehart, and Winston, 1977.

Krathwohl, D. R., Bloom, B. S., & Masia, B. B. *Taxonomy of Educational Objectives. Handbook II: Affective Domain*. New York: McKay, 1964.

Mager, R. F. *Preparing Instructional Objectives,* 2nd ed. Belmont, Calif.: Fearon, 1975.

CHAPTER THREE

DESCRIPTIVE REWARD STATEMENTS

This chapter develops teacher skills in building and presenting verbal reward statements. As a management technique for teachers, reward statements are positive consequences readily available for changing student behavior. As consequences for students, they describe important social and academic behaviors and focus student attention upon other relevant present and/or future consequences resulting from the behavior. Because consequences determine future occurrences of student behavior, skills in properly using verbal reward statements are essential elements of any successful classroom management system.

THE FUNCTION OF VERBAL REWARD STATEMENTS

The following three principles describe the function of verbal reward statements in changing student behavior.

1. The occurrence of an appropriate instance (e.g., condition-behavior match) provides an opportunity for delivering a reward statement.
2. Delivering a reward statement increases the future probability of the represented class of behavior.
3. Delivering a reward statement increases the future probability of the represented class of condition statements setting the occasion for the referenced class of behavior.

The first principle is one of technology or application. It specifies the contingent use of a reward consequence: only when an instance of behavior matches the conditions. The second and third are principles of behavior. They indicate the effect of using the reward consequence upon any condition-behavior pair. Such use increases the probability (chance) of the class of behavior of which the instance of behavior was a member; it also increases the probability that future occurrences of an instance of the class of conditions will set the occasion for (evoke or bring forth) an instance of the behavioral class exhibited. The third principle indicates a direct link (relationship) between the reward consequence and the conditions. The combined three principles ensure the increase of behavior in the context of matching conditions. If the teacher applies reward consequences to condition-behavior nonmatches, the result would increase the probability of the conditions setting the occasion for inappropriate or nonmatching behavior. Thus, we see the reason for the principle of technology, which stresses the necessity for a condition-behavior match before the delivery of a reward consequence. The following examples illustrate the elaborate forms of reward statement consequences considered in this chapter:

STUDENT: (*John reads a difficult passage with only one error and has seldom done so.*)

TEACHER: Your reading keeps improving, John, you read all the hard vocabulary words correctly. I'm proud of you. Trying so hard has really paid off.

STUDENT: (*Zelda finishes all the worksheet problems on time.*)

TEACHER: Zelda, this is the first time you have gotten three of the four worksheets done on time for a whole week. This is the best week you have had for turning in work. I bet you feel good. I knew you could do it.

When presented contingent upon a condition-behavior match, these verbal reward statements increase appropriate behavior within established classroom conditions. To have a cumulative effect across time, the procedures for building reward statements must be followed to ensure that crucial features of student behavior and behavior change are referenced consistently. The illustrations focus student attention upon important behavioral changes across time. In John's case, the teacher notes that the student has continued to improve in reading, has performed well on hard words, and has succeeded by trying hard. The latter is a self-management behavior on which the other two student performances are historically dependent. For Zelda, the teacher points out that the student has achieved a new level of successful performance, the student should feel good about her own accomplishment, and the teacher believed the student could work hard. This chapter presents an analysis of verbal reward statements and procedures to ensure that all the necessary statement elements are present during delivery.

TYPES OF REWARD CONSEQUENCES

Building and presenting reward statements in the classroom requires a broad view of what behavior consequences—both verbal and nonverbal—are. In general, consequences are changes following behavior that are either positive or negative to an individual. Positive changes are generally considered reward consequences; negative changes are often considered corrective consequences (although some forms are considered punishers). It is necessary to remember that positive consequences for one student are sometimes not positive for another. This section examines three distinct forms of change which can follow any instance of behavior.

Sensations, or Emotional Changes Sensations are the physiological changes individuals experience as a result of behavior. "Good feelings," the "wow" of a back flip, the "exhilaration" of a long walk, and the "fear" when confronting a bear are all emotional reactions to changes that occur as a result of behavior. Such individual reactions occur continuously, but some are more apparent than others. While describing such individual changes with precision is very difficult, they are generally easily labeled as positive or negative feelings which individuals want to repeat or to avoid.

A Newly Structured World Another result of behavior is to create environmental changes (consequences) that add new elements to the individual's world or remove old ones. Moving lumber and pounding nails in a planned fashion provide a new house. Moving earth and planting a seed yields a flower. Writing about an event produces a story. And a student's perfect paper promotes a teacher's smile. Each of these actions results in a positive environmental consequence. But some environmental changes are negative. Drunken driving results in another's death, and the slip of a knife in a cut finger. But, whether positive or negative, all the above cases produce a newly structured world. In real life, some environmental changes are more obvious and/or rewarding than others. In the classroom, teachers' verbal statements are rewarding consequences that *amplify* positive environmental changes occurring because of student behavior.

Access to Different Events or Activities Often behaviors allow access to events or activities which provide an environment in which an individual behaves differently. Such access-allowing behaviors are changed by the new activities they allow. When the new activities are positive, the behaviors required for gaining such access are strengthened. Some possible examples include raking a lawn to obtain a bicycle ride, handing in homework to obtain extra free time, shopping to eat dinner, and being nice to others in order to be invited to take part in enjoyable social activities.

All three classes of reward consequences are or become closely related. For example, students often initially complete academic tasks in order to gain access to preferred activities. However, as academic behavior is rewarded by access to other events, the academic behavior itself becomes additionally reinforcing. The academic products (e.g., completed worksheet, finished drawing), as new changes in the world, and the individual's emotional reactions are associated with both academic behaviors and the activities they allow.

In addition, one or all of these three consequences can increase or maintain student behavior at any time. For example, writing a story can produce emotional changes during its production, the story's completion implies a restructured world which produces positive emotional changes, and the publication of the story allows access to new events that produce positive affective consequences (e.g., giving a lecture or talk). Identifying the specific forms of natural consequences that increase appropriate classroom behavior and focusing student attention on them via reward statements is a major skill of classroom management.

THE ELEMENTS OF COMPLETE REWARD STATEMENTS

A complete or ideal reward statement consists of three elements describing (1) appropriate behavior, (2) behavior change over time, and (3) consequences of behavior. Systematic use of all three elements with all students is an essential part of classroom management, even though teachers cannot expect to use all three elements in every reward statement they make. For effective classroom use, teachers must practice building and using complete reward statements. The outcome of building and using verbal reward statements is one of teaching's most "creative" activities and allows the establishment of a naturally positive classroom environment.

Describing Appropriate Behavior   The description of appropriate behavior mirrors the analysis presented in Chapter 2 by referencing an observable class of behavior. But referencing a large class does not provide the necessary descriptive detail. For example, reading, drawing, writing, experimenting, working with others, or bringing materials are all large inclusive classes of social or academic behavior. None of them focus the student on what is correct or appropriate about the behavior. The specification of relevant quantitative and/or qualitative attributes forms a descriptive class, which focuses on the exact behavior that the teacher would like repeated. For example, the student could be reading accurately, drawing with complementary colors, writing concisely, experimenting according to safety procedures, sharing materials with Sam, or bringing required texts to class. Each of these describes for the student what is correct and what is to be repeated. The following series of examples and nonexamples (i.e., inappropriate statements) clarify how verbal statements describe an observable class of behavior with relevant quantitative and qualitative attributes identified.

The easiest statements to deliver to students describe only a single behavior and do not require the teacher to consider its relationship to other behaviors (see Chapter 7). A number of important considerations apply to describing even a single behavior. Consider the following example:

> **Examples:** "John, you _read those words rapidly._"

"Reading those words" is the observable behavior, and "reading" is the most inclusive behavior class. The term "rapid" is an added description of behavior quantity and identifies the behavior subclass "rapid reading" for the teacher to reward. In providing such detailed information, the statement tells John what is correct about his reading performance.

> **Nonexample:** "John, you're a _wonderful student._"

This is not a satisfactory behavioral description because "wonderful" does not communicate a specific behavior. To do so, the teacher would have to describe the specific behavior and behavior class being referenced. In fact, the term "wonderful" expresses the teacher's feelings toward the student. Thus, this statement expresses teacher approval, but is not a detailed behavioral description.

> **Example:** "You all have my congratulations for _finishing your worksheets on time._"

"Finishing a worksheet" is an observable academic class of behavior. In addition, the quality "on time" defines a subclass of finishing the worksheet which provides additional information for the students. Thus, the behaviors being congratulated by the teacher are clearly described for the students.

> **Nonexample** "Everyone, that was an _excellent workbook session._"

This is a nonexample because no specific student behavior is described. Rather, students are being informed that something was "excellent" during the workbook session. Rather than describing behavior, this statement identifies the activity and conveys the teacher's feelings about it.

Substituting an activity and consequence for an accurate behavioral description is a common form of reward error.

> ***Example:*** "I am impressed; this whole group *read with faultless expression*. Everyone's expression fit his part."

The behavior is clearly specified, with "oral reading" being the class of behavior. In the example, "faultless expression" qualifies the behavior and is, in turn, qualified by "Everyone's expression fit his part." Thus, student attention is focused upon the behavior subclass that is being rewarded: "fitting one's expression to the part."

Describing How Behavior Has Changed Over Time Most changes in classroom behavior are not instantaneous, but occur through a slow evolution. Thus, a teacher will come in contact with a behavior over a long period of time. During such long-term behavior change, the teacher needs to show students how they have changed or are changing. In doing so, the students' attention is focused on how their behavior has changed relative to themselves or others.

There are several basic ways teachers can express student behavior change over time. Some of those are:

1. The *first time* for the behavior (e.g., "This is the first time you have scored 90 percent in spelling.").
2. The *xth time* for the behavior (e.g., "This is the third time you have scored 90 percent in spelling.").
3. The *xth time in a row* (e.g., "This is the fourth time in a row you have scored 90 in spelling.").
4. *Improving more each time* (e.g., "You are getting more spelling words correct each day.").

Each of these expressions is tied to a changing quantitative or qualitative attribute of a class of behavior. As behavior changes across time, teachers describe the progression the students are going through. Frequent reference to these changes not only provides the student with a picture of how she or he is changing but also increases the probability that the behavior will continue to evolve. The following examples illustrate descriptions of behavior changes for social and academic behaviors.

> "Joan, your reading is *getting faster every day*. Your reading is now rapid."

"Getting faster each day" tells how the class of "reading faster" has changed across time. The term "rapid" further describes the behavior. In effect, the student has become a rapid reader by becoming a little faster each day.

"Everyone's work has been checked and there was not one error; *that is a first*. What accurate readers!"

In the above example, the teacher is telling the students that they have achieved errorless reading as a group for the first time. Chapters 4 and 5 will show how verbal condition statements can be used with this type of behavior change description to set the occasion for, or motivate, student behavior.

"Mary, you have tried seven problems in the first 10 minutes of seat-work; you are *doing more each day*. Keep it up!"

"Doing more each day" informs the student of progress that has been made. That the behavior class is "trying problems," rather than "working problems correctly," raises an important point: Teachers may have to qualify a great deal, but can always say some truthful positive thing to students.

"Vernander, it's great that you have had 10 correct problems on your worksheet for *three days in a row*."

"Three days in a row" represents a change over time. Used repeatedly as a continuing daily reflection of student performance, this form of behavior change can be combined with other verbal statements presented in this chapter to improve student performance.

In summary, the use of the change-over-time element in reward statements requires teachers to know what social and academic behaviors their students have been progressing toward. As indicated in Chapter 2, only an analysis of the curriculum will provide the extensive list of behavior classes necessary for effective management. With practice, teachers can construct change-of-behavior elements for reward statements to cover a wide range of student performance improvement.

Describing Consequences of the Behavior Each of the three forms of reward consequences—emotional reactions, access to different events or activities, and a newly structured world—can be related directly to students or to others (teachers, peers, parents). As a consequence of their behavior, students gain a new addition to their world, engage in a different activity, and experience a positive emotional change. In addition, others may experience similar types of consequences as a result of students' behavior. Thus, as a consequence of students' behavior, teachers, peers, or parents may gain a new addition to their world, be able to engage in a different activity, and experience emotional change. Altogether, these combinations provide six different forms across academic and social classes for describing behavior consequences—a large set of consequences for the teacher to describe. Examples of each, grouped on the basis of whether they relate to the student or others, follow.

    Consequences Related to the Student. The consequences can be related to single or multiple behaviors performed by the student. This chapter provides examples with a single behavior; Chapter 8 provides examples with multiple behaviors.

    "Martha, reading so clearly must really *make you feel good.*"

Here the teacher is inferring that the student's "good feeling" exists. Many private events are learned in this way. Even a very young student can recognize the emotional reactions that are part of learning once they have been described. This form of description should be used often with younger and older students.

    "Martha, reading so clearly has earned you *a chance to collect the books.*"

"Clear reading" describes the behavior consequence that is an opportunity for the student to collect books. Assuming that collecting books is a positive activity desired by the student, it serves as a reward consequence for clear reading. Paired with the reward consequence, the teacher's verbal statement describing the consequence becomes a powerful management tool.

    "Martha, this story has power; just look at how the verbs are working. Action is everywhere! *This will get you an A for the assignment.*"

The "A for the assignment" provides the student with a newly structured world as a consequence of her writing behavior. From the student's viewpoint, the A was not there until she completed her writing.

    Consequences Related to What the Student Does for Others. The following examples explicate the type of rewards that students can produce for others.

    "Valencia, your continued improvement in reading has *made me feel like a very effective teacher.*"

The student's improved reading has caused a positive emotional state for the teacher. The teacher's verbal statement to the student describes this effect. Such teacher approval is a powerful form of reward for student academic and social behavior.

    "Rendella, thank you for helping John find his paper; *that will allow him to go to recess on time.*"

Cooperative behavior by the student has produced access to a desired activity for a classmate. In general, consequences to other students are highly effective rewards. They occur often enough to be frequently described.

> "Nancy, *your parents should take a lot of pride* in the fact that you have completed all your assignments this week. They can see you are taking on more responsibility."

The teacher's description calls attention to the parents' possible emotional reaction to the student's performance. As with teacher approval, parental reactions prove to be powerful rewards.

> "William, your hard work in solving the mathematics puzzle *has won a surprise for everyone in the class.*"

The behavior of working hard has produced a newly structured world for all of William's classmates. The teacher's calling attention to this consequence would generally be a highly positive reward.

The consequences identified for use with older and younger students also differ. The best consequences for older students can include almost anything that is "reality based." But, for older students, elements that emphasize consequences for other students and focus on student behavior in the future are most effective. For younger students, the consequences in verbal statements should relate to the present more than to the future. Rather than ignore the future, teachers of younger students have to develop students' ability to delay consequences. The first step is to bring together the immediate and the distant consequences. Students in the middle grades and remedial students typically accept a mixture of the immediate and the distant. The two examples that follow illustrate different types of consequences in reward statements for older and younger students:

> "Harpo, if you keep getting 95s on your math homework, I would suggest *you go into accounting or actuarial work of some kind.*"

> "Harpo, another high scoring math paper that *gets you an A!* Keep getting these every day."

The first example is geared to the older student and the second to the younger one. The first is descriptive and considers the future consequences the behavior will allow the student to participate in. The second relates to a short-term consequence, the grade of A.

> "Kristina, you have control of this lathe; all of the parts turned are within tolerance. You have learned to operate the machine very quickly. *You have a knack for this type of work.*"

This example for older students describes the behavior and tells how the teacher knew that the behavior existed. The consequence suggests a career direction. The effect of the behavior upon the teacher is not addressed in this presentation.

> "Mabel, you have shown concern for others by coming to class on time; thus, *we can get started on time and continue without interruption.* You are doing that more and more often and *everyone appreciates it.*"

This example would be appropriate for any student—young, old, or remedial—who is having trouble performing the basic social behavior of coming to class on time. The first consequence points out that the student's behavior has made access to academic events a little easier, and the second delineates the emotional state the teacher and students have because of the behavior.

COMPLETE REWARD STATEMENTS

The three basic elements of reward statements can be combined by teachers to form complete reward statements. In dealing with students, teachers will find that complete reward statements are highly positive and very powerful reward consequences within the classroom. In effect, complete reward statements allow the influence of all three basic elements to affect student behavior simultaneously. A routine for building complete reward statements and practice exercises are provided at the end of this chapter. This section provides examples of complete reward statements for study. In the series of examples, each of the different elements is labeled as follows: (1) description of observable behavior—single underline; (2) change in behavior over time—double underline; (3) behavior consequence—dashed underline. In the following four examples, no distinction is made between behavior consequences that relate to the student and consequences that relate to others; many examples reference both.

> "Marc, this is the first day you have marked your workbook when directed. That helps earn an A for today and gives me pride in your accomplishment."

> "This is the third day in a row that the class has made less than six errors on the group reading. That should make us all proud. What a fine accomplishment."

> "This is a first, Costella; you have gotten every problem correct on your math worksheet. Your parents will be proud of you."

> "Sally, this is wonderful! Your experimental notebook shows that you followed all the experimental steps in breaking down the compound. Since you continue to do it consistently, you have the makings of an expert chemist."

While these examples only include the three basic elements presented earlier, their combined use in the classroom is quite dramatic. Some special points in the examples also call for comment. The first example illustrates the use of two types of consequences: First, "earn an A" represents a restructured world for the student, and then "gives me pride" is an emotional reaction by another (in this case, the teacher). The second example has some extra wording. The phrase "What a fine accomplishment" could be considered a consequence for the student. But, more important, the example clearly emphasizes the consequence "That should make us all proud" from the perspective of the teacher. The latter is clearly another emotional consequence for the teacher. The third example's description of behavior is both quantitative, "every problem," and qualitative, "correct." Together, these provide a valuable focus for student attention across time. Finally, the fourth example has a compound consequence. The first part, "this is wonderful," relates to the teacher, and the second part, "makings of an expert chemist," relates to the student and involves a restructuring of the student's world.

When analyzing or constructing complete reward statements, teachers may be unsure what function a particular part plays. Quite often it is functioning in more than one way. In practice, such functioning presents no problem. In fact, when teachers reach the point of seeing and explaining possible dual functioning, they have gained a clear grasp of reward statement content. However, in some cases, an emotional reaction by the teacher (e.g., "good thinking") may be erroneously substituted for an observable behavioral description of the student (e.g., "You answered these word problems quickly"). Thus, teachers must be certain that reward statements that include teacher approval also include an adequately described student behavior.

THE PARTIAL REWARD STATEMENT

Often, time constraints do not permit the delivery of complete reward statements. In fast-paced instruction, complete statements may be counterproductive. In such situations, the short or partial reward statement, containing one or two of the reward statement elements, can be used during the activity, lesson, or class. However, teachers must adhere to certain safeguards.

The element describing appropriate behavior has priority in the construction and use of partial reward statements. The primary reason is that the behavior description tells the student what to continue doing. Another is that the description of behavior helps the teacher to refer to behavior change over time, the element of second priority. The following examples simply describe behavior:

1. "Clear reading, John."
2. "That is the correct answer."
3. "Thanks for sitting quietly, Gloria."
4. "Everyone has met the reading criteria today."
5. "Sue, you are writing with clear, even strokes."
6. "Errorless spelling."
7. "You have divided the math problem correctly."

The one-word statements teachers use in most classrooms typically do not constitute reward statements. Words such as "yes," "fine," and "OK" usually only tell the student to stop or continue some unspecified behavior. These words specify conditions for future behavior, rather than serving as reward consequences. Other single-word statements such as "good," "great," "excellent," and "fantastic" are primarily emotional reactions by the teacher and, thus, are consequences of student behavior. While important, they are not considered descriptions. Since one-word statements almost always fail to describe behavior, they give the student no clear future path to follow.

DIRECTING REWARDS

The audience for reward statements consists of any individual or group present in the classroom. All statements in the above examples were directed toward individuals or groups within a classroom. Such groups could consist of a row of students, a reading group, a math table, a portion of the class in a special activity area, or a team. In practice, teachers divide a class of students in any fashion that allows a contingent reward statement to address the student or students behaving appropriately. The more ways that can be thought of, the greater the chance teachers have to deliver reward statements and maintain reward statement variety.

WHEN TO PRESENT REWARD STATEMENTS

As indicated, reward statements are delivered contingent upon a condition-behavior match. Beyond this rule, teachers must determine when to use them within the flow of behavior that takes place during classroom activities. The complete reward statement is used best to relate socially and instructionally important behaviors to the activities necessary for student growth. This use of reward statements requires the teacher's analyzing a set of objectives to determine the disparity between them and existing student skills (see Chapter 2). Any such unacquired skills are of social and instructional importance and need to be addressed. For example, if students have trouble keeping their eyes on their own paper or cannot finish their work on time, they should be rewarded with statements for performing such behaviors (see Chapter 12 for details of solving classroom problems). Additionally, teachers must be aware of any future behaviors of students that may require special attention (i.e., potential problems). Another use of reward statements is at the end of an activity period to review important student behaviors. In such cases, reward statements, including multiple behaviors, are often mentioned. At the end of an activity, a teacher might say in review:

> "Demian, not only did you *read without an error,* but you *completed your workbook on time* and *corrected it when asked.* You have begun to do these things more often in the last few weeks and I appreciate it."

The different classes of behavior (in italics) represent procedural steps which the student has followed. This verbal statement reviews the steps expected of the student, what he did, and how his following the steps of the procedure has changed over time. (Chapter 8 covers the form and use of multiple behavior reward statements.)

Partial reward statements can be used at almost any time during an activity, lesson, or subject. These statements are designed to keep instruction or independent work flowing, yet reward social and academic behavior effectively. For example, during independent work, teachers would not want to excessively interrupt students who are working hard on math problems. At the same time, some verbal rewards are needed to keep students working hard. To meet both requirements, teachers can deliver short reward statements as they observe students' work. For example, they might say, "Bob, your division problems are correct," or "I appreciate this row working hard to finish its problems." However, when teachers privately confer with students during independent work, complete reward statements are more effective.

During instructional activities that involve frequent student-teacher interaction, the partial reward statement is also useful. In these situations, teachers interject short reward statement for academic behavior whenever students respond to a question, or teachers tell students how their social behaviors are following the classroom rules. For example, a teacher might say, "Joan, your answer shows comprehension of the text," or "I appreciate everyone following rule 3." At the end of such instructional activities, a complete reward statement is highly effective as a review.

These guidelines for when to use complete or partial reward statements are important, but there are exceptions. For example, when students need powerful rewards, complete statements should be used if at all possible. Or short reward statements should be used to help pace instruction for remedial students who typically require both fast-paced instruction and frequent rewards. The most important rule overall for using reward statements is: *Whenever there is a condition-behavior match, a reward statement of some form should be given.*

In following this rule, teachers must first consider what knowledge students need about their behavior, its change, and consequences; then, teachers should include these elements in the reward statement that best fits the situation. Here are a few more examples that target important student behavior but use only one or two elements:

1. "Gilda, you are reading faster than ever."
2. "Thank you, everyone, for passing your papers quickly for workcheck."
3. "Let's all smile, you have once again completed your projects on time."
4. "Tanya, you cleaned up your art materials quickly."

The biggest problem in using complete or partial statements relevant to ongoing behavior is the considerable preparation needed for their quick and smooth presentation. Thus, structured practice with reward statements is of major importance. Practice is provided at the end of this chapter.

HOW TO PRESENT REWARD STATEMENTS

This chapter has outlined the elements that make reward statements an effective classroom management tool. However, using reward statements also requires teachers to master the social skills necessary for their effective presentation. As a starting point, all statements to students should be truthful and sincere. The elements in the verbal reward statement should directly reflect the teacher's belief in the importance of what the student has done, how the student has changed or is changing, and/or the behavior consequences the student has produced or will produce. In general, teachers should smile when they present statements. Initially, practice may be required in order to "reward with a smile"; however, most teachers will find that a smile is a natural part of delivering a verbal reward statement once appropriate student behavior has been associated with it. The verbal rewards should be presented in a natural tone of voice as a direct statement, loud enough to be clearly heard by the individual or group of students being addressed. Finally, teachers should maintain eye contact when presenting reward statements. In the case of a group reward, teacher eye contact can be maintained by scanning the group being addressed. A common teacher presentation error is to look away from a student while saying, "That was pretty good reading." Instead, the teacher should look at the student and say, "John, that was clearly read with expression." The latter example references the behavior that caught the teacher's attention.

In addition to the general presentation skills discussed, some social presentation styles are critically important in dealing with students of different ages. With older students, grades 8 through 12, teachers should be low keyed and descriptive when presenting reward statements. For most older students, overly enthusiastic expressions of how the teacher feels about the student's behavior (i.e., teacher approval) should be communicated individually out of the range of peers. This adjustment may also be required for socially and emotionally advanced younger students. The content of the reward statement is the same, except for the modification of the teacher's approval, which is more a matter of presentation than content. Thus, for older students, verbal rewards are more "reserved"; and warm, friendly contact, such as a pat or handshake, is also generally absent from older students. On the other hand, with younger students, especially those in grades kindergarten through 3, emotion and enthusiasm are as important as behavioral descriptions are for older students. Here, friendly social contact in the classroom is often present, with a hug and handshake helping to ensure student attention to statement content. Typically, the teacher smiles because the student does.

All the preceding rules of thumb can be broken, depending upon the individual students involved. To some degree, the style a teacher adopts is a personal preference within the bounds of it proving effective. In general, a reserved, descriptive manner is effective across all types of students. Thus, teachers should take a conservative approach with a new group of students. Later, when a teacher comes to know the students and has determined what they like or will accept, the delivery style can be changed to fit the situation. Also, the longer and more intensely students have been rewarded, the more they will accept variations in styles and, thus, be rewarded by the content of statements.

CONSISTENCY AND PERSISTENCE IN DELIVERING CONTINGENT REWARD STATEMENTS

Reward statements are presented contingent on a condition-behavior match. Previously, the text stressed that teachers must achieve consistency in using rewards accurately (i.e., deliver them contingently). But more than consistent accuracy in presenting contingent rewards is needed. Another element is teacher persistence in the continued presentation of contingent consequences. Teachers cannot only reward a behavior one, two, or three times. Rather, teachers must reward a behavior repeatedly on many occasions—sometimes over months—before reducing the reward frequency. Even then, rewards do not really stop. Rather, teachers become able to reward new behavior classes that include "old" subclasses. For example, consider students sitting in their seats doing math problems. At first, a teacher might have to reward sitting before being able to switch to rewarding the number of math problems completed. In effect, rewarding completed math problems also rewards the behaviors that the student uses to complete them correctly. Taking consistency and persistence together, an important classroom management principle is, *Teachers must be persistent and consistent in using contingent verbal reward statements.* Chapters 8 and 9 further outline how to be persistent and consistently contingent.

BUILDING AND DELIVERING REWARD STATEMENTS

The reward statement describes to students the important behaviors they have exhibited, how their behavior has changed over time, and the behavior's consequences. Delivering reward statements that make these features obvious to students requires teacher practice in building and using them. Such practice can be done anywhere. Teachers can practice generating statements while walking or driving to work or even sitting in front of the television. But it is important during the early stages of practice to write the statements down and check them against the statement-building routine presented below. As with most skills, extensive practice is necessary to present effective reward statements.

Reward Statement Building Routine To practice constructing reward statements, teachers should ask themselves the following building routine questions. After practice, the routine will be easily remembered.

1. *What activity is of immediate interest?* The answer gives the teacher part of the context in which to frame questions 3 through 5.
2. *To what individual or group should the statements be directed?* The answer provides the rest of the context from which to build statements. After building several statements, the teacher needs to see if there is a bias towards or away from some of the students.
3. *What class of behavior does the student perform that matches the conditions?* The answer is arrived at by examining the instances remembered. Further considerations include:
   a. *Is the behavior social or academic?*
   b. *What are the qualitative and quantitative attributes of the class as evidenced by the instances?* This answer facilitates thorough description.

4. *How has the class of behavior changed over time?* Considerations should include the following:
   a. *Have there been any qualitative changes in behavior?*
   b. *Have there been any quantitative changes in behavior?*
   c. *How often have the changes occurred?* Is it the first, *x*th, *x*th time in a row, most times ever, that the change has shown itself?
5. *What consequences could occur?* Considerations should include the following:
   a. *Are the consequences of the social or academic behavior related to emotional changes, access to activities, or a restructured world?*
   b. *Are the consequences related to the student(s) or others?*
   c. *Are the consequences in the immediate future or distant future?* This answer is related to the older and younger students.

In using the routine to build complete or partial reward statements, teachers will find that statements "flow" rather easily after several weeks. Further, their use will result in a classroom environment that is a warm and happy one both for students and teachers.

Reward Statement Delivery Checklist During practice and classroom presentation, careful consideration must be given to the delivery of reward statements. If practice and planning are not done, many statements—no matter how well structured—will fail to be effective. By considering and practicing statements in the context of the following questions, the teacher will gain the skills necessary to maximize the potential effectiveness of reward statements.

1. *Does the behavior match the conditions?* The reward statement is delivered contingent on a condition-behavior match.
2. *Does the statement or the teacher's presence unambiguously reference the group or individual the statement is intended for?*
3. *When would the statement be most effectively used?* Consider the following facets:
   a. *Is the behavior new or a problem?* If the answer is yes, the complete reward statement is appropriate.
   b. *Do the students have extensive social or academic skill deficits?* If the answer is yes, deliver reward statements at a high rate.
   c. *Is the statement to be presented at the start or the end of an activity?* If the answer is yes, the complete reward statement is appropriate.

    d. *Is the aim of the statement to keep the behavior occurring throughout the activity?* If the answer is yes, then the partial statement is appropriate.

4. *How would the statement be most effectively presented?* Again, many facets are present.

    a. *Is sincerity present?* Believing that the behaviors and consequences are important is essential.

    b. *Is the smile present?* Again, believing that the behaviors and consequences are important is essential.

    c. *Does the voice have enough volume and tonal qualities (nonmonotone)?* If so, the teacher has a higher chance of keeping student attention.

    d. *Is eye contact made during the statement's presentation?* This will ensure that the student attends to the statement's presentation.

    e. *Is the statement delivered quickly without redundancy or repetition of content?* If the answer is yes, there will be little interruption of instruction.

PRACTICE ACTIVITIES

1. Generating descriptive reward statements (pp. 47, 53)
   1.1 Identify elements of reward statements for delivery practice. Present examples for group critique and discussion.
   a. Select two examples of a complete reward statement from the text—one for social behavior and one for academic behavior.
   b. Use each example as a starting point in listing each of the following elements of reward statements for academic and for social behavior (modify the examples as necessary):
   (1) Behavior description (instance/class name, quantity/quality attributes)
   (2) Change in behavior (first time, xth time, improvement in quantity/quality attribute)
   (3) Consequence to student (emotional, newly structured world, access to activities)
   (4) Consequence to others—parents, teachers, peers (emotional, newly structured world, access to activities)
   c. Using the above, list an example of a partial reward statement for social and for academic behavior, including (in order) a behavior description, consequence to student, consequence to others. Write it out in a form you would say it.
   d. For each example, add a change-in-behavior (i.e., improvement) reference. Write the expanded statement in a form you would say it.
   1.2 Practice effective delivery of reward statements using specific examples and variants. Use a mirror, tape recorder, or other media aid to guide practice. Then have classmates critique final level of performance. (p. 60)
   a. Practice effective delivery of each statement in 1.1(a) to a hypothetical student. Maintain eye contact; smile; act sincere; have adequate vocal volume/intonation; give quick, relaxed presentation.
   b. Expand and practice each social and academic reward statement by varying each of the behavior change descriptions as follows (p. 49):
   (1) "First time."
   (2) "The xth time this week."
   (3) "Any improvement in a quality attribute."
   If necessary, write the three versions of each social reward statement and then the three versions of each academic reward statement. Practice effective relaxed delivery of the six statements in 30 seconds or less.
   c. Return to the original two complete reward statements 1.1(a). This time, vary the consequences to students so that each form of consequence is referenced in a statement in the following order (p. 50):
   (1) Emotional student consequence.
   (2) Newly structured world.

(3) Access to activities.

If necessary, write each expanded statement. Practice effective delivery until relaxed. Allow five seconds per statement.

d. Return to the original two complete reward statements 1.1(a). This time vary the consequences to others so that each different type of consequence is referenced in a statement in order (use peers, parents, or teachers, as desired) (p. 50):

(1) Emotional consequences to others.

(2) Newly structured world.

(3) Access to activities.

If necessary, write each expanded statement. Then practice effective delivery until relaxed.

1.3 Practice generating examples of complete reward statements. Then present examples for group critique and discussion. (pp. 53, 59)

a. List ten descriptions of behavior—five social behaviors and five academic behaviors. Try to make the behaviors as different as possible from each other.

b. Read through each behavior on the list, identifying an example of an attribute of the behavior that might change across time as the behavior improved. Read through the list again, identifying an example of a consequence to the student. Read through again and identify a possible consequence to others. This time, do not write any of these elements down.

c. Next, for each behavior on the list, orally generate a complete reward statement that includes the behavior description, a change in behavior, and a consequence to the student and to others. Practice delivering the ten statements effectively and unhurriedly.

d. Work through the list faster and faster, until all ten statements can be delivered effectively within 60 seconds. Don't worry about remembering each specific element, just concentrate on producing an example of the element in the standard order.

1.4 Practice variations in generating complete reward statements. Present examples for group critique and discussion.

a. Select one of the preceding examples. Then practice the following variations:

(1) Consider how the behavior could change across time for a given attribute. Generate a series of complete reward statements tracing the change in behavior. (p. 49)

(2) Repeat the statement, varying a reference to each of the three student consequences in a single statement. (p. 51)

(3) Repeat the statement, but vary a reference to each of three consequences to others. (p. 51)

b. Practice the variations for a single example from the list, then select a new example and repeat the process until you achieve a relaxed presentation.

1.5 Practice originality in generating complete reward statements. Present examples for group critique and discussion.

a. Select one of the preceding examples of a complete reward statement.

    b. See how many different ways you can phrase the statement, including all elements (e.g., reorder elements, paraphrase). Next delete one or more of the elements to see how many different examples of partial reward statements you can construct.

2. Delivering descriptive reward statements in school classrooms.

  2.1 Visit a school classroom. Identify condition-behavior matches for student *social behavior* and simulate delivery of reward statements. Try to look at the behavior, prepare a statement, then say the statement out loud or to yourself. Don't forget to add a referent for the group or individual performing the behavior. (p. 59)

    a. Identify an appropriate student social behavior occurring frequently in the classroom (e.g., listening). Scan the classroom regularly, noting which students are engaging in appropriate behavior.

    b. Imagine you are a teacher. Observe the students and, to yourself, present a partial reward statement to students behaving appropriately with the following elements: behavior description, consequences for the student (emotional, newly structured world, or access to activities). Try to "present" approximately four reward statements per minute. If possible, use a tape recorder in the rear of the room or behind a one-way glass.

    c. Achieve variety in presentation by using different consequences for students' elements and adding consequences to other statements.

    d. Add a change in behavior reference. Once complete reward statements can be delivered effectively, you are ready to work with students in a classroom.

  2.2 Identify condition-behavior matches for student *academic behavior*, and simulate delivery of reward statements. Try to look at the behavior, prepare a statement, then say the statement out loud or to yourself. Do not forget to add a referent for the group or individual performing the behavior.

    a. Identify an appropriate student academic behavior occurring frequently in the classroom (e.g., completing worksheets). Scan the classroom regularly, noting which students are engaging in appropriate behavior.

    b. Imagine you are a teacher. Observe the students and, to yourself, present a partial reward statement to students behaving appropriately with the following elements: behavior description, consequences for the student (emotional, newly structured world, or access to activities). Try to "present" approximately four reward statements per minute. If possible, use a tape recorder in the rear of the room or behind a one-way glass.

    c. Achieve variety in presentation by using different consequences for students' elements and adding consequences to others.

    d. Add a change in behavior reference. Once complete reward statements can be delivered effectively, you are ready to work with students in a classroom.

2.3 Deliver reward consequences to students in a controlled classroom setting. Try to have another individual rate your behavior on the checklist in the text and critique your performance.
    a. Arrange to work as a monitor for student seatwork in a regular classroom.
    b. Identify in advance classes of appropriate student social and academic behavior. Scan the classroom for student condition-behavior matches. Present complete or partial reward statements for student academic and social behavior. Always reference the student being reinforced. Vary reward statements across students and groups. Try to achieve a reward statement rate of 2–4 per minute.

2.4 Deliver reward consequences to students in a classroom setting. Try to have another individual rate your behavior on the checklist in the text and critique your performance.
    Make arrangements to take over a teacher's class for one half-hour. Identify in advance classes of appropriate social and academic behavior for the activities planned. Present reward statements to students at a rate of 2–4 per minute within the context of regular classroom activities.

REFERENCES

The terms "feedback," "praise," "social reward," "attention," and "reward statements" have all been used to describe teacher-delivered verbal consequences to students. The following references show the effect verbal consequences can have on student behavior. These references represent research that took place in the classroom and emphasize the use of verbal statements to change behavior. The positive effect of teacher attention on both social and academic classroom behavior is impressive.

Allen, K. E., Henke, L. B., Harris, F. R., Baer, D. M., & Reynolds, N. J. Control of hyperactivity by social reinforcement of attending behavior. *Journal of Educational Psychology,* 1967, *58,* 231–237.

Ayllon, T., & Roberts, M. D. Eliminating discipline problems by strengthening academic performance. *Journal of Applied Behavior Analysis,* 1974, *7,* 71–76.

Becker, W. C., Madsen, C. H., Arnold, C. R., & Thomas, D. R. The contingent use of teacher attention and praise in reducing classroom behavior problems. *Journal of Special Education,* 1967, *1,* 287–307.

Chadwick, B. A., & Day, R. C. Systematic reinforcement: Academic performance of under-achieving students. *Journal of Applied Behavior Analysis,* 1971, *4,* 311–319.

Clark, C. A., & Walberg, H. J. The influence of massive awards on reading achievement in potential urban dropouts. *American Educational Research Journal,* 1968, *5,* 305–310.

Ferritor, D. E., Buckholdt, D., Hamblin, R. L., & Smith, L. The noneffects of contingent reinforcement for attending behavior on work accomplishment. *Journal of Applied Behavior Analysis*, 1972, *5*, 7–17.

Goetz, E. M., Holmberg, M. C., & LeBlanc, J. M. Differential reinforcement of other behavior on noncontingent reinforcement as control procedures during the modification of a preschooler's compliance. *Journal of Applied Behavior Analysis*, 1975, *8*, 77–82.

Harris, F. B., Johnston, M. K., Kelley, C. S., & Wolf, M. Effects of positive social reinforcement on regressed crawling of a nursery school child. *Journal of Educational Psychology*, 1964, *1*, 145–153.

Hasazi, J. E., & Hasazi, S. E. Effects of teacher attention on digit-reversal behavior in an elementary school child. *Journal of Applied Behavior Analysis*, 1972, *5*, 157–162.

Rosenfeld, G. W. Some effects of reinforcement on achievement and behavior in a regular classroom. *Journal of Educational Psychology*, 1972, *63*, 189–193.

Smith, D. E. P., Brethower, D., & Cobot, R. Increasing task behavior in a language arts program by providing reinforcement. *Journal of Experimental Child Psychology*, 1969, *8*, 45–62.

Chapter 3 expands verbal consequence description by outlining their form and content. This expansion is based on research showing that teacher consequence behavior in the classroom is not naturally performed at a significant rate, and training teachers in this behavior is not the simplest of tasks. The following references provided the authors with direction.

Cooper, M. L., Thomson, C. L., & Baer, D. M. The experimental modification of teacher attending behavior. *Journal of Applied Behavior Analysis*, 1970, *3*, 153–157.

Cossairt, A., Hall, R. V., & Hopkins, B. L. The effects of experimenter's instructions, feedback, and praise on teacher praise and student attending behavior. *Journal of Applied Behavior Analysis*, 1973, *6*, 89–100.

Hall, R. V., Fox, R., Willard, D., Goldsmith, L., Emerson, M., Owen, M., Davis, F., & Porcia, E. The teacher as observer and experimenter in the modification of disputing and talking-out behaviors. *Journal of Applied Behavior Analysis*, 1971, *4*, 141–149.

Horton, G. O. Generalization of teacher behavior as a function of subject matter specific discrimination training. *Journal of Applied Behavior Analysis*, 1975, *8*, 311–319.

Kazdin, A. E., & Klock, J. The effect of nonverbal teacher approval on student attentive behavior. *Journal of Applied Behavior Analysis*, 1973, *6*, 643–654.

White, M. A. Natural rates of teacher approval and disapproval in the classroom. *Journal of Applied Behavior Analysis*, 1975, *8*, 367–372.

CHAPTER FOUR

CLASSROOM RULES AND ACTIVITIES

C lassroom rules clarify what student behaviors are appropriate for classroom activities. As a condition statement within classroom contingencies, rules have an integral role in facilitating condition-behavior matches. But, to be effective, rules must be adequately formulated and used. This chapter presents the requirements for establishing effective classroom rules.

THE FUNCTION OF RULES

Two principles describe the function of rules (condition statements):

1. Condition statements reference and precede an instance of an appropriate behavior class.
2. Delivering condition statements increases the present probability of occurrence of an instance of the referenced class.

The first is a principle of technology. It describes the ordering of three elements: (1) rules (as condition statements) always reference (describe) a behavior; (2) the referenced behavior always matches (is appropriate to) the rules; and (3) the rules must precede the behavior. Given this, the second principle predicts the outcome of delivering a rule: the increase in the present probability of an instance of the referenced behavior. Referencing inappropriate behavior (condition-behavior nonmatch) results in an increase in that behavior. Failing to reference appropriate behavior results in a decrease of that behavior. Such results are not the goals of an effective technology. From the point of view of the classroom, rules set the occasion for the student social behavior necessary for effective academic instruction to occur. Thus, rules facilitate student condition-behavior matches.

CLASSROOM ACTIVITIES

All subject areas or classes—whether language arts, mathematics, social studies, art, science, or physical education—consist of a *cycle* of classroom events. Each event within that cycle is called an *activity*. The activities, for example, in an art class might be a teacher demonstration, distribution of materials, independent work, teacher evaluation, and cleanup. A cycle, in most cases, is complete when all its activities have been performed. A cycle may take one day or a week. For example, a teacher demonstration may occur about twice a week, and students' independent work may occur daily. When all activities have been performed, the activity cycle is complete. This set of activities represents the first level of conditions established by the teacher in the classroom setting. It provides an operational structure or general set of conditions for students and teachers. (How activities are patterned within a cycle is covered in Chapter 11.)

Rules define the social behaviors necessary for each activity. As the behaviors specified by the rules are performed and repeatedly reinforced by the teacher and other students, they become linked with the regular cycle of classroom activities. Once this connection occurs, the instructional program can be presented as effectively as teacher presentation skills and the program's design allow. The outcome is no inappropriate student behavior interfering with the presentation of instruction.

FORMULATING RULES

In formulating effective classroom rules, five steps are followed:

Define the Class Activities Because rules are relative to classroom activities, defining such activities is the first step in formulating rules. To determine the activities for a class, teachers should list all the events in which teachers and/or students engage. For early elementary, self-contained classrooms, the list of activities is long because several subject areas are covered. But the cycle of the events is short: All events are repeated daily. For most subject-specific classes, especially the sciences, there is a short list of activities which can have various patterns of presentation. These cycles can cover many days and are often defined by some area or unit of subject matter. To establish classroom rules, teachers must identify only the different activities in a cycle, *not* the pattern of the activities. (Chapter 11 outlines considerations in patterning the activities of a cycle by considering what activities should precede or follow other activities.) If teachers group students, it is necessary to consider the activity only once since the rules for each group are essentially identical. (How groups are managed in relation to activities and rules is discussed later in this chapter.)

In listing activities, special individual events such as sharpening a pencil, going to the bathroom, or asking for help should not be included. These are done by individuals, not the class or some instructional group. Special academic events (e.g., a pop quiz or once-a-week spelling test) that happen outside the cycle should be noted, but not listed with the main cycle events. Activities that could be considered as part of a regular cycle are shown in the following examples:

Physical education—gym

1. Dressing
2. Class roll call
3. Group warmup (calisthenics)
4. Sport instruction
5. Sport or game practice
6. Showers and dressing

On some days one or two gym activities will be changed or replaced by a physical fitness exam. The rules that evolve from the listed activities would cover the necessary social behavior for these special academic events. Clear sets of condition statements (see Chapter 5) are needed to outline the procedures for these events.

Mathematics

1. Turning in homework
2. Teacher presentation (review and new materials)
3. Individual seatwork (workbook)
4. Seatwork (workbook) check

Although turning in math homework is listed, assigning homework is not. The homework may be assigned at the end of the teacher presentation or following the seatwork check. A math test may occur once a week and could take the place of the teacher presentation and the individual seatwork. Again, the rules for individual seatwork would cover the social behaviors required of the students' math tests.

Language arts—sixth grade

1. Teacher language presentation
2. Teacher spelling presentation

3. Teacher reading presentation
4. Observing/remediating student independent work
5. Work check
6. Cleanup

The teacher may or may not teach the language or reading in groups, but the multiple use of the same activity for different groups would not require that the activity be changed. Therefore, the same list of rules would be used. Special activities may include spelling tests, movies, assemblies, or field trips. The last three activities may require a special set of rules because of the diversity of social behaviors involved.

Self-contained class—first grade

1. Opening activity
2. Teacher reading presentation
3. Reading worksheet—independent
4. Language presentation
5. Language worksheet—independent
6. Recess
7. Teacher math presentation
8. Math worksheet—independent
9. Lunch
10. Penmanship
11. Spelling
12. Science/social studies
13. Closing activity

In the first grade, students are learning as much about social behavior as they are about academic behavior. Thus, it is important to include lunch, recess, an opening activity, and a closing activity. The latter two are used to review rules, daily activities, and student social and academic accomplishments. Rules should be defined for each of these areas.

Chemistry—eleventh grade

1. Teacher presentation (lecture)
2. Short worksheet
3. Workcheck of worksheet
4. Laboratory
5. Unit examination (full class period)

The cycle for this set of chemistry activities may cover one or two weeks, depending on the topic. The teacher may continuously present lectures for the whole unit's material, with daily short worksheets covering the previous day's material followed by a workcheck to give students feedback about their performance. The laboratories could be given several times throughout the unit or could be given as a block of experiments just before the unit exam. The important point is that the activities can be performed in different patterns within a cycle. No matter what pattern is chosen, the rules and social behaviors for the activities remain the same.

Determine the Social Behaviors Necessary for Activities   In identifying social behaviors, teachers must ask what students do to accomplish the activity. A list of appropriate social behaviors should follow. At the same time, teachers should ask what students do that is inappropriate for the activity. Considering inappropriate behaviors often directs teachers to important socially appropriate behaviors. Here are some examples of appropriate behaviors for the preceding activities:

Game practice—physical education

1. Playing the position assigned
2. Accepting player substitution
3. Substituting when asked
4. Accepting mistakes of others
5. Accepting one's own mistakes
6. Speaking appropriately to others

Speaking appropriately to others is a social behavior that is often overlooked.

Group reading—language arts

1. Sitting in seat
2. Following along (keeping place)
3. Accepting turn to read
4. Listening to others
5. Accepting the mistakes of others
6. Accepting one's own mistakes

The last two items, (accepting the mistakes of others and accepting one's own mistakes) have implications for the development of strong attitudes and self-concepts.

Teacher presentation—mathematics

1. Sitting in seat
2. Looking at the board (or teacher)
3. Answering questions when asked
4. Listening to others' answers
5. Accepting mistakes by others

Listening to others answer is also a social behavior that is often ignored.

Individual seatwork—mathematics

1. Sitting in seat
2. Looking at own work
3. Finishing seatwork
4. Turning in seatwork

The social behavior of looking at one's own work might not be considered without thinking about some of the inappropriate behaviors that often occur during an individual academic activity.

Seatwork check—mathematics

1. Exchanging work as directed
2. Checking work accurately
3. Marking grade or points as directed
4. Returning work as directed
5. Commenting positively about others' grades
6. Accepting the grade given

For any of these examples, other excellent alternatives exist. The important point is to define social behaviors sufficiently so that (1) the students know what to do and (2) the teacher knows what to correct and reward. More will be said about correcting and rewarding in the section on using examples and nonexamples. (Chapters 3, 6, and 8 cover rewards and corrections in detail.)

Determine Which Activities Need a List of Rules Four guidelines help to determine if an activity needs a set of rules:

1. The activity has a long list of necessary social behaviors.
2. The activity requires a long time to do (10 minutes or more).
3. The general classroom rules (discussed below) do not cover the majority of social behaviors.
4. The activity is, or has been, associated with social behavior problems.

Any one of these four criteria is sufficient for developing a set of activity rules. For example, the preceding activities for the mathematics subject area do not all need separate sets of rules. Turning in homework does not require a separate set of rules. For turning in homework, students may just be presented with the procedure (i.e., putting the homework in a box marked "homework" at the beginning of each period).

Sometimes a subject area like language arts may contain similar activities. For example, teacher presentation activities in reading, grammar, and spelling typically require the same student social behaviors. Therefore, rather than rules being required for each, all three areas would have the same set of "teacher presentation" rules. This principle also holds for independent seatwork and workcheck activities. Guideline 4 is aimed at the special events such as assemblies and field trips. These rules will be practiced daily, a week or two before the activity.

Make a Set of Rules for the Selected Activities   The set of rules for each selected activity adds further structure in which the student operates. The result over time is a coordinated flow of movement between student and teacher that indicates a "well-managed" classroom. Here are some sample rules for the mathematics activities listed above.

Math Presentation

1. Sit quietly
2. Pay attention to teacher
3. Answer questions when asked
4. Listen to others
5. Accept mistakes by others

Math Worksheet

1. Work in your seat
2. Do your own work
3. Try hard to finish
4. Turn in worksheet
5. Raise hand for help

These examples illustrate five characteristics of effective rules discussed below.

Rules describe the social behaviors necessary to accomplish an activity. This principle has been discussed in the section on identifying the social behaviors necessary for an activity. Although behaviors can sometimes be classified as either social or academic, this should not stop teachers from targeting the behaviors in question. For example, "trying hard to finish" could include aspects of both social and academic behavior. If problems in classroom routines arise when using a rule, teachers should simply change the rule after clearly informing students of the change.

Keep rules short. All of the rules shown above have no more than four words. Here are some examples and nonexamples of short rules:

Examples

1. Look at blackboard.

2. Turn in worksheet.

Nonexamples

During teacher presentation look at the blackboard.

Turn in your own worksheet at the end of the seatwork activity.

3. Raise hand for help.

Do not talk unless you get permission from the teacher.

Phrase the rules in a positive way. Notice that all of the above examples are positive. This reminds teachers what to reward and tells students what to do. A nonexample (i.e., an inappropriate rule) would state the rule as a negative command. Here are some examples and nonexamples.

Examples	*Nonexamples*
1. Work hard.	Don't play around.
2. Be friendly.	Don't hurt others.
3. Accept others' mistakes.	Don't laugh at others.
4. Raise hand for help.	Don't yell for help.

The rules must be observable. If the rule specifies observable behavior, teachers can reward students when the rule is followed and correct them when it is broken. A quick test for observable rules is to ask, "Can I see if the rule is followed or broken?" If the answer is yes, the rule is observable. Some examples and nonexamples of observable rules follow:

Examples	*Nonexamples*
1. Sit quietly.	Know how to act.
2. Listen to others.	Comprehend others.
3. Answer questions when asked.	Believe that you should answer questions.

Limit the number of rules to five. In most cases, for each activity, rules should be limited. Use the fewest number of rules required to keep behavior manageable.

Make a Set of General Activity Rules General activity rules help teachers prepare for appropriate or inappropriate behavior that is unanticipated. If the student behavior is appropriate, the teacher is not forced to think of a novel reward statement, but can use a reward statement that reflects the broad classes of behavior on which the general rules are founded. The same is true for inappropriate student behavior. Correction consequences also follow from specifying general classes of behavior. Should a particular type of behavior become frequent, teachers will have had time to prepare specific reward and correction statements or procedures (Chapters 3, 6, and 11 give specifics).

Most student social behavior fits into three general classes of behavior. First, there is the behavior related to what the student does in terms of his or her academic work. Second, there is the behavior related to peers. And, third, there is the behavior related to the teacher. A general rule should be constructed for each of these classes of behavior. Thus, three general rules are needed. General rules apply to *all* activities. Some examples of how to phrase rules in each class are given below:

Student	*Peers*	*Teacher*
1. Work hard.	1. Be friendly to others.	1. Follow teacher directions.
2. Be diligent.	2. Cooperate with others.	2. Listen to teacher.
3. Try hard.	3. Be considerate of students.	3. Work with the teacher.
4. Make an effort.	4. Be congenial to others.	4. Cooperate with the teacher.

SELECTING RULES

In certain situations, both general rules and activity specific rules are not needed. First, if the subject area has only two or three activities and they are similar, the use of a general set of rules may be enough. But problem behaviors may exist that a specific activity rule or rules may help eliminate. If this is the case, activity rules should also be used. Second, for the older students, only general rules may be needed, especially if the list or pattern of activities is not too complex and the students do not cause management problems. If only general rules are used, teachers must perform three tasks: (1) outline for students the full sequence of events within classroom activities; (2) reward students for appropriate social behaviors, including transitions from one activity to another; and (3) present numerous examples and nonexamples of each rule.

INTRODUCING AND USING RULES

Formulating rules generates (1) a list of activities, (2) a list of social behaviors for each activity, (3) a list of rules for each major activity, and (4) a list of general rules to cover all activities. Once teachers have these lists, the next step is to introduce and use rules effectively in the classroom. Some guidelines for introducing and using classroom rules follow:

Stress the Importance of Rules When introducing the rules, it is important to motivate students to follow them. How this is done depends on the age of the students. For younger students, teachers should make a "big deal" about the rules. The condition statements (see Chapter 5) used to introduce the rules should include elements such as how proud teachers and others would be if students follow the rules. Students should be asked how much they would like to follow the rules, or if they are ready to follow the rules. Here are some examples of statements introducing rules to young students:

> "These rules are important. Following them shows me that you have gained self-control and can cooperate and work with others. I like individuals who can do things for themselves and others. That makes me proud of you."

> "Since these rules are so important, how many of you would like to follow them?" (Students reply.) "That is great; I hope all of you can do it. I will tell you when you are following them."

> "I hope you all can follow the rules and make me proud of you. These are important things to do. Your parents would be proud to see that you can follow them. How many can show me the self-control needed to follow these rules?" (Students reply.)

For older students, a more direct presentation should be used. Give students a rationale that stresses the positive consequences of following the rules (see this section and Chapters 3, 8, and 10 for a fuller discussion of consequences and their use). An adult, matter-of-fact presentation, which stresses the teacher's own belief that following the rules is helpful, is best for the older students.

Give and Ask for Examples and Nonexamples of Rules This principle should be followed for both general and specific activity rules. During the introduction and early stages of rule use, teachers should prompt student responses by presenting a few examples and nonexamples of each rule. After a few days of prompting, students should be able to easily generate examples and nonexamples. An important point is never to spend over one minute presenting any set of rules. Rather, ask students to think of new examples and then call on a few individuals to give specific examples and nonexamples. If students have trouble following a particular rule, teachers must ask for examples and nonexamples of the rule. A student who is having trouble following a rule must be asked for examples and nonexamples.

Rules	*Examples*	*Nonexamples*
1. Try Hard.	Doing the problems assigned.	Talking to one of your classmates.
2. Do your own work.	Looking only at your paper.	Asking Mary for the answer.

3. Accepting the mistakes of others.	Being quiet when one misses a problem.	Laughing at someone for missing a problem.

Inform Students of the Rewards for Following Rules Informing students of potential rewards is especially important during the introduction of the rules. (Chapters 3, 8, and 10 expand on potential rewards.) Here are some examples of students' rewards for following rules:

1. Learn more.
2. Feel good about themselves.
3. Make others feel good (e.g., the teacher and principal).
4. Make their parents proud of them.
5. Finish assigned tasks faster (which leaves more time for their own projects).

Conspicuously Post and Review Rules Daily In order to be consistently effective, teachers must repeatedly set the occasion for appropriate behavior. This should be done very quickly and in different ways as often as possible. On some days, individual students can be asked to read one or all of the rules; on other days, students, as a group, might read them together. Also, on certain days, teachers may emphasize only part of the rules (e.g., those broken most often) or ask only for examples. The important principle is to call students' attention to the rules daily.

During the early phase of rule use, the teacher should make sure that students know what rules apply for what activity. This typically requires reviewing the rules before each activity. Review is especially important for remedial students who exhibit socially inappropriate behavior.

Give Reward Statements When the Rules Are Being Followed Students may be rewarded before, during, and after an activity or class. Students should be told descriptively how they followed the rules and, when possible, asked how they feel about behaving appropriately. Teachers should be certain that what is said is "true" to the best of their knowledge. Thus, teachers' observation skills become a critical classroom management tool. Here are some examples of reward statements used at different phases of classroom activities:

At the end of an activity or class

1. "Everyone in the first row followed all the rules and I feel good about that. How do you feel?"
2. "Thank you, class. You are all getting much better at following rule 3."

3. "The first three rows did a perfect job of following all the rules. Let's give ourselves a hand."
4. "Mark, Mary, and John followed the rules for the entire class. In fact, I am happy about everyone's performance today. How do you feel?"

During an activity

1. "John, I like the way you are sitting in your seat. I appreciate that."
2. "Look at this row pay attention to what I am saying; they will learn a lot."
3. "You really tried hard on these problems, Harriet. You must enjoy doing math."
4. "Ricardo, that right answer showed me that you were really paying attention and learning more."

Chapter 3 presented introductory forms of reward statements, and more advanced forms are given in Chapter 8. The examples here illustrate how reward statements are needed for effective rule use.

SPECIAL EVENT RULES

Special events such as field trips and assemblies have a particular structure and, thus, require a set of social behaviors different from those of the classroom. To handle these events, the teacher can take one of two directions. The first is to key the activity's social needs from the general activity rules. Here examples and nonexamples (i.e., inappropriate instances) would be used with the general rules to cover the particular differences between the classroom and the special event. The second is to make up a set of specific rules for each special activity event. For both procedures, the teacher has to go over the rules for the events a week or two in advance. It is frequently necessary to practice some of the pieces of social behavior required for the event. This can often be done in the context of other events, as the following examples show:

"Look at the way you are waiting quietly while you stand in line. This is the way you will have to do it when we go to the symphony next week. Who thinks he can wait as patiently there as here?" (Students reply.) "I am looking forward to it."

"The way you are paying attention to me is exactly how you will have to pay attention to the speaker at next week's assembly. Who can do it?" (Students reply.) "If you can, you should have an interesting time."

The rule about special events is this: State the necessary social behaviors, practice them, and use statements referencing them.

USING RULES WHEN TEACHING MULTIPLE GROUPS

Working with multiple groups can occur in almost any subject area. Different groups work on at least two different types of activities: One is teacher directed, and the other is some form of independent work. Thus, with multiple groups, teachers must observe that each group is following the rules established for its assigned activity. The guidelines presented above remain relevant, but two need to be modified slightly:

1. Before the start of simultaneous activities, review the rules for each of the activities taking place at the time (i.e., cover both teacher-directed and independent group rules).
2. Present reward statements to the group(s) not working independently. (Just comment across the room if necessary or take a moment to walk around to the other groups and give statements.)

TRANSITIONS FROM ACTIVITY TO ACTIVITY

The use of rules helps set the occasion for an activity. But teachers have the problem of transitions from one activity to another. The best approach to this problem is to (1) determine how long it should take for the students to transition (change) and what supplies are needed for the next activity, (2) specify these to the students (see Chapter 5 for details), and (3) deliver reward statements to students for taking necessary supplies and for doing so within the time specified (see Chapter 3 and 8 for details). If problems persist, "transition" rules, which specify the necessary social behaviors for the transition, can be used.

THE TESTING OF RULES

Students will always test established classroom rules. If students can obtain reward statements for not following the rules, they will do so. Thus, teachers must learn to observe students' social behavior as they teach. The students' rule-following behavior is the condition for teachers' reward behavior. With practice, teachers' observation skills should become as automatic as automobile driving. Above all, teachers must be *persistently and consistently contingent* in presenting consequences for the behavior related to the rules.

STRUCTURING THE CLASSROOM SETTING

The classroom setting provides the context in which classroom management procedures are used to facilitate the delivery of instructional activities. To ensure effective instruction, it is necessary to arrange the setting to help implement management procedures. The following two guides facilitate implementation:

1. Make simultaneous activities as independent as possible.
2. Within an activity, make students as independent as possible.

The first guide addresses settings in which two or more groups are engaged in different activities at one time. To encourage students to work independently and not bother others, teachers often turn desks to face in opposite directions or use some form of partition. Here, distance and reduced visual contact can facilitate management. But the problem with establishing distance and visual separation is that it imposes limits on the teacher's ability to apply management procedures. If the students are separated in terms of distance or vision, so is the teacher. The best overall approach is the combined use of rules and reward statements with classroom arrangements involving just enough turning and partitioning so that independent student behavior can be promoted, but observation is not hindered.

The second guide can also be accomplished through a combination of distance and rules. To crowd students, especially young ones, at a table for a reading or language activity creates management problems. But if separate desks are used, along with rules for independent behavior, the chance for instructional success will be maximized. In the long run, the rules and reward statements promote appropriate social behavior. Also, students need the opportunity to communicate and cooperate with others. An early start to promote such behavior will cause each succeeding year to require less management effort and, thus, allow more time for instruction.

BUILDING AND USING CLASSROOM RULES

The following rule-building routine and checklist for using classroom rules summarizes the procedures in this chapter for setting up and using effective rules.

Rule-Building Routine Like the other routines throughout this text, the rule-building one presents a list of questions which the teacher needs to answer during the process of building rules:

1. *What are the classroom activities?* The answer is arrived at by examining the major instructional events involving teachers and/or students. Further considerations include the following questions:
   a. *What is the activity cycle?* Do the activities repeat themselves every day (fixed cycle) or at differing times (variable cycle)? This helps the teacher answer the next question.
   b. *What special events take place?* Activities that are not part of the regular cycle should be noted, but are not included in the list of rules unless potential social behavior problems exist.
   c. *Are groups being used?* If the answer is yes, remember not to repeat activities since the rules will be the same.
2. *What social behaviors are necessary for each of these activities?* Think of the things the student must do in order to engage in academic behavior.
3. *Which activities need a list of rules?* To answer this question, two considerations are required.
   a. *Is the activity*
      (1) Socially complex?
      (2) Especially long?
      (3) Associated with a history of behavior problems?
      (4) For younger students for whom the general activity rules are not sufficient?
      If the answer to any of these questions is yes, then a set of rules is necessary for the activity.
   b. *Do several activities require similar social behaviors?* If the answer is yes, only one set of rules for these activities should be made up.
4. *What should be considered when making a set of rules for selected activities?*
   a. *Do the rules describe the social behavior necessary to accomplish an activity?*
   b. *Are the rules short?* Short is four or five words.
   c. *Are the rules positive?* They should be.
   d. *Are the rules observable?* The teacher should be able to tell when a rule is broken.
   e. *How many rules are there?* About five is the limit per activity.
5. *Is there a set of general activity rules?* Such rules would deal with the following:

a. *Is there a rule that describes the individual student's academic work?* There should be.
b. *Is there a rule that describes the relationship between peers?* There should be.
c. *Is there a rule that describes the desired relationship between students and the teacher?* Again, there should be.

Rule-using Checklist When introducing and using rules, the following questions need to be asked:

1. *Has the importance of rules been emphasized?* This should be true for both the introduction of rules and their daily use.
2. *Have examples and nonexamples been asked for?* This needs to be done during both the introduction and daily use of rules.
3. *Have the students been informed of the rewards for following the rules?* Some mention should be made when the teacher reviews rules and gives reward statements.
4. *Have the rules been posted?* This should be done in an obvious place.
5. *Are the rules reviewed daily?* For extreme social behavior problems, review may have to be done at the start of each activity. All the instructional groups need to know what rules apply to their specific activity.
6. *Are the students being rewarded when the rules are followed?* Reward statements should reference the rules followed and specify some of the consequences.

PRACTICE ACTIVITIES

1. Establishing classroom activities, social behaviors, and rules

   1.1 Determine activities and social behaviors for individual students. Present examples for group discussion. (pp. 68, 71)

     a. Obtain a schedule of classroom activities for an elementary (grades K–6) or a secondary (grades 7–12) classroom. For a two-hour block of time in the elementary classroom or a one-hour block of time in the secondary classroom, list all student activities. Distinguish between teacher-directed and independent student activities, as appropriate.

     b. For each activity, list the student social behaviors required to perform the academic behavior tasks.

     c. For each activity in sequence, list the social behaviors required for students to transition (i.e., change) from one activity to the next.

   1.2 Formulate rules for the activities identified. Present examples for group discussion. (p. 73)

     a. For each activity and each transition, list up to five rules specifying the key social behaviors required. Refer to the steps for construction of rules presented in the text.

     b. Write a set of general activity rules that apply to all of the activities above. Write at least one rule for student behaviors, one for peer relationships, and one for teacher relationships. (p. 74)

   1.3 Generate examples that reward rules for group critique and discussion: Make up verbal reward statements for students who follow rules to be used during and at the end of each activity. Include a behavior description and consequences to students for following rules. Practice the effective delivery of two rules for each activity and for each general activity rule. (p. 77)

   1.4 Generate examples for introducing rules to students for group critique and discussion: Prepare a three-minute introduction to students of the rules for one of the above activities. In the introduction, accomplish the following: (p. 75)

     a. Post and state the rules in a serious manner.

     b. Inform students of the consequences of rule following to students, to peers, to teachers.

     c. Give and ask for examples and nonexamples.

2. Establishing rules in regular classrooms

   2.1 Determine classroom activities and rules. Present examples for group discussion. (p. 81)

     a. Observe the scheduled activities for a two-hour block. Specify an activity schedule for student groups and required social behaviors. Review the activities and social behaviors with the classroom teacher.

     b. Construct rules for each activity. Review rules with classroom teacher.

     c. Construct general activity rules for students, peer relationships, and teacher relationships. Review rules with classroom teacher.

2.2 Implement classroom rules in a school classroom over a three-day period. Try to have an observer critique the rule introduction and delivery
of verbal reward statements. (p. 82)

    a. Prepare a poster with rules; prepare verbal reward statements for
use with activity rules and general activity rules. Prepare a three-
minute introduction for rules following the three-step procedure in 1.4
a–c above.

    b. Introduce classroom rules to students. Present verbal reward state-
ments for appropriate rule-following behavior during and at end of
activities. Try to achieve 2–4 statements per minute. Use the consequences emphasized by the rule introduction.

    c. Introduce rules for all subsequent activities, following the procedures
above.

    d. Repeat procedure for days 2 and 3, but substitute a two-minute re-
view for the original introduction.

REFERENCES

B. F. Skinner and Robert Gagné present the theoretical rationale for the use of
rules. Skinner speaks in terms of the necessity to "prompt" new behavior and
"set-the-occasion" for the behavior that matches the contingencies. Gagné, on the
other hand, talks about the use of "external conditions" that facilitate student
attention. But the clearest guidelines for the practical content of rules and their
application to specific learning activities is provided by Stephen Yelon. These and
the references on the application of rules to classroom use guided the authors in
construction of the chapter.

Emmer, E., Evertson, C., & Anderson, L. Effective classroom management
at the beginning of the school year. *Elementary School Journal,* 1980, *80,*
219–231.

Gagné, R. M. *Conditions of Learning,* 3rd ed. New York: Holt, Rinehart and
Winston, 1977.

Glynn, E. L., & Thomas, J. D. Effects of cueing on self-control of classroom
behavior. *Journal of Applied Behavior Analysis,* 1974, *7,* 299–306.

Kazdin, A. E. Role of instructions and reinforcement in behavior changes in
token reinforcement programs. *Journal of Educational Psychology,* 1973,
64, 63–71.

Kounin, J. & Gump, P. Signal systems of lesson setting and task-related
behavior of preschool children. *Journal of Educational Psychology,* 1974,
66, 554–562.

Madsen, C. H., Becker, W. C., & Thomas, D. R. Rules, praise and ignoring:
Elements of elementary classroom control. *Journal of Applied Behavior
Analysis,* 1968, *1,* 139–150.

Medland, M. B., & Stachnik, T. J. Good-behavior game: A replication and systematic analysis. *Journal of Applied Behavior Analysis,* 1972, *5,* 45–51.

Skinner, B. F. *The Technology of Teaching.* New York: Appleton-Century-Crofts, 1968.

Skinner, B. F. *Contingencies of Reinforcement: A Theoretical Analysis.* New York: Appleton-Century-Crofts, 1969.

Yelon, S. L. *Learning and Liking It.* East Lansing, Mich.: Michigan State University, Learning and Evaluation Services, 1976.

CONDITION STATEMENTS

Developing teacher skills in building and presenting verbal condition statements is the aim of Chapter 5. Thus far, classroom conditions have been considered in two different ways. First, they were defined broadly as a series of repeatable instructional activities. Chapter 4 introduced the notion of required classroom "activities," whose specification was dependent upon the academic content and teaching methodology within an instructional program. Second, conditions were defined as classroom rules which reference the student social behaviors required for the instructional program's effective delivery. Chapter 4 also outlined procedures for using classroom rules that facilitate classroom activities. The present chapter expands the notion of conditions by providing teachers with procedures for constructing and using verbal condition statements that clarify contingencies within classroom activities by referencing the desired social and academic behavior of students. The organization and content of this chapter parallels Chapter 3 to emphasize the correspondence between condition and reward statements.

THE FUNCTION OF VERBAL CONDITION STATEMENTS

The principles that describe the function of verbal condition statements are the same as those for rules (principles 1 and 2 below). Rather than elaborating on these separately, we describe the complementary function of condition and reward statements. The following combines the principles presented in Chapters 3 and 4, with examples added in order to illustrate this relationship.

1. Condition statements reference and precede an instance of an appropriate behavior class.

> TEACHER: Zelda, I would like you to do nine of ten problems correct on your mathematics worksheet. I know you can do it and earn an A.

2. Delivering a condition statement increases the present probability of occurrence for an instance of the referenced class.

> STUDENT: (*Zelda gets nine of ten problems correct.*)

3. The occurrence of an appropriate instance (e.g., condition-behavior match) provides an opportunity for delivering a reward statement.

> TEACHER: Zelda, that's the first time you have gotten nine of ten correct. You have earned an A. I am proud of you.

4. Delivering a reward statement increases the future probability of the represented class of behavior.

> STUDENT: (*Over the next several days Zelda obtains nine of ten problems correct on her mathematics worksheet, receiving an A each time.*)

5. Delivering a reward statement increases the future probability of condition statements setting the occasion for the referenced class of behavior.

> STUDENT: (*Over the next few days, each time the teacher asks Zelda to perform an academic or social behavior, she does so. As often as possible, the teacher delivers a reward consequence for following instructions.*)

The verbal condition statement accompanying the first principle facilitates the condition-behavior match required for the verbal reward consequence by referencing the behavior, its change, and its consequences (both verbal praise and an A grade). As a result, the probability of future appropriate student behavior increases (principle 4). In addition, future verbal condition statements by the teacher also become more likely to directly influence *any* future student behaviors they reference (principle 5). These effects occur because the verbal condition statement, as a class, is associated with the reward consequences. Without this association, condition statements very quickly lose their effect on behavior; with it, the statements can affect any class of behavior the teacher focuses on. By using verbal condition statements, teachers gain another powerful management tool for efficiently managing student classroom behavior throughout classroom activities.

ELEMENTS OF A COMPLETE
CONDITION STATEMENT

A complete condition statement consists of three elements: a description of the desired behavior, a description of possible consequences, and a motivational challenge to the students. These elements effectively increase the present probability of student behavior.

Describing the Desired Appropriate Behavior Procedures for describing behavior logically follow the steps for analyzing behavior outlined in Chapter 2. Once important classes of academic and social behavior have been analyzed, teachers are able to build the descriptive component of complete condition statements. Here are some examples and nonexamples of describing behavior in the context of setting conditions.

>   *Example:*   "John, let's see if you can *read these words rapidly.*"

"Reading" is the class and "word reading" the subclass. "Rapidly" is the quantitative element of word reading that makes it an unambiguous behavior. The student knows what behavior is expected.

>   *Nonexample:*   "John, let's see how *good your reading is.*"

"Good" does not clarify the behavioral class "reading." Even after an informal association with unambiguous descriptions (e.g., good reading is rapid, accurate), "good" has limited descriptive value and functions more as a *potential* emotional consequence of the teacher.

>   *Example:*   "Everyone, I would like to see you *finish your worksheets before the end of the period.*"

The statement's description is unambiguous because "finish your worksheet" is further clarified by "before the end of the period," a quantitative characteristic.

>   *Nonexample:*   "Everyone, I would like you to have an *excellent worksheet session.*"

The ambiguity comes from "excellent." The student is being asked to do something with the worksheet, but this something is not contained in the description.

>   *Example:*   "I would like to be impressed by this group's *reading with faultless expression* and would like everyone's expression to fit her part."

The class of behavior is oral reading, which is qualified by "faultless expression." "Everyone's expression to fit her part" descriptively defines the qualification. The statement could be expressed with a greater economy of words, but it is a detailed description.

Description of Possible Consequences This element mirrors the description of consequences in reward statements (Chapter 3). Thus, the consequence elements of condition statements describe the *possible* emotional changes, access to different events or activities, and/or a newly structured world for the student or others resulting from social and/or academic behavior. Also, the specific possible consequences described will depend upon the ages of the students.

　　Possible Consequences Related to the Student. The following examples identify student consequences from successful performance of the appropriate behavior.

> "Remember, everyone, clear reading *really makes you feel good.*"

"Feeling good" is an emotional change resulting from reading clearly. Thus, the teacher is pointing out that an academic behavior will make the student "feel good."

> "Jim, if you can build that project according to the class standards, you *will get an A.*"

"Getting an A" represents a newly structured world that is a consequence of "building that project according to standards."

> "If this group finishes early and gets 9 out of 10 math problems correct, there will be *time for working on your individual projects.*"

Here, a social behavior, "finishes early," and an academic behavior, "getting 9 out of 10 math problems correct," together result in access to an activity. In this example, the teacher is pointing out that multiple behaviors (detailed in Chapter 8) are required for the consequence.

　　Possible Consequences Related to What the Student's Behavior Does to Others. The following examples illustrate this form of consequence.

> "Everyone, remember if you work on your own paper, you will be *helping others get their work done.*"

If others "get their work done" the student who "works on [his or her] own paper" has helped other students maintain their efforts to complete their work.

> "Marina, a high score on your math homework would *make me feel like an effective teacher.*"

In this example, the student could produce an emotional change in the teacher.

> "I would like to see everyone *attend academic award time* by scoring 90 percent or better on their spelling and reading this week."

How the students can gain access to an "academic award activity" by performing the specified academic behaviors is stated.

Like reward consequences, different types of consequences are effective in condition statements with older and younger students. The consequences for older students can include almost anything that is reality based. But for older students, the most effective consequences (1) emphasize possible changes for other students or (2) focus on future student behavior. Immediate consequences, especially those involving other students, should also be used frequently. Other effective immediate consequences are the emotional changes that result from engaging in the desired social or academic behavior. For younger students, the consequences in condition statements should relate more to the present than the future. But rather than ignore the future, teachers must develop the ability of younger students to work for future consequences. A key step is for the teacher to use condition statements with both immediate and distant consequences. Typically, older students also accept mixtures of immediate and distant consequences. The two examples that follow illustrate different types of consequences in statements for older and younger students:

> "Owen, let's see if you can get twelve or fifteen correct on your math worksheet; it will indicate that you have a chance at being successful on the college entrance test coming up."

> "Owen, let's see another twelve problems correct on your math worksheet. It will get you an A for today in math."

The first example is appropriate for an older student and provides a future opportunity with only some probability of happening. The second is for the younger student and is much more immediate.

> "Eleanor, do you think the painting could have the qualities we talked of?" (*Student replies.*) "If it does, it will indicate the potential you have as a commercial artist."

> "Eleanor, do you think the painting could have the qualities we talked of?" (*Student replies.*) "If it does, it will certainly impress me."

Again, the first example is for older students, and the second for younger students. In the second example, the consequence identified is both immediate and related to another, the teacher.

Motivating the Desired Appropriate Behavior The motivating component sets the occasion for, or attempts to get, the desired behavior started. Motivation involves (1) establishing a student commitment to the desired appropriate behavior and (2) having the teacher acknowledge support for the student's trying. Establishing a student commitment usually takes place in the context of two basic types of "motivational challenge." The commitment is not a command statement from the teacher, but involves choice on the part of the student. The teacher's support of the student can be expressed in many ways. The examples presented are only suggestive. Also, this aspect of motivating the student is part of the teacher's general enthusiasm for seeing students perform the desired behavior. The following examples distinguish between the two types of challenges, with the examples in each emphasizing the teacher's motivational support of the students.

Open Challenges. In the open challenge, the teacher asks students if they can or will perform the appropriate social or academic behavior specified. The following examples illustrate different open challenges.

> *"Who think they can* do their problems by the end of the period? *Raise your hands if you think you can." (Students reply.) "Great! I will be watching."*

The teacher directs the motivational component toward a group by asking the question, "Who think they can. . . ," and indicates that he or she will be watching to see if the students can do it.

> *"Joseph, I think you can do it. Can you?" (Student replies.)*

Now the teacher challenges the student with, "Can you do it?" and then adds his or her support by saying "I think you can do it." (The student behavior would be specified by the teacher in some other part of the statement.)

> *"Melanie, your past work indicates to me that you can do it if you try hard. I would like to see you try hard* and do all these fraction problems correctly."

This example indicates that the student will have to "try hard" to do all the fraction problems correctly, and the teacher would like to see the student try. The teacher does not give the student a choice; however, as in the other examples, there is no direct command from the teacher. Rather, the challenge is presented in a positive fashion to indicate the teacher's commitment to support the student.

Modeled Challenges. Modeled challenges relate to what others have done or are doing. This form of challenge presents another individual (or group) as a model for the students to imitate. The aim is not to cause competition between individuals or groups, but to show the student what the teacher considers an appropriate change in behavior and that the student can accomplish this change. These challenges can be made to individuals or groups. Each involves what others have done or are trying to do. Some examples follow:

> "Everyone, *the first class* had everyone turn in all their homework today. *Can you do it tomorrow?*" (Students reply.) "*I think you can, so give it a try.*"

Here the challenge is related to what "the first class" did, and is setting conditions for "tomorrow." The statement is completed with teacher support.

> "Hugo, *Harriet is going to try* to get all her sentence analysis worksheet completed and correct today. *Do you think you can do the same?*" (Student replies.) "*OK, give it a try.*"

This challenge asks the student to try what another student, Harriet, has made a commitment to try. "OK, give it a try" indicates the teacher's support.

> "I would like to see you pay attention while others are reading. *John and Mary did it yesterday. Can you do it today, Kirk?*" (Student replies.) "*Excellent, I will be watching.*"

Kirk is asked to commit to what John and Mary did yesterday. "Excellent, I will be watching" functions as the teacher's support. If John and Mary could hear this statement, they may also be influenced to pay attention again and, thus, the present probability of their behavior and Kirk's will increase.

EXAMPLES OF COMPLETE CONDITION STATEMENTS

The three condition elements (behavior description, possible consequences, motivational challenge) are combined to form complete condition statements. Complete condition statements clearly set the occasion for appropriate student behavior and, when paired with reward statements, will consistently and reliably influence student behavior in the classroom. In effect, the three elements combine to "focus" student atten-ion upon appropriate behaviors that are important for the teacher and the student. In this regard, verbal condition statements serve as "road signs." If the behavior specified by the statement is rewarded, the statement becomes even more likely to be followed. If the behavior is performed and not followed by reward statements (or other forms of reward), the statement becomes less effective. A routine for building complete condition statements and practice exercises is provided at the end of this chapter. The following section provides examples of complete condition statements for study. In each example the different elements are labeled as follows: (1) description of the desired behavior—single underline; (2) possible reward consequences—dashed underline; (3) motivating the desired behavior—double underline.

The labeling makes no distinction between behavior consequences' motivational types. These and other distinctions are made in the discussion of the examples.

"Everyone, you know we all could feel fantastic today. All you would have to do is get fifteen problems correct on your worksheet. That would get you an A. Can you do it? (*Students reply.*) "OK, let's give it a try!"

"Michael, John followed each of the rules for reading yesterday. And what happened? He got an A and made me happy. Can you do it today and get an A? (*Student replies.*) "The challenge is yours, let's see you do it."

"Connie, can you do twelve of the fifteen division problems correctly on today's worksheet? I would like to see it." (*Student replies.*) "I know you can do it, but remember to do the subtraction portion of each problem. OK?" (*Student replies.*) "Go to it!"

"I can see this math group is ready to work independently on the members' individual assignments. Martha, Jolly, Zelda, Terrence, Jennifer, can you each work independently?" (*Students reply.*) "Remember to raise your hand if you really get stuck on a problem. Then I will help you, and it will help you to let others continue working independently. So, go to it and give your best."

The first example starts to set the occasion for "doing 15 problems correct" by having the students consider the positive emotional consequence of "feeling fantastic." Then the students are asked to make a commitment to performing the behavior. The second example shows the student the consequences by way of another student's past behavior. This technique demonstrates that the possible future consequence for the student and others is realistic: another student has in fact "gotten an A" and "made the teacher happy." These first two examples are straightforward. The third and fourth illustrate some variations, and two behaviors: the behavior class the teacher is most interested in *and* a supporting subclass that makes the students' accomplishment of the behavior class more probable. In the third example, "doing 12 of 15 division problems correctly" is aided by the subclass "doing the subtraction portion of each problem." In the fourth example, students' "working independently" is facilitated by other students "raising their hands for help." The consequence in the third example relates only to the important class of behavior ("doing division") and describes a possible emotional change for another, the teacher. In the fourth example, the two consequences relate to the class ("raising hands"), with the first focusing on others (the teacher), and the second on each of the students. Finally, the motivational challenge in the last two statements consists of two parts. This occurs because there are two separate behaviors in each example. However, the commitment question for students follows the primary behavior of interest in both cases. Generally, many alternative grammatical forms can be used to construct complex condition statements, but the teacher's emphasis must always relate the desired behavior with the student's commitment to accomplish it.

DEALING WITH NEGATIVE REPLIES TO CHALLENGES

The examples above all assumed a positive (i.e., affirmative) student reply to the commitment element of the condition statements. But this is not always the case. Sometimes the student does not think he or she can perform the behavior for whatever reason. The teacher's response in these cases is critical because it bears directly upon the student's positive attitude and self-concept. The first rule for the teacher is *not* to enter into a discussion of why the student gave the negative reply. The teacher does not want to reward the student's negative class of behavior ("I can't do it") with attention. Instead, the teacher needs to emphasize that the student can do it. Here are some examples of possible replies:

"But I think you can, so give it a try."

"You have shown me in the past you can do it, so just try."

"I think you are ready to do it, so give it your best."

"Most of you feel you can and I know that you will help the others by setting a positive example. Let's all try hard."

The statements "I think you can," "You have shown me in the past you can," and "I think you are ready to do it" all emphasize that the teacher has a positive view of the student as someone who can accomplish the behavior. Thus, the reply is essentially an expansion or extension of the teacher support within the motivation component of the condition statement. The fourth example is directed to a group response containing some negative replies. Here the reply focuses on the positive students' response and points out how these students can help others who are not so positive about their skill to perform. (Important student-student relationships are covered more fully in Chapter 10.) In all cases the teacher ends the statement with a positive request.

The second rule for dealing with, and eliminating, negative replies while building a positive student attitude and self-concept is to reward appropriate behavior when it occurs. From the perspective of Chapter 3, on reward statements, this rule has three aspects:

1. There is almost always something appropriate about a student's behavior.
2. Seek and reward even the smallest appropriate change.
3. Reward as often as possible.

The following short, quick reward statements can be used in response to a negative reply to the conditions, once the student is behaving appropriately.

"Three problems already done. I knew you could do it!"

"You are trying hard, Zarrella. That is the first step in showing me you can do the assignment."

"The first four sentences have been capitalized correctly. Keep it up and you will succeed."

"Now that is a positive start, Joan. In two of the first three passages you have found both the contradiction and what it contradicts. Let's look at the second problem."

These examples all "point back" to the teacher's reply to the student's negative response and confirm the teacher's judgment of what the student can do. Further, each example indicates the student's accomplishments thus far, demonstrating that the student can do the assigned task. The fourth example does even more by showing the student that part of her behavior is an example of appropriate behavior and establishes positive conditions for additional instruction (i.e., correction) to firm the student's skill.

PARTIAL CONDITION STATEMENTS

As with reward statements, there is often not enough time to deliver complete condition statements. During fast-paced instruction—especially in practicing a rote skill such as memorizing mathematics facts—interrupting the activity to give complete statements can be counterproductive. In these situations, partial condition statements, containing one or two elements, can be used across the entire activity. There is one requirement to ensure that the partial condition statement will operate effectively. The element describing appropriate behavior must be included in the partial condition statement, because this description tells the student what is expected. In addition, descriptions help "set up" the motivation element so that student commitment to the behavior can be secured.

Traditionally, the simple descriptions of behavior have been considered as "directions" or "instructions" for the student to follow. Here are some examples:

> "Class, please open your text to page 37 and answer the comprehension questions."

> "Start editing the passage by first finding the capitalization, punctuation, and spelling errors; then cross out the redundant sentences."

> "I would like you all to finish your assignment by the end of the hour. Do you all understand?"

Each of these examples is a description, but educational history has shown that directions or instructions will soon fail to set the occasion for (evoke) the appropriate behavior unless they are linked to reward statements over time. The third example attempts to confirm that the students know what behavior to perform, but does not ask students for a commitment to achieve the behavior (e.g., "Can you do it?").

After a description of behavior, the motivation challenge should be included within partial condition statements. Once students know what to do, the next most important thing is for them to commit themselves to doing it. Often, the behavior description can be embedded into the commitment question, saving time. Some examples follow:

> "Angus, can you find nine out of ten of the punctuation errors on this section of the worksheet?" (*Student replies*.) "That's the spirit."

> "Who think they can follow rule 4 and study independently for the next 15 minutes?" (*Students reply*.) "Great!"

> "Wolfgang, do you think you can incorporate perspective into the still-life assignment?" (*Student replies*.) "OK. Remember the steps for doing so are listed over the blackboard."

With the addition of the motivational element, the chances of the desired behavior occurring increase. The more elements the condition statement includes, the more powerful it will be in setting the occasion for appropriate behavior. But the above examples, which combine the commitment question with the description of the behavior, will set the occasion if time is limited.

DIRECTING CONDITION STATEMENTS

The audience for condition statements (and reward statements) consists of any individual or group that is present in the classroom. All the statements in the above examples are directed to this audience. Groups can consist of a row of students, a reading group, a math table, students in a special activity area, or a team. As long as the students in the group are about to engage in the same class or classes of behavior, a condition statement can be directed toward them. Often the teacher may focus on the total class (as when going over the class rules at the beginning of a period or activity) and then deliver subsequent condition statements to individual instructional groups engaged in different assignments.

WHEN TO PRESENT CONDITION STATEMENTS

Once condition statements can be constructed, teachers must determine when to use them within the flow of classroom behavior. From a behavioral perspective, complete condition statements should be used whenever possible to amplify all new socially and instructionally important behaviors required during activities. As with reward statements, following this principle with condition statements requires the teacher to analyze the instructional objectives and the social behavior necessary for the instructional activity (see Chapters 2 and 4). Complete condition statements also are required for the behaviors, social or academic, with which students have the most difficulty. For example, if students have trouble "paying attention to their own work" or "not carrying to the next column," condition statements should be used to set the occasion for students to perform these tasks. To set the occasion for problem behaviors, the teachers must always attempt to anticipate them through prior study of student strengths and weaknesses (see Chapter 12 for detailed procedures for examining a problem).

From a time perspective, complete condition statements are best used at the beginning of an activity to stress necessary social behaviors. For example, covering activity rules (see Chapter 4) provides teachers with an excellent opportunity to go beyond simple description in monitoring students.

> (*After having the students read the rules.*) "Who can follow each of these rules?" (*Students reply.*) "That's what I thought. You know them and can do them. That will help each of you get an 'A' for today. Let's show yourself again today."

If a new procedure is to be used for academic or social behavior, it is very important to use a complete condition statement at the start of the activity:

> "The first activity requires you to edit the passage on your worksheet. Remember, first find the capitalization errors; second, the spelling errors; third, find the redundant sentences and cross out all but one of the redundant parts; fourth, rewrite the passage, combining the redundant sentences; fifth, put in all necessary punctuation; and, sixth, check the passage over for each of the things you did. Raise your hand if you think you can do that." (*Students reply*.) "That's what I like to hear, positive students. Go to it."

This statement is long, but the behavior is complicated. If the students are just learning to edit material, they would need this complete management condition statement, along with specific instruction designed to teach them the procedure's behaviors. As an alternative presentation, the teacher could have the students give the steps of the procedure.

Another effective place to use complete condition statements is at the end of an activity. In this case, the condition statement sets the occasion for the next day's behavior.

> "Tomorrow, we will again follow these rules. Let's read them together." (*Class reads rules*.) "Remember, by following them you are taking a large step towards making an A and making your parents proud of you. Raise your hand if you think you can follow them tomorrow." (*Students reply*.) "I will look forward to seeing you all do it."

> "Newell, will you be able to practice your piano lessons with the necessary diligence tomorrow?" (*Student replies*.) "You know when you do, your playing gains a flow and ease which each musical score requires. I will look forward to listening to your playing after you practice."

These statements both focus student attention toward the future. Thus, they represent an early stage of teaching the students to plan activities.

Partial condition statements can be used almost any time during an activity in which appropriate behaviors are firmer or less problematic. These statements are designed to keep instruction or independent work flowing, while setting the conditions for changes in various subclasses of behavior. Such applications should not interrupt the working student, but facilitate important behavior changes. In meeting both requirements, teachers can deliver short condition statements as they observe students working:

> "Bertha, can you remember the next step in your editing of the passage?" (*Student replies*.) "You got it."

> "Red group, remember to turn in your worksheets when you finish."

> "OK, Marsha, I bet you are about to do these subtraction problems without forgetting to borrow when necessary."

These partial statements will prove effective in helping the student achieve success in much of his or her work. The biggest problem for teachers using relevant partial condition statements is that considerable planning and practice is needed to implement them consistently and persistently in the classroom.

Although these principles are important to follow, there are exceptions. For example, when students have extensive academic or social behavior deficits, it is often necessary to use complete statements throughout the activity, presenting them as fast as possible without slowing the rate of instruction. A rule about when to use condition statements, complete or partial, might state:

> Whenever it is time for an instance of behavior change, some form of condition statement should be given.

The most important instances are related to a newly acquired class of behavior or to persistent problem behavior. Thus, the more the teacher knows about the student's academic and social behavioral history, the more the rule can be followed in the classroom.

HOW TO PRESENT CONDITION STATEMENTS

The presentation skills required to maximize the effectiveness of condition statements are very similar to those used to present reward statements. Teachers must always try to be sincere in their presentations. Thus, statement elements should directly reflect the teacher's belief that the requested behavior and its possible consequences are important, and that the student can perform the behavior. The alternative belief by the teacher that the behavior, its consequences, and the student performance are impossible or unimportant will be obvious to the students. However, the teachers' sincerity should be revealed if teachers examine student behavior (as outlined in Chapter 2), search for relevant consequences for the behavior, and construct statements that are within the limits of change students can make. The more the teacher is involved in the analysis and construction of condition statements, the more the unimportant and trivial aspects of the student's behavior in the classroom will be discarded, with only the important and possible aspects remaining and being believed. The teacher's involvement in the construction of management practices is usually followed by a second general presentation skill: delivering statements with a smile. After the teacher sees the effectiveness of condition statements in setting the occasion for appropriate behavior, the smile is almost guaranteed because most teachers enjoy seeing students learn. Third, the condition statements also should be presented in a positive tone of voice, avoiding the monotonous droning that puts students to sleep. This tone can be practiced with another teacher or a tape recorder that gives an accurate voice representation. At the same time, teachers need to be sure that their voice has enough volume to be heard by all to whom it is directed. Finally, teachers should maintain eye contact while presenting condition statements. When the statement is directed at a group, eye contact can be made by scanning the group being addressed. If the statement is addressed to a group but intended for one or two members, teachers should look at the targeted students for the greater part of the scan. A common presentation error is to look away from a student while saying the condition statement. Such deflection gives the statement an air of unimportance. Instead, the teacher simply should look at the student and present the statement.

Teacher presentation skills also depend upon the age of the students. With older students, in grades 8 through 12, teachers should be low keyed and descriptive in their delivery. Specifically, teachers need to get student commitments, but the follow-ups to students' positive replies must not be exclamatory; phrases such as "I would like to see it," "very good," or "I will look forward to it" are adequate. This adjustment may also be required for socially and emotionally advanced younger students in grades 5 through 7. Thus, verbal condition statements for older students are reserved. But with younger students, especially those in grades kindergarten (K) through 3, emotion and enthusiasm are as important as their lack is with older students. In keeping with this manner, the warm, friendly contact of a pat or handshake are often present during and at the end of the condition statement to help ensure younger students' attention to the contents.

The preceding rules of thumb can all be broken, especially after teachers have been setting conditions and rewarding students for some time. As long as it is effective, the style a teacher adopts can largely be a personal preference. In general, a reserved, descriptive manner is effective for all, and especially with a new group of students. The best approach is conservative at the start. Later, when the teacher knows the students and has determined what they like or will accept, the delivery style can take a different direction. But the teacher needs to remember that the longer the students have been in a setting where conditions and rewards have been consistently and persistently set and delivered, the more the students will accept variation in the presentation of statements.

PERSISTENCE AND CONSISTENCY IN DELIVERING CONDITION STATEMENTS

In the present context, "persistence" is defined as the continued presentation of condition statements, and "consistency" is the accurate presentation of condition statements. Persistence and consistency in delivering condition statements require the same elements as does their use in delivering reward statements: Teachers must set the occasion for the instances of a class of behavior repeatedly, over many activity opportunities. An important classroom management principle is to *persistently and consistently deliver condition statements when students have to change their behavior (i.e., when a different condition-behavior match is required)*. Chapters 9 and 10 outline how to follow this principle.

CHECKING HOW CONDITION STATEMENTS ARE WORKING

Teachers may often wonder how their condition statements are working. As with reward statements, the success of condition statements can be determined in three basic ways. The first is to take a quick look at the student or group to whom the statement was directed a moment or two after you turn (physically) to something else. Rather than turning the whole body and cueing the student, teachers should turn their head quickly to see the expression and/or gestures being made. If the student is working or smiling, the style of the statement was satisfactory. However, if the student's behavior is inappropriate and the statement was more than descriptive and low-keyed, the statement may not have been effective. At the same time, students' inappropriate behaviors often have more to do with the group or individual's conflict at responding to contingencies involving peers (Chapter 10 provides techniques for establishing compatible contingencies between teachers and students.) A second procedure to see how the statements are working is to have an observer watch student behavior following statements. Finally, a third way is to sample older students by asking a question about a statement following its delivery:

"Marilyn, does that request seem appropriate?"

"Does everyone in the group consider these consequences important?"

"Eamon, how do you like being asked about doing the task?"

Notice that each example refers to an element of a complete condition statement. It is important not to overdo such statements and to restrict them to individuals or small groups—at least until the teacher gets acquainted with the students.

BUILDING AND DELIVERING CONDITION STATEMENTS

The major objective of the condition statement is to describe what behavior should be exhibited, what consequences are possible, and to motivate the student to perform the behavior. To achieve this multifaceted objective, teachers must practice building and delivering condition statements. Such practice can be done anywhere; teachers can practice while walking or driving or even sitting in front of the television. But it is important in the early phases to write the statements and check them for completeness. The more practice teachers get, the better they will become in presenting effective condition statements in the regular classroom setting. Teachers will find that using verbal condition statements effectively becomes one of teaching's most creative activities. To facilitate such practice, statement-building routine and statement delivery checklists are provided.

Condition Statement Building Routine   To practice constructing statements, teachers need to ask themselves the following questions:

1. *What activity is of immediate interest?* This gives the teacher a context for the answering of the rest of the questions.
2. *Who can the statement be directed at?* This asks to what groups or individuals can the statement be appropriately addressed.
3. *What behaviors are appropriate?* Once a behavior has been identified, the teacher must clarify it and put it in perspective. The following behavior-related questions help:
   a. *Is the behavior social or academic?*
   b. *What are the qualitative and quantitative aspects of the behavior?* This question facilitates thorough description.
4. *What consequences could occur?* This question can be broken into the following subquestions:
   a. *Are the consequences for academic and social behavior related to emotional changes, access to activities, and/or a restructured world?*
   b. *Are the consequences related to the student or others?*
   c. *Are the consequences in the immediate future or in the far future?*
5. *What can be said to motivate the student to perform the behavior?*
   a. *What can be said to have the students acknowledge that they can do it?* The commitment is the form employed to get student acknowledgement. There may be others.
   b. *What can be said to acknowledge that the teacher believes the student can do it?* These are partial condition statements such as, "I agree," "I know you can," or "It's up to you."

6. *What can be said in response to a negative acknowledgment by the student?* Instead of dwelling on the negative behavior, teachers should emphasize that the student can do it.

After using this procedure to build complete or partial condition statements, teachers will find that statements will "flow" rather easily after a few weeks. Further, their use will result in a classroom environment that is a warm and happy one for both students and teacher.

Condition Statement Delivery Checklist During the practice phase of developing condition statements, teachers need to carefully check the important aspects of delivery. If careful consideration is not given in the practice and planning stages of classroom management, contingency errors become highly likely. The following questions can help the teacher assure the effective delivery of statements in the classroom.

1. *Does the statement or the teacher's presence unambiguously reference the group or individual the statement is intended for?*
2. *When can the statement be most effectively used?*
   a. *Is the behavior to be performed new or a problem?* If the answer is yes, the complete condition statement is appropriate.
   b. *Do the students have extensive social or academic skill deficits?* If the answer is yes, the use of complete statements is appropriate.
   c. *Is the statement to be presented at the start or end of an activity?* If the answer is yes, the complete condition statement is appropriate.
   d. *Is the aim of the statement to keep setting the occasion throughout the activity for the appropriate behavior?* If the answer is yes, the partial condition statement is appropriate.
3. *How would the statement be most effectively presented?* Again, many facets are involved:
   a. *Is sincerity present?* Believing that the behaviors and consequences are important is essential.
   b. *Is the smile present?* Again, believing that the behaviors and consequences are important is essential.
   c. *Does the voice have enough volume and tonal qualities (nonmonotone)?* If the answer is yes, students will more likely attend.
   d. *Is eye contact made during the statement's presentation?* This will help ensure that the student attends to statement content.

    e. *Is the statement delivered quickly, without redundancy or repetition of content?* If the answer is yes, there is less chance of boring students or letting the condition statement become a lecture.

The answer to many of these checklist questions will depend on how long the students have been in a classroom with positively set conditions and delivered rewards. Teachers' delivery styles will be determined by this consideration and the teachers' own skills at building and delivering statements.

PRACTICE ACTIVITIES

1. Generating condition statements
   1.1 Identify elements of condition statements for delivery practice. Present examples for group critique and discussion. (pp. 88, 92)
       a. Select two examples of complete condition statements from the text—one for social behavior and one for academic behavior. Using the examples as a starting point, list each of the following elements of condition statements (modify the examples as necessary):
           (1) Desired behavior description (instance/class name)
           (2) Possible consequences to student (emotion, newly structured world, access to activity)
           (3) Possible consequence to others (peers, teacher, parent)
           (4) Motivational challenge (student commitment question/ teacher support)
       b. Using the above examples, list two partial condition statements for student social behavior and two for academic behavior, including, in order, a behavior description and motivational challenge. Write each partial condition statement in the form you would say it. (p. 95)
       c. For each partial condition statement, add the elements of consequences for students and for others to form complete condition statements. Write each complete condition statement in the form you would say it.
   1.2 Practice delivery of the examples from 1.1. Use a mirror, tape recorder, or other media aid to guide practice. Have classmates critique your delivery. (p. 103)
       a. Practice effective delivery of each statement to a hypothetical student or another member of your group. First practice partial, then complete, statements. Maintain eye contact, smile, act sincere and enthusiastic, provide adequate vocal volume and intonation, and achieve a quick, relaxed presentation.
       b. Expand and practice complete statements by varying them to show the two forms of motivational challenge: (p. 91)
           (1) Open challenge
           (2) Modeled challenge
           Note that an open challenge asks students, "Can you do it?" and requires a choice response from students indicating commitment. A modeled challenge adds, "Student X can do it" to the open challenge procedure. If necessary, write out the two open and modeled versions of each example. Practice effective, relaxed delivery of the four statements in 30 seconds or less.
       c. Return to the original complete condition statements in 1.1 and vary the possible consequences to the student, so that each form of consequence is referenced in order: (p. 89)
           (1) Emotional consequences to the student
           (2) Newly structured world
           (3) Access to activities

If necessary, write out each expanded statement. Practice effective delivery until relaxed.

    d. Return to the two complete condition statements in 1.1 and vary the possible consequences to others (e.g., peers, teachers, parents) so that each form of consequence is referenced in a statement in order: (p. 89)

        (1) Emotional consequences to others

        (2) Newly structured world

        (3) Access to activities

    If necessary, write out each expanded statement. Then practice effective delivery of the statements until relaxed.

1.3 Practice generating examples of complete condition statements. Present examples for group discussion. (p. 99)

    a. List ten descriptions of desired student behavior—five social and five academic. Try to make the behaviors as different as possible from each other.

    b. Read through each behavior on the list, identifying an example of a motivational challenge, an example of a possible consequence to the student, and an example of a possible consequence to others. Do not write these examples.

    c. Next, for each behavior on the list, generate a complete condition statement that includes the desired behavior, consequence to the student and others, and motivational challenge. Practice delivering the ten statements effectively and unhurriedly. (As a standard format, first state the desired behavior, then a consequence to student or others, and finally the motivational challenge.)

    d. Work through the list faster and faster until you can deliver all ten statements effectively within 60 seconds. Don't worry about remembering each element, just produce an example of the element in the standard format.

1.4 Practice variations in generating complete condition statements. Present examples for group critique and discussion. (p. 92)

    a. Select one of the preceding examples, then practice the following variations:

        (1) Repeat the statement, changing from an open challenge to a modeled challenge.

        (2) Repeat the statement, varying the reference to each of the three student consequences in a single statement.

        (3) Same as variation (1), but vary reference to each of three consequences to others.

    b. Practice variations for a single example from the list, then select a new example and repeat the process until you achieve a relaxed presentation.

1.5 Practice originality in generating complete condition statements. Present examples for group critique and discussion. Start by selecting a preceding example of behavior. Generate a complete condition statement. Now, see how many different ways you can phrase the statement while including each component. Change the order of elements in the statement, or paraphrase different elements and re-lationships among them. To begin, try writing all the versions you can think of. Then try to generate alternative wordings, given a behavior.

2. Delivering condition statements in school classrooms
   2.1 Identify social behaviors and activities for condition statements and for simulating delivery of condition statements. (p. 102)
   - **a.** Observe the scheduled activities in the same regular classroom used in Chapter 4. Refer to the activities, social behaviors, and rules. Determine where condition statements should be used.
   - **b.** Imagine you are the teacher. Within the structure of the activities (i.e., beginning, during, end), present a partial condition state-ment, to yourself, to set the occasion for future student behavior with the following elements:
     (1) Desired behavior.
     (2) Motivational challenge.
     Try to "present" one to four statements per minute. If possible, use a tape recorder in the rear of the room or behind a one-way glass.
   - **c.** Next, present simulated verbal reward statements to students who exhibit appropriate social and/or academic behavior targeted in the condition statements. Try to present up to four statements per minute, with a ratio of one condition statement per three reward statements.

   2.2 Deliver condition statements to students in a controlled classroom setting. Try to have another individual rate your behavior regarding condition and verbal reward statements, using the condition state-ment delivery checklist in the text. (p. 103)
   - **a.** Arrange to work as a monitor or teacher in a regular classroom.
   - **b.** Identify in advance activities and appropriate student social and academic behaviors desired.
   - **c.** Anticipate desired student behaviors. Present complete or partial condition statements for student social and academic behaviors. Follow advance plan for presentation of condition statements before, during, and at the end of activities.
   - **d.** Vary condition statements across students and groups. Try to achieve a rate of one to two per minute as appropriate (i.e., without interfering with student performance during task). Follow up with reward statements for appropriate student social and academic behavior within the activities, especially those tar-geted by condition statements.

REFERENCES

The theoretical background for the use of verbal condition statements is the same as for activities and rules in Chapter 4. Recent studies have correlated the use of teacher directions and comments prior to instruction or independent work and have found a strong relationship between the directness of these statements and the degree to which the students are on task. These studies show that clear, direct condition statements by the teacher are an important component of effective management.

Borg, W. R., & Ascione, F. R. Classroom management in elementary main streaming classrooms. *Journal of Educational Psychology*, 1982, *74*, 85–95.

Borg, W. R., & Ascione, F. R. Changing on-task, off-task, and disruptive pupil behavior in elementary classrooms. *Journal of Education Research*, 1979, *72*, 243–252.

Borg, W. R., Langer, P., & Wilson, J. Teacher classroom management skills and pupil behavior. *Journal of Experimental Education*, 1975, *44*, 52–58.

Emmer, E. T., Evertson, C., & Anderson, L. Effective classroom management at the beginning of the school year. *Elementary School Journal*, 1980, *80*, 219–231.

Evertson, C. M., & Emmer, E. T. Effective management at the beginning of the school year in junior high classes. *Journal of Educational Psychology*, 1982, *74*, 485–498.

Kounin, J. S., & Gump, P. Signal systems of lesson setting and the task-related behavior of preschool children. *Journal of Educational Psychology*, 1974, *66*, 554–562.

Rosework, S. Goal setting: The effects on an academic task with varying magnitudes of incentive. *Journal of Educational Psychology*, 1977, *69*, 710–715.

In the selection of condition statement components, the necessity of the motivation element is supported by the research on commitment in behavior analysis as well as in social psychology. In behavior analysis research, the work by Howard Rachlin and Leonard Green stands out. They consider commitment as a choice that guides future behavior and limits future choice. They point out that one's values are different in the present than they will be in the future, and only by agreeing to a commitment can one ensure that one will act in accordance with one's present values when the future arrives. Social psychology research indicates that commitment and volition (choice) are related to individuals' attitude changes. Charles Festinger's cognitive dissonance research forms a foundation for the later work by Jack Brehm and A. R. Cohen. Today, every text in social psychology covers the extensive research done in this area. Both fields try to explain the extent to which commitment changes behavior. There is also a long history in psychology regarding the term "choice." E. C. Tolman, for example, argued that all behavior involves choice.

Brehm, J. W., & Cohen, A. R. *Explorations in Cognitive Dissonance*. New York: Wiley, 1962.

Festinger, L. *A Theory of Cognitive Dissonance*. New York: Harper & Row, 1957.

Rachlin, H. *Behavior and Learning*. San Francisco: Freeman, 1976.

Rachlin, H., & Green, L. Commitment, choice, and self-control. *Journal of the Experimental Analysis of Behavior,* 1972, *17,* 15–22.

VanderZanden, J. W. *Social Psychology*. New York: Random House, 1981.

CORRECTION PROCEDURES

T his chapter provides teachers with the procedures and skills to correct inappropriate student behavior. Rules, condition statements, and reward statements set the occasion for or reward appropriate behavior. But, often students enter the classroom with an extensive repertoire of inappropriate behavior. Teachers cannot wait for appropriate behavior to occur and then reward it. Inappropriate behavior often disrupts activities so that neither the inappropriately nor the appropriately behaving students receive effective instruction. If instruction is to proceed, inappropriate behavior must be stopped as quickly as possible. Only then can effective teaching occur. Thus, the procedures outlined in this chapter are necessary requirements for effective management.

THE FUNCTION OF CORRECTIVE STATEMENTS

Three principles describe the function of corrective consequence statements:

1. The occurrence of an inappropriate instance of behavior (e.g., condition-behavior nonmatch) provides an opportunity for delivering a corrective statement.
2. Delivering a corrective statement decreases the future probability of the inappropriate class of behavior.
3. Delivering a corrective statement decreases the future probability of condition statements which set the occasion for the inappropriate class of behavior.

As with reward statements, the first principle is one of technology. It indicates that the use of a corrective statement is contingent (dependent) on a condition-behavior nonmatch. The other two are behavioral principles: they indicate a decrease in the probability of the class of (inappropriate) behavior and the class of conditions setting the occasion for (evoking or bringing forth) the (inappropriate) behavior. Thus, they are the reciprocal of reward statements.

But to stop inappropriate behavior as fast as possible and replace it with appropriate behavior requires much more than corrective statements. The teacher must use corrective procedures that combine both condition and consequence statements arranged over time in order to effectively stop inappropriate behavior.

The greater the nonmatch between conditions and behavior, the greater the demand upon the corrective procedures to rapidly decrease and replace the inappropriate behavior. On the other hand, use of the most powerful technique to correct the least obtrusive form of inappropriate behavior (e.g., daydreaming or passing a note) could result in decreasing even the appropriate behavior. Thus, corrective procedures must be adjusted to the degree of condition-behavior nonmatch. Each of the corrective contingency variants differs, but each contains a full complement of contingency elements which encompass the application of all eight principles of behavior and technology specified in Chapters 3, 4, and 5 and here.

This chapter focuses on the elements of one academic and four social behavior correction procedures, and considers the implementation features required for their correct application to inappropriate behavior.

ELEMENTS OF CORRECTIVE STATEMENTS

The elements of a corrective consequence statement parallel those of a reward. The three corrective elements are (1) the description of the inappropriate behavior, (2) how it has changed over time, and (3) the consequences of such behavior. But the corrective statements teachers make to students seldom contain all three elements. Instead, some or all of these elements are spread over the course of a corrective procedure. There are two reasons for this: First, there is a need to stop the inappropriate behavior with as little teacher-student interaction as possible; second, the corrective statement does not inform the student of what behavior to perform. Corrective procedures are designed to meet these two requirements. There is little use for complete or partial corrective consequence statements. Rather, this chapter focuses on the corrective procedure in which corrective consequence elements may appear.

FOUR SOCIAL CORRECTION PROCEDURES FOR THE CLASSROOM

This section considers four social correction procedures: ignore-reward, warning, separation, and office referral. Which is used depends on (1) the degree to which student behavior deviates from established conditions, and (2) the length of time the inappropriate behavior has persisted or endured. The greater the deviation or persistence, the more extreme is the procedure used to stop the behavior before it interferes with the instructional presentation or with the learning of other students.

The Ignore-Reward Procedure The ignore-reward procedure is the first step in dealing with inappropriate behavior. Although it does not contain a corrective consequence that reflects the condition-behavior nonmatch, this procedure is exceedingly effective in stopping mildly inappropriate behavior. Thus, this procedure is used for *inappropriate behavior that does not disrupt the instructional presentation or harm others.* This class of behavior includes such things as looking at a math book during a reading worksheet, gazing out the window during instruction or independent work, doodling during a teacher presentation, playing with various objects during independent work, or dozing during a lesson. From the teacher's perspective, the ignore-reward procedure aims to make the student's inappropriate behavior a cue for rewarding another student for the appropriate behavior that the first student is not displaying. From the student's perspective, the procedure aims to describe the appropriate behavior to be performed and indicate that its performance is rewarding. The procedure may have as many as six steps, depending on how the student's behavior changes with each implemented step:

1. Ignore the individual displaying the inappropriate behavior.
2. Overtly reward a second student who is displaying the appropriate behavior (so that the first student sees a model of the appropriate behavior and that it is rewarded).
3. If the first student starts to display the appropriate behavior, reward after a short time.
4. If the first student does not display the appropriate behavior after a short time, try steps 1 and 2 two more times.
5. If the first student does not display the appropriate behavior after repeating steps 1 and 2, go to the warning procedure (described below).
6. For the next activity or day, set the conditions for the desired behavior and go back to step 3 or 4 (whichever is appropriate).

"Ignore" in step 1 refers to the teacher not overtly attending to the student. In step 2, the rewarding of another student models the appropriate behavior for the first and indicates that its performance is rewarded. For step 3, a short delay between appropriate behavior and reward is imposed because if the teacher rewards the behavior immediately, the student may learn the misrule "If I am inappropriate and then appropriate, I will receive the teacher's attention (reward)." If this happens, inappropriate behavior will increase, not decrease. Step 4 simply indicates that the procedure must be given a chance to work. Step 5 is a means to stop an inappropriate behavior that continues to persist. If it is not stopped, the student will miss instruction or practice activities. The final step represents an attempt to firm the appropriate behavior and is precautionary. Here are some examples, with the step of the ignore-reward procedure being implemented indicated in parentheses:

Example 1

STUDENT: (*Barbara stares out the window.*)

TEACHER: (*Talking to Mark who sits close to Barbara.*) Mark, I like the way you are sitting up and paying attention to the lesson. (*Steps 1 and 2.*)

STUDENT: (*Barbara turns and attends to lesson.*)

TEACHER: (*After a short time.*) Barbara, I appreciate your paying attention. Thank you. (*Step 3.*)

Example 2

STUDENT: (*Verbin does not open his book for math.*)

TEACHER: The rule is to follow directions and I can see that Marc and the rest of row 3 have their books open and are ready for the lesson. Good going. That's the first step toward an A for today. (*Steps 1 and 2.*)

STUDENT: (*Verbin, who sits next to row 3, opens his book and follows along.*)

TEACHER: (*After all students in Verbin's row have their books open.*) "I appreciate everyone in row 2 following along in their book. I can see everyone wants to learn more about long division." (*Step 3.*)

In both examples the ignore-reward procedure worked the first time. At the start of the next day, setting conditions through verbal conditions would help prevent the onset of the inappropriate behaviors. The third example indicates a failure of the ignore-reward procedure.

Example 3

STUDENT: (*Sedric is drawing during an independent worksheet activity.*)

TEACHER: (*Turning to Alice, who sits behind Sedric.*) "Alice, you are pointing to each word as it is read. That is what I like to see." (*Steps 1 and 2.*)

STUDENT: (*Sedric continues to draw.*)

TEACHER: "Everyone in the front of the room is pointing as the group is reading. That will help you all keep your place. Mary, continue reading." (*Step 4.*)

STUDENT: (*Sedric continues to draw.*)

TEACHER: (*After another student reads.*) "You all must be enjoying this story. Just look at how all but a few are pointing and paying attention to the story." (*Step 4.*)

STUDENT: (*Sedric continues to draw.*)

TEACHER: (*Uses the warning procedure—Step 5.*)

Continued failure to get the student back on task moves the teacher to implement the warning procedure.

The Warning Procedure The second correction procedure employs corrective consequences. This warning procedure is used for *inappropriate behavior that disrupts the instructional presentation or nondisruptive behavior that continues to occur.* Disruptive behaviors include talking out of turn, tickling others, laughing at another, yelling obscenities, throwing spitballs, popping papers, and flying paper airplanes. Continuing nondisruptive behaviors include those defined for the ignore-reward procedure, but which have not been stopped by its application. Warnings are most effective if given at the start of the behavior (even continuous nondisruptive behavior has numerous starting and stopping points). This prevents the student's behavior from being rewarded by other students (see Chapter 9 on establishing compatible contingencies in the classroom). The following steps constitute the warning procedure:

1. At the start of the behavior, warn the student.
2. If the student starts to behave appropriately, reward the student after a short time.
3. If after a short time the student does not behave appropriately, use the next stronger correction procedure, separation (see the following section).

A "warning" statement describes both the inappropriate and the desired appropriate behaviors, along with the consequences for continuing the inappropriate behavior, including the loss of positive behavior consequences. The "reward after a short time" in step 2 is, again, to avoid the contingency error described as rewarding the student behavior of, "If I am inappropriate and then become appropriate, I will be rewarded." Step 3 moves the teacher to a stronger procedure to stop the disruptive or continuing nondisruptive behavior. If the student's inappropriate social behavior continues, then instruction of the group will suffer. In many ways, stopping inappropriate behavior not only allows instruction to continue for others and ensures that they are not pulled off task but also helps the students see teachers as effective, take-charge instructors who follow established contingencies. Some examples of the warning procedure, follow. The first continues the last example from the ignore-reward procedure, where the inappropriate behavior persisted.

Example 1

STUDENT: (*Sedric continues to draw even after repeated application of the ignore-reward procedure.*)

TEACHER: Sedric, this is a warning. Continued drawing during reading is not appropriate. If you continue, you will be separated from the group and lose your chance for an A today.

STUDENT: (*Sedric starts to read as directed.*)

TEACHER: (*After a short time and perhaps after giving a reward statement or two to others.*) Sedric, you're reading clearly and I appreciate your following along. Your chances for an A today are improving.

Notice that the warning was issued directly: The teacher started off with "Sedric, this is a warning" and then described the appropriate and inappropriate behaviors and their accompanying consequences. Often it is sufficient to identify the student and say, "This is a warning." This is especially appropriate when the students have been in a classroom that uses correction procedures persistently and consistently, and have gone over examples and nonexamples of inappropriate behavior and its consequences. But the full procedure should be used often. The accompanying reward statement first directs attention to the appropriate academic behavior, "reading clearly," before acknowledging the appropriate social behavior. The next two examples focus on disruptive behavior.

Example 2

STUDENT: (*Ramella talks out during a teacher presentation.*)

TEACHER: Ramella, this is a warning. Talking out is not acceptable. If you do not attend to the presentation, you will be separated from the group and lose the privileges that come with following the rules.

STUDENT: (*Ramella stops talking immediately and starts to attend to the group presentation.*)

TEACHER: (*A short time later the teacher calls on Ramella to answer a question, and the correct answer is given.*) Ramella, that's correct. It shows me that you are paying attention. I appreciate it.

Example 3

STUDENT: (*Fernando laughs at another student's errors.*)

TEACHER: Fernando, this is a warning. Laughing at others is not permitted. The rule is to accept the errors of others. If you continue laughing, you will be separated from the group.

STUDENT: (*When another student makes an error, Fernando laughs and mocks the student.*)

TEACHER: (*Uses the separation procedure.*)

Fernando's continued inappropriate behavior requires the teacher to move to a more powerful social correction procedure: separation from the group.

The Separation Procedure   Warnings usually stop much of the disruptive behavior that occurs in the classroom, especially after the correction procedures have been in operation for a time. But often a few students' social behavior is inappropriate enough to stop instruction or put others in danger. The separation procedure is used when a student's *inappropriate behavior puts others in danger or continues disrupting the lesson.* Dangerous behaviors include hitting others, throwing objects, or extreme emotional outbursts that have the potential to put others in danger. The behaviors that fit into this class depend on the classroom situation. The separation procedure, like warnings, is most effective if used at the first occurrence or reoccurrence of the behavior. In these cases, the teacher stops other possible dangers or disruptions to the lesson. The separation procedure's steps are as follows:

1. Tell the student that the behavior is unacceptable.
2. Separate the student from the rest of the class for a predetermined time.
3. When the time is up, ask the student if he is ready to return and participate.
4. If the student's answer is yes, let the student return and after a short time reward him for appropriate behavior.
5. If the student's answer is no or he does not reply, have the student remain separated for another period and return to step 3 at the end of this time.

The statement given to separate the student from the group includes a description of the inappropriate and the desired appropriate behaviors. Both of these behaviors are put in the context of being separated and what the student should think about during the separation time. For example:

"Wolfgang, hitting others is unacceptable and separates you from the group. Go to the separation area and consider what is appropriate during reading and what you have lost because of your present behavior."

There is no need for great variation here. The teacher must be direct and return to the lesson. The preceding statement takes about 8 to 10 seconds. Since correction procedures are established in the same way as classroom rules are (discussed in detail below), the students will know what to do as the teacher continues the interrupted instructional activities.

Separation involves the student going to a predesignated place, such as a chair in the back of the room. The important element is that the student not engage in any social or academic behavior that could be rewarding or rewarded during the separation time. The student should not be allowed to play with objects or do any academic work that would receive credit. Often teachers put students in halls unattended. Here students are given the chance to talk to passers-by, view any activity that may take place there, or play with some object they have procured or already had in a pocket. The duration of the separation time can vary, but is best linked with the length of one class activity. For example, if a student continues to disrupt or put others in danger at the beginning of an activity, the separation time should be for the length of the activity. If the behavior occurs at the end of an activity, the separation should span the next activity. During separation, the student must lose out on all possible academic and social rewards related to appropriate behavior. The student should not be able to earn academic credit for work missed, even if the teacher thinks that the work should be made up. In other words, the student's social behavior has an impact on the student's scholastic (grade) achievement. The following examples clarify the use of the full procedure. The first starts where the last warning procedure example left off.

Example 1

STUDENT: *(When another student makes an error, Fernando laughs and mocks the student.)*

TEACHER: Fernando, your continued laughing at others separates you from the group. Go to the separation area and consider what you should be doing when others make errors and the consequences of not doing so.

STUDENT: *(Goes to the separation area for the specified time.)*

TEACHER: *(After the specified time has passed.)* Fernando, do you care to join the group for the independent work part of the lesson?

STUDENT: Yes.

TEACHER: Then, please do so.

STUDENT: (*Works appropriately for a short time.*)

TEACHER: Fernando, the first section of your worksheet is entirely correct; I enjoy seeing you participate and do so well. Keep it up.

Example 2

STUDENT: (*Ursula hits another student during a presentation.*)

TEACHER: Ursula, hitting others separates you from the class. Go to the separation area and consider what you should be doing during the lesson and what you are losing for not doing it.

STUDENT: (*Goes to the separation area.*)

TEACHER: (*After the specified time has passed.*) Ursula, are you ready to return and follow the class rules?

STUDENT: (*Ursula does not answer.*)

TEACHER: Everyone, take out your books, turn to page 37, and do the problems listed on the board. Raise your hand if you need help and please remember the rest of the rules for the workbook activity.

STUDENT: (*Still in the separation area.*)

TEACHER: (*After the specified time is up for Ursula's separation*) Ursula, are you ready to return and follow the class rules?

STUDENT: Yes.

TEACHER: Then, please do so.

STUDENT: (*Works appropriately for a short time.*)

TEACHER: Ursula, look at this! It shows that you can really punctuate when you try hard. Can you do that for the rest of the problems?

STUDENT: Yes.

TEACHER: Excellent, I know you can, so give it a try.

In both examples the teacher does not waste words. Minimal interaction occurs. The teacher wants to spend time attending to appropriate, not inappropriate, behavior. The reward statements in both examples contain the condition statement's motivation element (see Chapter 8), which is important when keeping weak behavior going (setting the conditions in this way is a necessary and usually sufficient management procedure).

The Office Referral Procedure   Separating the student from the group and putting him or her in an unrewarding place will stop most inappropriate behavior in a relatively short period of time or reduce its occurrence to a very low rate. But sometimes the disruptive or dangerous inappropriate behavior continues to persist or consists of something the teacher or school defines as requiring more than separation from the group. This means separation or referral to the principal or to whoever is in charge of discipline problems. The following three conditions indicate when such a measure needs to be taken:

1. Some lesson-disturbing behavior continues in the separation area (after the student has been warned there).
2. The inappropriate behavior continues over several days.
3. The teacher or the school thinks the behavior is severe enough to warrant immediate separation to the office (no warning is given).

The first condition requires the application of a warning in isolation. This warning simply tells the student that if the behavior continues during separation, the student will be sent to the office. For example:

"Heldegard, if you continue to talk out, you will be sent to the office."

If the behavior does not stop in a very short time, the student should be sent to the office. In the office the same rules need to be followed as when the student is separated in the classroom: (1) No rewarding behavior should be engaged in and (2) no academic credit should be given, even if the student has to make up the work. Only in this way will the full consequences of the inappropriate behavior become clear to the student.

If the student must repeatedly be sent to the office, the last step is to separate the student from school or set up a parent conference. Generally, a parent conference is effective when a student has been sent to the office twice or if the behavior has been defined as one requiring a parent conference for the student to stay in school. All schools have procedures and behaviors related to parent conferences. The important concern is that these be congruent and consistent with classroom management.

ADJUSTING SOCIAL CORRECTION PROCEDURES FOR INDIVIDUAL STUDENTS

In general, the correction procedure used depends on two factors: (1) the severity of the behavior and (2) the length of time the behavior has continued. With the latter, only consideration has been given to the student's inappropriate behavior being resistant to correction and requiring a stronger procedure (e.g., separation instead of warning). But teachers also need to consider the student who typically exhibits appropriate social behavior over an extended period, but on some rare occasion behaves inappropriately. In such cases, the correction procedure used can be less extreme (e.g., a warning instead of a separation). For situations requiring stronger or weaker correction procedures, the teacher's statements need to indicate to the student that the usual procedure is not being followed.

This is especially true of cases using a weaker procedure. The following two examples cover both types.

> "Derek, because your talking out has continued for several days, I am sending you to the office."

> "Astrid and Bernice, because you both have behaved appropriately in the past, I am only going to separate you at the back of the room for fighting. Please go there and consider what you should have been doing and what you have lost."

Adjustments like those in the second example should be used *only once* and only when students have a long history of appropriate behavior. The second time inappropriate behavior occurs even in the span of a semester, teachers should use the standard correction sequence.

A GENERAL ACADEMIC CORRECTION PROCEDURE

Whenever possible, a student's academic errors should be corrected without delay. Errors practiced by students ultimately require greater effort for remediation, both in terms of teacher classroom activity and instructional planning time. This section presents a general procedure to facilitate quick and efficient academic corrections.

Academic corrections lie in the transition area between classroom and instructional management because they often repeat some portion of the instructional procedure used to establish the behavior. Thus, the content of academic corrections is often program specific. But the varieties of corrections have enough in common to allow a general correction procedure to be used effectively and efficiently. The foundation for a general academic correction procedure has been established in Chapter 2, which presents teacher-specific procedures to define the desired student behavior, and in Chapters 3 and 5, which show how to build condition and reward statements for such behavior. The steps of this general procedure are the following:

1. Indicate what is incorrect (inappropriate).
2. Model the correct (appropriate) behavior.
3. Have the student perform the problem or give the answer on his or her own.
4. If the behavior is correct, inform the student.
5. If the behavior is still incorrect, return to step 1.
6. Repeat the problem type or question at a later time.

In step 1, the teacher can indicate that something is wrong or point to a specific element that requires correction. The approach chosen depends on the type of behavior performed and the context of the error. If the student has misstated a fact or principle, the teacher indicates what is incorrect by a simple "No" or "The correct answer is . . . ." The latter is preferable, since giving the correct answer covers steps 1 and 2 at one time. If an error occurs in the context of similar problems, some of which are answered correctly, the teacher needs to say something like, "Look at number 6 carefully." Often the student will return to the problem and correct it; if so, the teacher will have progressed through step 3. The behavior in this case is usually part of a procedure containing multiple behaviors (see Chapters 7 and 8), one of which the student performed incorrectly.

The importance of step 1 depends on the form and context of the student response. If the answer is oral, the error is indicated by going quickly to step 2 of the correction procedure. Because the correction (step 2) immediately follows the incorrect behavior, the error is indicated clearly. If the incorrect behavior is in the context of other responses, which usually indicates a written form, the teacher must point out clearly what is incorrect. For example, during an independent worksheet, the teacher might say, "John, look at number 6," or "John, number 6 is incorrect."

In step 2, modeling the correct behavior, the teacher can simply give the answer or demonstrate the procedure. This approach is always effective for two general types of behavior: (1) stating or identifying (usually in oral or written form) an object, fact, rule, principle, or procedure; and (2) stating or identifying (usually in oral or written form) where, when, why, or how the object, fact, rule, principle, or procedure is used or applied. For these two types of behaviors, modeling the correct behavior consists of giving the answer. But modeling the correct behavior should be controlled in terms of degree and content for the third general class of behavior: (3) performing a procedure that requires the application of a fact, rule, or principle.

The modeling of a procedure requires demonstrating the steps of the procedure while providing a verbal description of each step being demonstrated. If the procedure involves the application of a fact, rule, or principle, the teacher must first find out if the student can state it by asking questions that require the correct identification. If the student cannot make the correct identification, the incorrect behavior is at least partly related to the first two general types of behavior and the correction is to give the answer. Only after the student is able to state the fact, rule, or principle can the procedural application be performed. Once the student can state the fact, rule, or principle, the teacher must describe and demonstrate the steps of the procedure. Often the procedure being demonstrated is less important than the rule. For example, the application of end marks (periods) to sentences involves finding the end of the sentence and placing the appropriate end mark there. The important behavior is related to the first two general classes of behavior listed above: (1) identifying the type of sentence and (2) identifying which end mark goes with that type of sentence. At the age students generally learn about using end marks, the procedure for putting them in the right place is less difficult than making the required identifications.

Often a student performs a procedure, with or without the application of facts, rules, or principles, in the context of other similar types, like on a worksheet. A teacher who sees an item is incorrect in the context of several similar correct items needs to point out the error, but the student should model the correct behavior. Because the student has achieved several correct responses in context, the student will generally demonstrate the correct behavior. The teacher-student interaction might be as follows:

TEACHER: Timothy, look carefully at number 3 of part A on your worksheet. (*Step 1.*)
STUDENT: (*Works the problem correctly—steps 2 and 3 combined.*)
TEACHER: Paying close attention helps get the items correct. Keep it up. (*Step 4.*)

Because of the context of other correct items, step 6 of the correction procedure need not be performed.

Steps 3 through 6 of the correction procedure (student performs behavior; if behavior is correct, student receives reward; if behavior is incorrect, return to step 1; repeat problem type at a later time) are almost self-explanatory. In step 4, the reward statement is either partial or complete. In step 6, the duration between the time of the correction and the repeating of the problem depends on the instructional program, the size of the class, and the structure of the activity in which the behavior takes place. The latter factor leads to a problem for teachers using academic corrections, since students often do some portion of work at home and the teacher corrects work outside the classroom and away from the student performing the behavior. Such teacher corrections only perform the first step of the academic correction. It would be a day or two more before the teacher discovered if the student corrections were correct. This delay is not important if the student gets 80 percent to 90 percent of the items correct on all skills covered. But if the student's error rate is high, there is a need to correct the behavior as fast as possible, so that the error is not practiced.

The best solution to the problem of delayed correction is to design the class with a daily workcheck or work correction activity (as suggested in Chapter 4 and elaborated in Chapter 11). In effect, if the behavior is important enough to teach, it is important enough to be mastered by the student. The time spent on correcting work will help ensure that mastery is taking place and the prerequisites for future behavior are present. Also, one of the best management procedures is effective instruction, which allows students to see the changes in their behavior. The time given to checking work in class aids this end.

Often during a workcheck or work correction activity, there is more to correct than the teacher can attend to in the time allowed. In such cases, the teacher needs to (1) sample a portion of the corrections done by as many students as possible and (2) use students who have mastered the material as assistant teachers. The job of the assistant teacher is to watch a student with problems and correct his work. If it is correct, the assistant tells the student, almost problem by problem. If it is incorrect, the assistant performs the steps of the academic correction procedure. The critical element is to teach the assistant the steps of the procedure and to watch the assistant use the procedure with another student who is having problems with the material. Teaching the procedure is simplified because the students are informed of it, as indicated in the section on introducing and using correction procedures. One last point: Each student should be given a chance to assist others, even if only in some small behavior he or she performs well.

HOW TO DELIVER CORRECTION PROCEDURES

The corrective consequence statement portion of the warning, separation, and referral correction procedures should be delivered in a neutral, nonemotional, but firm and brisk manner, so that the teacher avoids arguing about what was done and "reasoning" with the student. Such arguing or reasoning is unnecessary if the correction conditions have been set as indicated in the previous section. The best rule for delivering corrections is: *Follow the procedure.* The main idea is to make the correction quickly, so that the student does not get excess attention for inappropriate behavior and instruction can continue. The reward consequence statements for all three social correction procedures need to be delivered (as outlined in Chapter 3) with sincerity and a smile.

The corrective consequence statement of academic corrections should be approached with less authority and firmness than are social corrections. The former should be delivered as if the teacher saying, "Gee whiz, there is a little problem here; let's see if we can solve it." Because the teacher has gone over the form of the correction procedure with the students, they will see it as a positive event. In no way should the teacher make the correction threatening. The reward consequence portion of academic corrections need to be presented (see outline in Chapter 3).

INTRODUCING CORRECTION PROCEDURES

Like rules, correction procedures should be introduced and reviewed throughout the year. Because of the complexity of these procedures, some detail must be eliminated when presenting them to students.

When introducing correction procedures, the teacher should provide a positive perspective for viewing them and the consequences for using them. The best perspective is the reward procedure for appropriate behavior. This part of the teacher's introduction might include the following:

> "When you behave appropriately, I, as often as possible, try to describe what you have done, what its consequences are, and how you have improved over time. But there are times when we all make mistakes or do something inappropriately. Such things need to be corrected so they are, one, less likely to happen in the future and, two, because it will help you learn. Here is what I will do when you make errors."

Social Correction Procedures Next the social correction procedures should be introduced. It is important not to present social corrections in a negative way, but positively in a matter-of-fact voice. For example:

> "Also, there are times when one does not behave in an appropriate social way, that is, follow the class rules. As with the academic error, I will do one of several things."

For the social correction procedures, students need to be aware of five steps:

1. The teacher may at first ignore some behavior that does not bother others.
2. If the behavior continues or disrupts the lesson, the student will be warned.
3. If the behavior continues or puts others in danger, the student will be separated from the group for the rest of the activity and not receive credit for the academic work that he or she must make up.
4. If inappropriate behavior continues during the separation or the student continues to be separated, the student will be removed to the office and a parent conference set up.
5. When the student's separation time is up, he or she will be asked to return to the group. If there is no answer or a refusal, the student will remain separated and continue to lose academic credit.

These steps cover all four social correction procedures. Teachers should refer to these five steps to correct inappropriate social behavior. In the first three steps, the teacher gives and asks for examples and non-examples of the behaviors that require a particular social correction. Continuing from the above example, the teacher-student interaction might be as follows:

TEACHER: For inappropriate social behavior, up to five steps can be taken to correct the behavior. First, if the behavior does not bother others, I *may* ignore it for a short time, thinking that the student will correct him or herself. Some of the things that do not bother others include sleeping during a presentation (unless you snore) and gazing out the window during a worksheet activity. What are some other behaviors that you could do that would not bother others?

STUDENT: *(Teacher calls on individuals to reply.)*

TEACHER: Second, for nonbothering behavior that continues or behavior that disrupts the lesson, the student will be warned. The warning informs the student of what was inappropriate and what was expected of him or her. Disrupting the lesson includes talking out of turn, calling out obscenities, and flying paper airplanes. What are some other behaviors that you could do that would disrupt the lesson?

STUDENT: *(Teacher calls on individuals to reply.)*

TEACHER: Third, if these behaviors continue or the behavior puts others in danger, the student will be separated to the back of the room or, fourth, to the office. Dangerous behavior includes hitting others or throwing objects. *For this type of behavior no warning will be given.* I will determine if the separation is to the back of the room or to the office. During this separation time you will receive no academic credit for your work, but you will have to make work up. Finally, at the end of your separation time you will be asked to return. If you do not answer or say no, you will remain separated and continue to lose academic credit and all other benefits of working with the group.

During this presentation, it is important to show the students the place for separation, explain and model a warning for them, and role-play a student being warned and separated. Once this portion of the introduction is complete, the teacher should use the motivational element of the condition statement to challenge and commit students to behaving so that the procedures do not have to be used:

"How many of you think these procedures make sense? (*Students reply.*) How many think they can follow the rules so that these procedures do not have to be used? (*Students reply.*) I think you can if you try hard; let's give it a try."

The rules and the social correction procedures are again related: Following the rules indicates the appropriate behavior required to avoid the use of the correction procedures.

During this introduction it is important to have four of the five points posted, as with rules. These should be short and might be as follows:

1. Warn
2. Separate—room
3. Separate—office
4. Return and participate

The introduction is essentially one large condition statement describing (1) complex condition-behavior nonmatch relationships, (2) the consequences of such behavior, and (3) the commitment by students to try to avoid such nonmatching behavior.

Academic Correction Procedures Academic correction procedures should be introduced after social correction procedures. This introduction should cover the first five steps of the procedure. For younger students, the wording should be simplified, and for older students, it can be left relatively unchanged and the sixth step added. The points should be written out like the class rules (see Chapter 4). This part of the introduction might be as follows:

"For academic errors, errors related to your class assignments, I will do the following five things." (*Pointing to the list of points.*) "First, I will indicate what is incorrect. Second, I will model the correct behavior. Third, you will perform the behavior or answer the question. Fourth, if you are correct, I will inform you. Fifth, if what you have done is still wrong, I will start over."

At this point it is most effective to demonstrate by having a student role-play making an error. If time permits, teachers should demonstrate two different errors, one oral and one written. The contents of the demonstration will depend on the subject being taught. For elementary teachers, basic skills demonstrations are best.

USING THE CORRECTION PROCEDURES

Five important elements are necessary for the successful use of correction procedures in the classroom.

Posting and Reviewing Correction Procedures Posted procedures provide the teacher and the student with a referent that can be easily pointed to during review. The review should be done daily during the first few weeks of the procedure's use. After the first two or three days, review should take less than a minute and need only detail the points that are giving students the most trouble. Essentially, the posting and reviewing of correction procedures follows the procedures used for rules (see Chapter 4). Most important in reviewing social correction procedures is asking for examples of inappropriate behavior that fit the different correction procedures.

Setting Conditions and Rewarding the Students for Not Making Errors Reward statements should emphasize "doing it right the first time." They should be given for both academic and social behavior. Some examples follow:

> "Everyone, I appreciate your following the rules today. Doing it right from the start saves us all a lot of time and effort and shows you are gaining maturity. I hope you enjoyed the day."

> "Jerry, your math homework problems were all correct. There is no need for us to take time to correct work if it is done right the first time. Keep it up."

> "Alta, you did it right the first time, again. This certainly shows you are trying hard and cooperating. Because you know how to do these types of problems, could you help Nathan with his?"

Examples 1 and 3 not only indicate doing it right the first time, but relate the class of behavior to others, showing the student or students what larger classes of behavior (e. g., cooperation) they are developing by "doing it right the first time."

Informing School and Parents of Correction Procedures If all concerned parties are aware of the teacher's specific classroom consequences, there is a greater chance for understanding and cooperation if action needs to be taken for inappropriate behavior. When introducing the consequences to parents or school, the teacher should be careful to stress not only corrections but also rewards. This dual emphasis provides all parties with a balanced perspective on what occurs in the classroom.

Informing the school usually means contacting the principal or assistant principal. When this contact is made, the teacher should not only talk over the procedures but write them out. At this meeting, the teacher and school official establish the general office procedure, which must adhere to the basic rule of separation: minimize the student's chance of reward. The behaviors that involve suspension from school or setting up parent conferences must be clearly delineated. There will always be variance, but it should be reduced as much as possible.

Once the school procedures have been established, the parents can be informed of the consequence procedures to be used. This is best done with a letter and/or a phone call follow-up. The letter is easiest for the elementary teacher with a self-contained classroom. A prudent step is to have the letter contain a return slip on which the parent acknowledges the procedures and agrees to them. The contents of the letter should, again, cover both rewards and corrections, with the former being stated first. (Chapter 11 contains a sample letter to parents, with an accompanying acknowledgment slip, and the contents of this letter are clarified in Chapter 10, when supplemental rewards and point systems are discussed.) A clear delineation of rewards and corrections for students, parents, and school promotes student growth and positive teacher-school-community relations.

Keeping Records How often has the student been warned, separated, or removed to the office? This is an important concern when the teacher decides what correction to make for persistent problems (see Chapter 12) or when parents ask for information about their child's inappropriate behavior. Specific details will relieve many of the emotional side effects that generally accompany interaction with the student or parents when extreme corrections must be made (i. e., parent conference or a school suspension for inappropriate classroom behavior). If the teacher can tell the parent the extent to which other corrections have been tried, the effect of a specific statement will be apparent. Compare the following specific (1) and general (2) statements that a teacher might make to parents:

> "Over the last month I have had to warn Oscar 20 times. That is once per day on the average, and I have separated him 10 times because he did not stop disrupting the class. I believe that his behavior is distracting from the instructional time of others too much and, thus, requires this parent conference."

> "Oscar has been so inappropriate lately that I have had to stop the class on numerous occasions to remove him from the group. This cannot continue, because I am being distracted from teaching the other students."

The first statement describes the continuity of the student's inappropriate behavior (remember that the parents have been informed of the procedures and the types of behaviors each involves) and the consequences for others that result. At this point, a foundation has been laid for the teacher and the parents to start considering what must be done to stop the behavior. On the other hand, the second example will most likely lead the parents to ask for specifics, because their child's story probably was different from the teacher's.

Another advantage of keeping records is that parents can be shown the extent to which their child has changed since the last teacher-parent meeting, allowing the procedures decided on to be evaluated. Without the details of behavior occurrence, the teacher has no real accounting of student change and, thus, teacher success. The details of keeping records are covered in Chapter 11.

Consistently and Persistently Using Correction Procedures Like reward and condition statements, corrective procedures must be used consistently and persistently. For corrections, consistency is the delivery of a corrective procedure contingent on a condition-behavior nonmatch. Consistency also includes the application of the correction procedure that fits the behavior's severity or duration. If either of these aspects of consistency is violated, the likelihood of the inappropriate behavior continuing increases. In order to achieve consistency, the teacher has to memorize the procedures and the behaviors to which they are applicable.

Persistence in correcting is the continued contingent application of the procedure each time the inappropriate behavior occurs. Thus, corrections must be maintained for the life of the inappropriate behavior. In general, such behavior will evolve from more severe to mild—a change that indicates the student's attempt to adapt. Even though the behavior is becoming less severe, the appropriate correction procedure must be applied without fail. For example, a student who started by hitting or kicking others will later sulk in his chair when things are not going right. The former behavior required the separation procedure, the latter behavior requires use of the ignore-reward technique. The student is moving closer to appropriate, rewardable behavior; and the ignore-reward procedure is designed to gently push the student in this direction. But if his milder forms of inappropriate behavior are rewarded and not corrected, they will persist and the student will fail to develop the social and academic behavior needed for future success. Thus, teachers must consistently and persistently correct inappropriate behavior.

Finally, the use of the warning or separation procedures is often observed to ignite further or more severe inappropriate behavior. If this happens, the only thing to do is to correct the new or more extreme behavior. This secondary behavior must be eliminated just like other inappropriate behavior. No matter what kind of correction procedures are used, such secondary misbehavior may appear. Although corrections are the most difficult procedures for the teacher to learn and apply, they are required for effective management.

BUILDING AND DELIVERING
CORRECTION PROCEDURES

In order to build and deliver the correction procedures described, the teacher must answer certain questions. Thus, the following building routine and delivery checklist are included.

Correction Procedure Building Routine   The following questions will help the teacher to utilize the correction procedures individually and as a whole.

1. *What subject area is of interest?* The area will provide a frame of reference for the following questions.
2. *What classes of behavior could and/or do the students perform that do not match the conditions?* The answer is arrived at by examining remembered instances.
    a. *Is the behavior social or academic?*
    b. *What are the qualitative and quantitative attributes of the class as evidenced by the instances?* This question facilitates thorough description.
    c. *What are some related classes of behavior?* The answers lead to other classes of inappropriate behaviors.

3. *For social behaviors, what correction procedure is applicable?* Considerations should include the following:
    a. *Does the behavior disrupt the instructional presentation or bother other students?* If the answer is yes, use the warning procedure. If the answer is no, use the ignore-reward procedure.
    b. *Does the behavior put others in danger or continue to disrupt the lesson?* If the answer is yes, use the separation procedure.
    c. *How long or how often does the inappropriate behavior have to continue before the student is sent to the office?*
    d. *How long or how often does the inappropriate behavior have to continue before a parent conference is called?*

4. *Has an office procedure been established?* This procedure needs to be carefully worked out with the principal and office staff.
5. *Have the parents been notified of the correction procedures?* Consider the following:
    a. *Has a letter and/or a phone been used?*
    b. *Have the rewards and other positive aspects of classroom procedures also been mentioned?* The teacher will want

the corrections to be well understood, but it is important that the parents see the corrections as part of a very positive system.
   c. *Is a permission or parental consent form needed?* The answer is probably yes.

6. *Have the steps of each procedure been memorized?* (Some hints and mnemonics are given below.)

If all of these questions are answered as completely as possible, the teacher is ready to practice and implement corrections in the classroom.

Correction Procedure Delivery Checklist   The delivery of each correction procedure must be carefully practiced to achieve maximal effectiveness. By practicing in the context of the following questions the teacher will increase the likelihood of success.

1. *Is there a condition-behavior nonmatch?* A correction procedure is delivered contingent on a nonmatch.
2. *For the ignore-reward procedure, is the initial statement overt enough for the inappropriate student to attend to it?*
3. *For the warning and separation procedures, is the delivery firm and brisk?*
4. *For the social correction procedures, is arguing or reasoning with the student avoided?*
5. *For the academic correction, is the delivery done in a cordial and nonthreatening manner?*
6. *Have the steps to each procedure been posted and reviewed with the students?*

Once these six delivery questions can be answered in the affirmative, the teacher is ready to deliver correction statements to the classroom students.

Memorizing Correction Procedures: Mnemonics and Hints   The teacher's use of correction procedures must become automatic, like walking and talking. The teacher must start and carry through a correction without hesitation. If not, effectiveness is lost and classroom instruction will be further interrupted. To correct students automatically, the teacher must (1) memorize each procedure, (2) repeatedly practice using each procedure, (3) memorize the behaviors that fit the different procedures.

Only individual practice and study will enable the teacher to become proficient. The methods of practicing these procedures are the same as are required for reward and condition statements: The teacher must act out, talk through, and write down an imaginary or real correction situation.

A set of mnemonics is given to help teachers memorize each procedure. The steps in parentheses refer to the steps of the procedure being described:

Ignore-Reward Procedure

1. Ignore and reward (steps 1 and 2)
2. Reward or try again (steps 3 and 4)
3. Reward or warn (steps 4 and 5)
4. Set conditions (step 6)

Warning Procedure

1. Warn (step 1)
2. Reward or separate (steps 2 and 3)

Separation Procedure

1. Inform and separate (steps 1 and 2)
2. Ask and reward (steps 3 and 4)
3. Ask and ask again (steps 3 and 5)

Academic Procedure

1. Inform and model (steps 1 and 2)
2. Perform and reward (steps 3 and 4)
3. Perform and try again (steps 3 and 5)
4. Repeat (step 6)

These mnemonics, if practiced with the steps of the full procedure, will help the teacher remember the details in practice and delivery. The main goal of practice is to get corrections to flow like reward and condition statements.

P R A C T I C E   A C T I V I T I E S

1. Correction procedures for social behavior
    1.1 Identify initial statement elements of warning and separation procedures for delivery practice. Present examples for group critique and discussion.
        a. Select an example of a warning statement from the text. Use the example as a starting point in listing each element in a warning statement: (p. 114)
            (1) Warning identification
            (2) Description of inappropriate behavior
            (3) Description of appropriate behavior
            (4) Consequences of inappropriate behavior
            (5) Consequences of lost appropriate behavior
        b. Using the elements above, give an example of a warning statement. Write it in a form you would say it.
        c. Select an example of a separation statement from the text. Use the example as a starting point in listing each element in a separation statement: (p. 116)
            (1) Description of inappropriate behavior
            (2) Statement of separation procedure
            (3) Statement of what student should attend to during separation (appropriate behavior, loss of appropriate behavior's reward)
        d. Using the elements above, give an example of a separation statement. Write it in a form you would say it.
    1.2 Practice effective delivery of warning and separation statements.
        a. Present examples for group critique and discussion. (p. 129)
        b. Practice effective delivery of a warning statement and a separation statement. Present in an emotionally neutral, firm, brisk manner.
    1.3 Practice generating examples of warning statements. Present examples for group critique and discussion. (p. 114).
        a. List ten student social behaviors inappropriate in a classroom setting. Try to make the examples as different as possible from each other. Remember that examples of social behavior problems for warning procedures (i. e., do not interfere with instruction or are mildly disruptive).
        b. Read through each behavior on the list, identifying desired appropriate behavior, consequences of inappropriate behavior, and positive consequences of the appropriate behavior lost. Do not write any of these elements.
        c. Next, for each behavior on the list, generate a warning statement. Practice delivering the ten statements effectively and unhurriedly.
    1.4 Practice generating examples of separation statements. Follow the procedure in 1.3 to generate separation statements. Practice delivering the ten statements effectively and unhurriedly. Remember that

inappropriate behavior for separation statements is disruptive or puts others in danger. (p. 116)

1.5 Practice steps for correction procedures: reward-ignore, warning, separation. Review steps in small group discussion. (p. 131)

    a. List each of the steps for the reward-ignore, warning, and separation procedures. Practice repeating the steps in order for each procedure until you can present them to another person quickly and in a relaxed fashion. First practice slowly, then speed up.

    b. Obtain nine 3″ × 5″ or similar index cards. Write the name of each procedure on three cards. Have a friend shuffle the cards and present six in order to you. When you hear the name on the card, present the steps for the procedure (or you can practice yourself).

1.6 Simulate decision making with the three correction procedures. Practice with a small group, followed by critique and discussion (p. 131).

    a. Have a classmate identify four different inappropriate social behaviors and their settings. Then, for each behavior, specify three different levels of severity:

        (1) Nondisruptive (reward-ignore)

        (2) Disruptive (warning)

        (3) Potentially dangerous (separation)

    b. Write the 12 different behaviors generated in 1.6a on an index card. Present cards in random sequence. Practice identifying which of the three procedures to use for the given behavior. Try to decide quickly. If necessary, obtain additional examples and repeat.

1.7 Simulate the implementation of the procedures. Practice three with a small group, followed by critique and discussion.

1.8 Repeat the exercise in 1.7, but this time act out the procedure as if you were role-playing with a student.

2. Academic correction procedure (p. 120)

    2.1 Practice the academic correction procedure's steps. List each of the six steps of the academic correction procedure in the text. Practice repeating the steps in order until you can present them to another person quickly and in a relaxed fashion. First, practice slowly and then speed up.

    2.2 Practice the academic correction procedure. Critique practice and discuss in a small group.

    List five examples of student academic errors. Make the examples as different as possible from each other. For each example, follow the first four steps of the academic correction procedure as if you were role-playing with another student. Repeat until you can complete the procedure quickly and in a relaxed fashion.

    2.3 Simulate implementation of the academic correction procedure. Critique simulation and discuss in a small group.

        a. Have a classmate identify ten short learnings tasks on which an error could or could not be made. The tasks can be different or similar, as desired.

      b. Have the classmate work the tasks and occasionally make an error while you watch. Use the academic correction procedure when an error occurs.

3. Using correction procedures in the classroom (p. 130)
   3.1 Identify inappropriate social and academic behaviors.
      a. Observe a regular classroom. Try to return to a classroom you have worked in before.
      b. Count the frequency of inappropriate social behaviors over a 10–20 minute period. Whenever an inappropriate behavior occurs, note whether a reward-ignore, warning, or separation procedure is required.
      c. Next, imagine you are the teacher. Observe the students and, to yourself, present the proper correction procedure to the student whenever an inappropriate behavior occurs. (Use only the initial parts, up to the point that student behavior can change.) If possible, use a tape recorder in the rear of the room or behind a one-way glass.
      d. Repeat the procedure in 3.1c, this time for academic corrections.
   3.2 Deliver correction procedures to students in a regular classroom. Have an observer critique your delivery, using the checklist in the text.
      a. Arrange to take over a teacher's class for one half-hour. Identify in advance appropriate social and academic behaviors for the activities planned.
      b. Present condition and reward statements as appropriate. In addition, follow the regard-ignore, warning, and separation correction procedures as necessary for inappropriate social behavior. Also follow procedures for academic corrections.

REFERENCES

The response to inappropriate social or academic behavior traditionally has taken two forms: remediation and corrective teaching. The former usually involves a teaching specialist, either in behavior problems or subject area, and the student's removal from the regular classroom for remedial instruction because of the problem's extensiveness. Corrective teaching, on the other hand, has been done by the classroom teacher when skill deficiencies have been identified for the class or a student subgroup. The present approach is concerned with corrective procedures used by the teacher to focus on individual instances of inappropriate social or academic behavior. The hierarchical set of procedures presented for socially inappropriate behavior operationalizes many of the practical suggestions contained in the work of Lee Canter and Marlene Canter, Rudolf Dreikurs, Haim Ginott, William Glasser, J. S. Kounin, and B. F. Skinner. This is especially true in the context of the previous chapters and Chapters 8 and 10.

Canter, L., & Canter, M. *Assertive Discipline: A Take-Charge Approach for Today's Educator*. Seal Beach, Calif.: Canter and Associates, 1976.

Dreikurs, R., & Cassel, P. *Discipline without Tears*. New York: Hawthorn, 1972.

Ginott, H. *Teacher and Child*. New York: Macmillan, 1971.

Glasser, W. *Schools without Failure*. New York: Harper & Row, 1969.

Kounin, J. S. *Discipline and Group Management in Classrooms*. New York: Holt, Rinehart and Winston, 1970.

Skinner, B. F. *Technology of Teaching*. New York: Appleton-Century-Crofts, 1968.

The correction of instances of inappropriate academic behavior is of recent origin. The general correction procedure presented rests on the detailed work of Siegfried Engelmann and his associate, Douglas Carnine. Their work is the first to focus on the technology of correcting students during the learning-teaching interaction of instruction and practice.

Carnine, D., & Silbert, J. *Direct Instruction Reading*. Columbus, Ohio: Merrill, 1979.

Englemann, S., & Carnine, D. *Theory of Instruction: Principles and Applications*. New York: Irvington, 1983.

CHAPTER SEVEN

ANALYZING BEHAVIOR: PART II

T he analysis of behavior presented in Chapter 2 provides a static language for picturing behavior and procedures for establishing behavioral content. The static language describes behavior in terms of classes and instances. Its procedures define the specific content of behavior classes through an analysis of objectives embedded in the structure of the curriculum. Chapter 7 continues the analysis of behavior by detailing the relationships among behavioral units (classes) and the processes of behavioral evolution. The chapter also outlines procedures for determining relationships among behaviors of interest. Once such relationships and the steps of evolution are defined, the construction of behaviors can begin in systematic fashion. The procedures in the chapters up to and following Chapter 7 provide the tools necessary to build behaviors of interest within the bounds of classroom management.

BEHAVIOR CLASS RELATIONSHIPS

Defining a class of behavior so that its members (instances) can be observed is an important step in analyzing behavior. An equally important second step requires representing the relationships among different behavior classes and subclasses. Defining class and subclass relationships is the first step in planning conditions and consequences to evolve and maintain behaviors over time. (Knowledge of these relationships will be used in Chapter 8 to build advanced statements useful in both management and instruction.) Two forms of behavior class relationships are considered: hierarchical and historical.

Hierarchical Behavior Relationships Hierarchical relationships among behavior classes and subclasses are similar to set-subset relation-

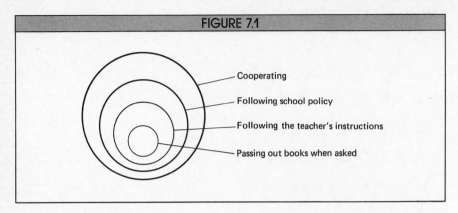

FIGURE 7.1

- Cooperating
- Following school policy
- Following the teacher's instructions
- Passing out books when asked

ships in mathematics. Just as a set of elements contains one or more subsets, a behavior class can contain one or more subclasses. In general, subclasses comprised of different behavioral instances can be related as members of a more *inclusive* class. Figure 7.1 illustrates inclusive subclass relationships involving cooperative social behavior.

Cooperation is the most inclusive class of student behavior in Figure 7.1, with "following school policy," "following the teacher's instructions," and "passing out books when asked" being subsets of each succeeding behavioral class. In effect, this series of subclass relationships means that a student who is passing out books is also following the teacher's instructions, following school policy, and cooperating. Thus, cooperation is a behavior that can be analyzed as a series of inclusive subclasses.

Knowledge of inclusive subclasses allows teachers to indicate to students any relationship a specific instance of a behavior subclass has to more general classes. For example:

> "Simon, passing out the books when I asked shows me that you are learning to follow instructions."

> "Simon, passing out the books is an excellent example of following instructions and really shows me that you can cooperate."

Each of these statements describes the student's behavior by going from a less to a more inclusive class (e.g., from "passing out books" to "learning to follow directions"). The subclass represents an example of the larger class. Such descriptions of behavior are critical elements in a management system because they indicate to the student how his or her behavior fits into a larger sphere of behavior.

Figure 7.2 also involves cooperative behavior, but illustrates how a broad behavior class can be separated into a group of *mutually exclusive* subclasses (i.e., the subclasses have no instances in common or, from another perspective, an instance is a member of only one subclass). Figure 7.2 is an initial analysis of cooperation in which all subclasses contain

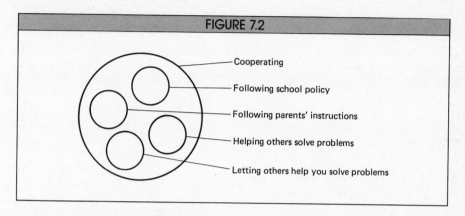

FIGURE 7.2

- Cooperating
- Following school policy
- Following parents' instructions
- Helping others solve problems
- Letting others help you solve problems

different instances of behavior (i.e., do not overlap). Unlike Figure 7.1, whether a student engages in one subclass has nothing to do with whether he engages in others. In a definitional sense, all Figure 7.2 instances are members of "cooperation," but not of the other subclasses. And in Figure 7.2, all of the subclasses are approximately at the same level of complexity.

Figure 7.3 illustrates that an equal level of complexity is not mandatory. Figure 7.3 shows how establishing subclasses in which the categories are not of comparable levels of complexity can obscure or confuse important class-subclass relationships.

In Figure 7.4, the same subclasses have been adjusted to represent equal levels of complexity and to indicate previously unidentified inclusive subclass relationships. It is evident in Figure 7.4 that the original (Figure 7.3) subclasses "taking one's turn to read" and "passing out books when asked" are subclasses of "following teacher instructions," which is approximately equal in complexity to "following parent instructions" and "helping others solve problems." The same two subclasses—"taking one's turn to read" and "passing out books when asked"—are clearly specified

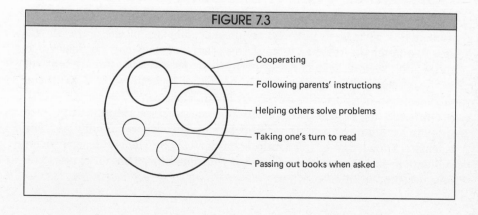

FIGURE 7.3

- Cooperating
- Following parents' instructions
- Helping others solve problems
- Taking one's turn to read
- Passing out books when asked

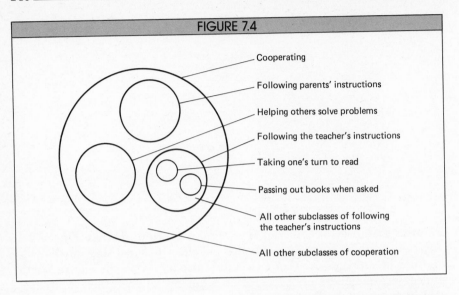

FIGURE 7.4

Cooperating

Following parents' instructions

Helping others solve problems

Following the teacher's instructions

Taking one's turn to read

Passing out books when asked

All other subclasses of following the teacher's instructions

All other subclasses of cooperation

in a qualitative form that allows accurate observation. The behavioral categories of Figure 7.3 would also require specification in observable terms. Such definitions, along with "following teacher's instructions," are examples of how subclass relationships help clarify important behavior relationships.

Knowledge of exclusive subclasses also allows teachers to indicate to students the relationship an instance of one subclass has to other subclasses within the same class. For example:

> "Ellen, passing out books shows me that you can follow my instructions, which indicates you can cooperate. Can you cooperate in the same way with your parents by following their instructions?"

> "Ellen, thank you for following my instructions, as I know you follow your parents'. Both show me you can cooperate."

Both statements refer not only to the behavior subclass and class the student has performed but also to another subclass of the class. In the first example, the teacher asks if the other subclass can be performed and, in the second, if it is being performed. As a result, the student receives a relational and descriptive picture of her behavior. Again, the subclass instances provide examples of the class.

Finally, as Figure 7.5 shows, similar subclass relationships also apply to academic as well as social behavior. As with social behavior, the teacher's knowledge of academic behavior can be clearly described for students in statements identifying the relationships behavior classes and subclasses have to each other:

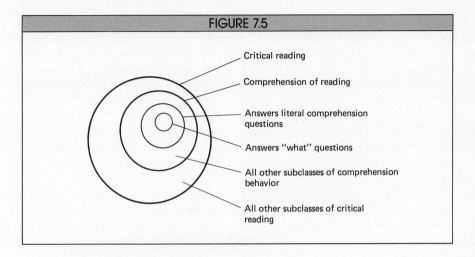

FIGURE 7.5

Critical reading

Comprehension of reading

Answers literal comprehension questions

Answers "what" questions

All other subclasses of comprehension behavior

All other subclasses of critical reading

"Tim, answering that 'what' question shows me that you can comprehend what you read."

"Tim, answering that 'deduction' question shows me you know how to comprehend. Now, can you do it for the inductive question?"

As with social behavior, the sample statements provide students with a relational and descriptive glimpse of their behavior. Since many general classes, such as cooperation and critical reading, are highly valued, showing how the performed subclasses are related provides a strong consequence for increasing the behavior.

Historical Behavior Relationships   Hierarchical relationships specify how behavior classes are defined in terms of component subclasses. Once a network of hierarchical relationships is established, teachers must determine whether specific behavioral classes and subclasses are interdependent. The term "historical" is used to describe relationships among behaviors in which some set of behaviors must exist in a student's repertoire before another class of behavior can occur. These relationships are called historical because the members of the class must enter the repertoire sequentially or separately. Thus, the component subclasses are taught separately and then put together. (The next section on behavior evolution clarifies this point.) The following mathematical behaviors illustrate a simple series of historical relationships:

1. Counting to 10 verbally.
2. Counting up to 10 objects.
3. Adding two or more groups of objects that total 10 or less.

Behaviors 1, 2, and 3 form historical relationships, since 1 is required prior to 2, and 2 is required prior to 3. Both 1 and 2 are required for 3. Thus, 1, 2, and 3 are interdependent. When teachers talk of "prerequisites" or "preskills" for behaviors, they are specifying historical relationships. Teachers who are able to "see" historical relationships can establish conditions and deliver consequences to build complex behaviors across time.

From the standpoint of classroom management, three important types of historical relationships can be distinguished: content interdependencies, procedural interdependencies, and performance dependencies.

Content Interdependencies. In content interdependencies, more inclusive behavior classes cannot be said to exist unless all of their component subclasses are present. In this regard, the presence of all subclasses together allows a *unique* behavior class to "emerge." For example, many different subclasses of behavior, including throwing a ball, hitting, catching, and following rules, are all required before an individual is said to be "playing baseball." Or, for a more academic example, a student's identification of a contradiction in an argument is not, in itself, an example of "argument analysis." The latter includes other behaviors such as identifying the meaning of terms, conclusions, unstated assumptions, evidence, the argument's form, and providing an overall evaluation of the argument. "Catching a ball" and "finding a contradiction" are, therefore, only parts of more inclusive classes for which all the parts are required before an instance of the inclusive class is considered performed. Again, these subclass relationships are historical because the subclasses are taught separately over time, rather than as a complex whole.

In using descriptive statements based upon content interdependencies, teachers cannot validly reference the occurrence of a class unless all other subclasses are known to be present. For example, it would *not* be accurate for teachers to say the following in regard to the previous examples:

> *"Mabel, finding contradictions sure shows me that you can analyze arguments."*

> *"Mabel, catching the ball that smoothly is all that playing baseball requires."*

Rather, teachers' knowledge of these content interdependent relationships would be expressed in the following terms:

> "Mabel, finding contradictions is one of the important elements of analyzing arguments. If you master the rest of the elements, you will be effective at analyzing arguments."

> "Mabel, catching the ball that smoothly is an important part of playing ball. If you can bat and field as well, you will be an effective player for any team."

These examples make clear the interdependent content relationships, so that students know what they do correctly, what correct behavior leads to, and what they need to improve. Unlike hierarchical relationships, in which the subclasses are examples of the class, historical relationships describe subclasses which are necessary components of the class.

Procedural Interdependencies. The second kind of historical relationship, procedural interdependencies, is similar to content interdependencies with the following requirement: All the behavior subclasses in the class must be performed *in a given order* for the behavior class to occur. Thus, in a procedural interdependency, initial behavior subclasses in a sequence are prerequisites for subsequent behavior subclasses. Some examples of procedural relationships can be identified for physical skills, such as pole vaulting, and for cognitive skills, such as mathematical strategies. For example, pole vaulting always starts with positioning the pole, running down the approach, placing the pole, and pushing off; this sequence is followed by body movements to help clear the bar and, finally, the bar release and vaulter's fall. In determining an answer to a mathematical problem, a standard sequence of steps may always be followed, although in certain types of problem some steps can be deleted. By comparison, the steps of (content interdependent) argument analysis need not be performed in a specific sequence. One may look for weak premises, conclusions, or contradictions in any order or virtually at the same time. The need to consider the subclasses in sequence is another indication of an historical relationship. Some examples follow:

> "Theron, you are following each step in the subtraction procedure and the result is a correct answer."

> "Theron, your lab notebook shows me that you followed the distillation procedure step by step. That is a new procedure and I am glad you learned it so fast."

> "Theron, I can see why you are getting the wrong answers in your subtraction problems. You are not changing the number you are borrowing from."

The knowledge of procedural interdependencies is required in the first two examples and is highly valuable in communicating to students. In addition, teacher statements can indicate the steps of a complex behavior the student missed, as is done in the third example, which relates to the correction consequences introduced in Chapter 1 and expanded in Chapter 6. Example 3 specifies the correct behavior, which is part of a complex procedure. Without knowledge of the procedural steps, the error, admittedly simple in this case, could not be communicated meaningfully.

Performance Dependencies. The third type of historical relationship is called a performance dependency. Students who are required to demonstrate a behavior must have nonsubject-area skills in their repertoire before they can perform the subject-related behavior. For example, in order to complete math story problems, students may be required to read at a certain level of difficulty. The students eventually must have a certain level of working vocabulary to perform successfully. The mathematics objective depends on requirements outside of the subject area. Content dependencies refer to *inter*dependencies between subject-area skills content and procedural dependencies concern intrasubject or skill dependencies. Knowledge of performance dependencies is required for constructing curricula and designing instruction. Performance dependencies also serve a purpose in management. Consider the following statements:

> "Quincina, writing numerals makes it possible for you to do addition problems on a worksheet. That new skill is already paying off."

> "Ethel, your improved skills in mathematics are allowing you to finish your accounting problems on time."

The dependency in the first example is "writing numerals" and in the second "math skills." Performance dependencies are what most teachers mean when they talk about "prerequisites," "preskills," or "aptitude."

As teachers define complex social and academic behaviors, an important goal is to clarify hierarchical and historical relationships among classes and subclasses, which are, in turn, defined as specific observable behaviors. Once such classifications of behavior are established, management systems can be outlined. When these systems are complete, teachers can systematically build increasingly complex behaviors from relatively simple subclasses. Without establishing such classifications through analysis, teachers are limited to dealing with each individual behavior in an uncoordinated, one-by-one fashion. Under these conditions, only the weakest and most inefficient management systems can be implemented.

THE EVOLUTION OF BEHAVIOR

The language of behavior classes and their relationships allows teachers to talk unambiguously about simple and complex behaviors. But they also require a language to describe the changes in behavior. Such a language describes the evolution of behavioral development. Three forms of behavioral evolution are considered: class refinement, class expansion, and class combination.

Class Refinement Given the existence of a class of behavior, there is often a need to refine one or more of its attributes. For example, a student's writing speed may need to be increased. While a teacher might consider all other attributes of this behavior satisfactory, slow writing may keep a student from functioning effectively in other settings, such as essay examinations.

Although behavior classes can be refined across many attributes, the emphasis here is on the quantity attributes of rate and duration. *Duration* is how long an instance of behavior occurs. Short durations are desirable for some behaviors, such as adding two numbers or writing a word. Long durations are important for other behaviors, such as in sitting in one's seat or following a classroom rule. *Rate* is the number of times an instance of a class is performed in a period of time. In most cases, teachers want academic behavior to occur at a fast rate, which means that the duration of each behavior instance is short. Thus, teachers' verbal statements within a management system continually refer to changes in rate or duration which reflect class refinement:

> "I am proud of this group. You have *listened to what I have said for over five minutes*."

> "Ralph, that is *the most problems you have ever done* on your worksheet. Please keep it up."

In the first example, the teacher references the duration of behavior ("for over five minutes"); and in the second, the change in rate ("the most . . . ever done"). Notice how the second example is similar to a change over time component of a reward statement. The procedures teachers use to refine a behavior class and the use of verbal statements in the refinement process are outlined in Chapter 9.

Class Expansion Class expansion involves making a class more complex by qualitatively broadening one or more of its subclasses. The behaviors of reading, writing, adding, and playing tennis are different for third graders and tenth graders. For example, reading becomes far more complex as new phonetic and morphographic units are added. As a result, students can read under a wider range of textual conditions. The same expansion process applies to physical skills such as playing tennis or baseball, for which subclasses are continually broadened by the addition of new strokes or techniques. Much general educational development is related to the process of class expansion.

Although the procedures for class expansion cover an extended time, isolated statements can indicate such change:

"Mary Ann, your compositions now have clear well-constructed paragraphs. Notice how each of them has a main idea and elaboration on that idea. You are mastering another element of written composition."

"William, your tennis game is improving. The spin you are now putting on the ball has helped the ball stay close to the net. Keep it up."

In each example, the expansion is represented by a behavioral relationship that has evolved over time. As a result, students are able to gain a clear picture of how their behavior has changed and its relationship to a larger class.

Class Combination   Behavioral evolution through class combination occurs whenever two or more existing classes are joined to form a new class. In terms of class relationships, the new class is more inclusive than the classes which make it up. Whenever classes are combined, the newly combined classes technically become subclasses. Students can, for example, learn all the subclasses for analyzing arguments (e.g., identifying evidence, finding conclusions, determining contradictions, outlining an argument's form) before being taught to put the behaviors together to establish the complex class of argument analysis.

As with class refinement and expansion, teachers can use descriptive statements to communicate the student's growth through class combination:

"Martha, by mastering the use of the microscope, you are one step closer to performing the analyses we will be doing in this course."

"Class, we have all learned how to look up a book in a card catalogue by author, title, or subject, and we have learned how books are shelved. Today, we are going to put those two skills together to find a book in the library."

The first example indicates that part of a "future" class has been achieved. The second example informs students they will be putting all the parts they have learned together so they can do something new.

The procedures that build behavior via class refinement, expansion, and combination are seldom used in isolation. Ordinarily, the evolution of behavior proceeds along all three courses of change. At any time, one class may be refined, expanded, and combined with others. In this way new and complex student behavior "emerges." Chapter 8 illustrates complex behavioral descriptions in advanced verbal statements, such as the ones above, which play a role in the procedures for behavioral evolution. Chapter 9 outlines procedures for facilitating the construction of complex behavior through the sequencing of verbal statements.

SUMMARY: A PERSPECTIVE ON BEHAVIOR

Chapter 2 and the present chapter have outlined a language for analyzing student behavior and behavior change. By applying this language, teachers are able to define, classify (i.e., identify relationships), and observe relevant student behaviors in their classroom. In addition, the language is necessary for a behavioral perspective that is an anchor point for constructing management systems.

The "unit" of student behavior is an unambiguously observable behavior class, rather than any specific instance of behavior. The teacher's aim is to define behavior classes so that the class membership of an instance can be accurately, reliably, and quickly determined. In this context, management and instructional procedures are applied to behavioral instances. Once classes of behavior have been defined, the relationships between classes must be established. The identification of hierarchical relationships across classes of behavior provides the teacher with knowledge of how behaviors are grouped, thus forming subclasses. Hierarchical relationships are structured arrangements of classes (inclusive and/or mutually exclusive) derived from an analysis of qualitative and quantitative attributes. Further, determination of historical relationships extends the teacher's hierarchical knowledge by representing the dependencies between related classes. Identifying these dependencies helps the teacher to effectively plan the sequential development of social and academic behaviors. Given the class relationships, the process of behavioral evolution can begin applying procedures to refine, expand, or combine classes of behavior. Along with the rest of the procedures outlined in this text, these three procedures represent an architecture of behavior. When this architecture is known and mastered, teachers have the critical skills to facilitate behavioral evolution. Thus, the teacher's task is formidable: the design and construction of an environment for changing human behavior. The remainder of this text attempts to make this task more manageable.

PROCEDURES FOR BEHAVIORAL CLASSIFICATION

The definition of behavioral relationships required for complex behavior evolution depends on three interacting elements: (1) the teacher's knowledge of the subject area, (2) the soundness of the curriculum's organization, and (3) the clarity of the objectives embedded in the curriculum. The first element is by far the most important—without it, successful analysis is impossible. If the teacher's knowledge is strong, weaknesses in the latter two elements can be overcome and a high level of success can be obtained. The following procedures are designed to facilitate the teacher's analysis of the curriculum's organization in order to discover its hierarchical and historical relationships. These behavioral classification procedures, in combination with those designed to clarify the objectives of the curriculum (see Chapter 2), help provide a complete picture of the behaviors of interest, the conditions under which they are performed, and their relationships to other behavior classes. Chapter 8 provides procedures for their use.

Establishing Hierarchical Relationships Hierarchical relationships are defined by examining the organization or structure of the curriculum. A curriculum can be any content organized into subcategories or subclasses. A formalized subject area curriculum usually has one or two subcategories under which the behavioral objectives are grouped. At times the curriculum is represented only by an adopted textbook. In this case, the text outline or table of contents represents the structure of the curriculum. The goal of a curriculum examination is the determination of hierarchical relationships. An examination of a mathematics curriculum for elementary students might include the classifications shown in Figure 7.6. Although they do not indicate behaviors, the classification names do represent them. Mathematics could be accurately called doing math. Addition could be called adding; multiplication, multiplying; and division, dividing. In this way, a sense of observability is retained. Subtraction, multiplication, and division could also be subclasses (like addition) for which the next level of classification provides more detail. As will be seen, such subclassification ordinarily provides the details required to

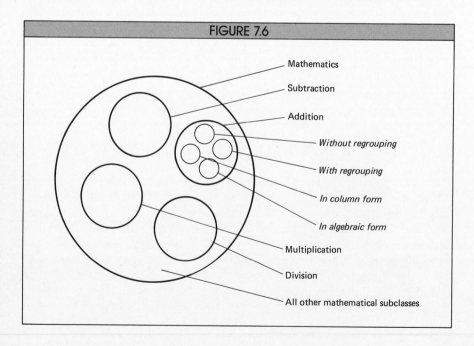

FIGURE 7.6

Mathematics

Subtraction

Addition

Without regrouping

With regrouping

In column form

In algebraic form

Multiplication

Division

All other mathematical subclasses

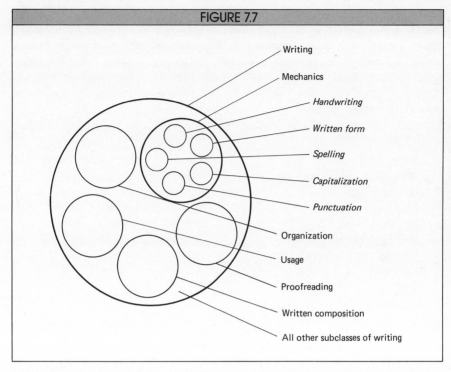

FIGURE 7.7

Writing

Mechanics

Handwriting

Written form

Spelling

Capitalization

Punctuation

Organization

Usage

Proofreading

Written composition

All other subclasses of writing

examine objectives and determine their historical relations. Figure 7.7 provides an analysis of a writing curriculum, with the major classifications including mechanics, organization, usage, proofreading, and written composition. In turn, each of these could be further classified as is mechanics. The objectives of the curriculum would be listed under the subcategories.

At times, and particularly in high school, subject areas or courses have only a list of objectives. If this is the case, teachers must look at the objectives and determine major categories that fit the objectives. At this point, subject-area knowledge is the teacher's only aid.

Social behavior hierarchical relations are established using procedures for the analysis of social behavior presented in Chapter 4. Given the necessary social behaviors of an activity, the first step is to ask: "What class of social behavior is more inclusive than the initial class?" For example, "participating in class activities" is more inclusive than "sitting quietly." Then, the question is repeated until no more inclusive classes can be identified. After this question has been asked for all the required social behaviors, a great deal of overlap will be found. The large inclusive classes will be related to most, if not all, of the initial classes (the necessary social behavior of an activity). But two general branches can always be identified: those related to group interaction behaviors and those related to self-management. In fact, many initial behaviors fit into either of these two large classes. "Sitting in seat," "looking at the board," "listening to others," and "accepting the mistakes of others" could all fall under the more inclusive classes of "cooperation" and "controlling one's self." The best management approach is to take both perspectives and build hierarchically related classes from each. The following is a list of more inclusive behavior classes for "accepting your turn," considered from both perspectives.

Group-Related	*Self-Related*
Following rules	Confident about answering
Accepting responsibility	Disciplining yourself
Helping others	Self-control
Playing your part	Self-management
Paying attention	Knowing yourself
Working with others	Self-restraint
Considering others	
Agreeing with assignments	
Cooperating with others	
Supporting others	

Essentially, these two large categories represent an initial analysis of social behavior. Because the English language does not clearly define the area of social behavior, it is almost impossible to determine which classes are more or less inclusive than others. However, even the rough analysis above provides the relationships needed to build effective statements.

"Kyle, sitting in your seat not only shows me you can follow instructions but can also manage yourself effectively."

"Ramella, taking your turn day-after-day demonstrates support for the group and your attention to your assignments."

There are a number of ways to express the relationships, singularly or in combination. Establishment of the relationships expands the variety of management tools available.

To determine important exclusive subclasses, the teacher should identify related settings for each of the more inclusive classes. The home, playground, other classes, playing at home, various kinds of stores, camping, and playing games are but a few settings where paying attention, showing self-control, and accepting responsibility can take place. In other words, the inclusive class is given qualitative attributes which separate it into subclasses. As with inclusive class analysis, exclusive class analysis provides an opportunity to deliver effective statements.

"Jose, taking your turn day-after-day demonstrates support for the group. I bet you do the same at home. Do you?"

"Buck, not only can you follow instructions in reading, but by sitting in your seat you are displaying this skill in math also."

These examples are reward statements, but the same forms can be adapted for condition statements.

Establishing Historical Relationships Uncovering historical relationships only has to be performed for academic behavior. There are two reasons for this. First, the attributes of social behavior classes for the regular and even remedial classroom are already known (e.g., most students can answer a question, sit in a chair, follow a direction). Only two things need to be changed in their social repertoire: where they do it and how often they do it. Reward statements, such as the above, address the "where" (Chapter 9 addresses procedures for changing the rate at which appropriate or inappropriate social behaviors occur in setting). Second, beyond the attributes that contribute to such classes as "sitting in seat," the behaviors are independent. So only the task of determining academic historical relationships remains.

Establishing Procedural Interdependencies. To determine procedural interdependencies, the objectives of a curriculum must be examined. In general, objectives do not indicate the procedural steps needed to perform a complex behavior. Thus, the teacher must ask two questions for each objective: (1) Are steps (subclasses) involved in performing this behavior? (2) What steps make up the procedure? The easiest way to determine if a procedure is involved is to perform the behavior and look for changes in movement or thought. Each of these changes usually requires that some smaller behavioral unit be stated as part of the full procedure. Beyond this, the recognition of an objective that has steps complex enough to be called a procedure or strategy is almost completely determined by the teacher's knowledge of the subject area. But, if recognition and explication can be accomplished, the advanced procedures covered in the remaining chapters become much more meaningful.

Establishing Content Interdependencies. Some content interdependencies are hidden within a single objective, so that as objectives are being examined for procedural interdependencies, teachers can also look for content interdependencies. The steps are identical, except that for content dependencies the steps are not performed in a specific sequence, even though all steps must be performed.

Often content interdependencies reference global behavioral classes such as football, soccer, argument analysis, or addition, which always cover a wide range of objectives. At this point, hierarchical analysis is useful because it breaks the objectives into related categories. Given a category, the teacher needs to ask, "What are the necessary elements that make up the global class?" The answer requires the examination of the objectives within the identified category. The most helpful analysis procedure is to perform the behavior, and the teacher's subject matter knowlege remains of paramount importance.

The above question can be asked for different sized subcategories in a subject area. In other words, the question is reapplied. For example, football can be analyzed for content interdependencies as well as for a procedural interdependency such as "passing," which has several types. Furthermore, each type of passing can be examined as a procedural interdependency. Thus, the application of content interdependencies leads to the discovery of procedural interdependencies.

Establishing Performance Dependencies. To identify performance dependencies the teacher must examine the desired objectives and student workbooks or texts. First, the objectives indicate the subject areas on which the behavior depends. Often, the conditions of a well-written objective will be the biggest help. These indicate the material that students are to use in performing the behavior. If students are to be given pencil and paper, writing is involved; if they are given a book, reading skill is required. The sciences require math skills. When objectives do not clearly specify the conditions required, key descriptive words in the objective can help. For example, *describe, demonstrate, perform, identify, list, point out, indicate,* are all descriptive terms that will help identify performance dependencies. Second, examining student texts and workbooks indicates the level of proficiency in other subject areas required as prerequisites for successful performance. Again, the only major aid teachers have is their knowledge of the subject matter.

In establishing relationships that are relevant to classroom management, the teacher must realize that there is no one set of correct outcomes. Two individuals will almost always arrive at different analyses, given the same objectives. Such differences are partly due to different individuals' degrees of subject matter knowledge. But these differences often occur because dependency is determined by instructional design and the skill and desire of the teacher to teach the behavior as an isolated class. Thus, no absolutes exist in the analysis of hierarchical or historical relationships, except that careful analyses are necessary for strong classroom management.

AN ANALYSIS ROUTINE FOR BEHAVIORAL CLASSIFICATION

The purpose of the following analysis routine is to assist teachers in determining behavior relationships that can be used as guides to construct complex behavior statements. Because the analysis of relationships must be preceded by an analysis of behavior, the present routine repeats the analyses presented in Chapters 2 and 4. Thus, the following outline presents the complete analysis of behavior routine required for managing the classroom.

1. *Identify the academic behavior classes.*
   a. *Identify the major classes of behavior in the curriculum* (e.g., reading, chemistry, mathematics).

    b. Within the curriculum class, *identify the grade level at which teaching is to occur.* This makes the number of objectives manageable.

    c. *Identify for each of the above objectives:*
        (1) *The behavior*—remember to define it in unambiguous terms if necessary.
        (2) *The conditions* under which the behavior occurs—it should provide further qualitative and/or quantitative attributes.
        (3) *The standard* of acceptable performance—this should also provide further qualitative and quantitative attributes.

    d. *Rate the observability of the objective by asking, "Can the behavior defined this way be reliably and easily observed?"* If the answer is yes, then the objective is unambiguous and appropriate to the teacher's management needs.

2. *Identify the social behavior classes.*

    a. *Identify the classroom activities.* Determine the major instructional events involving teacher and/or students.

    b. *Identify the necessary social behaviors for each of these activities.* What must the student do to engage in academic behavior?

3. *Identify the hierarchical relationships for social and academic behavior.*

    a. *For academic behavior, consider:*
        (1) The categories into which objectives are divided.
        (2) If there are no categories, group according to knowledge of subject area.

    b. *For social behavior, consider:*
        (1) *For each identified behavior, consider as many more inclusive classes as possible.* Think of the group and self-related classes.
        (2) *For each inclusive class, determine the exclusive classes.* Identify the settings in which the inclusive class can exist.

4. *Identify the historical relationships for academic behavior.*

    a. *For procedural dependencies, ask:*
        (1) *Are steps involved in performing the behavior?* Look for changes in movement and thought.
        (2) *What steps make up the procedure?* Often it helps to perform the behavior.

    b. *For content dependencies, ask:*
        (1) *What necessary steps make up the global classes of the established hierarchical relationships?*
        (2) *If content dependencies could exist in a single objective,*

> *ask the same questions as for procedural dependencies.*
> c. *For performance dependencies, consider:*
>   (1) *The conditions of each objective.* These will indicate materials needed and related to some other subject area.
>   (2) *The workbooks and textbooks the students are using.* This examination will indicate the level of proficiency required of the prerequisite subject area.

When teachers who have an adequate background in a subject area conduct the analysis and classification, they will gain not only some necessary elements to build a classroom management system but also skills to see behavior occur in the classroom. The basic analysis performed in Chapter 2 is helpful in this regard. But the help received by doing the present analysis is even greater. It is important for teachers to understand that while such analyses should be conducted with careful consideration, they do not require the degree of precision that a curriculum writer or instructional designer must achieve. Also, the task can be shared by those teaching the same curriculum. This begins to establish consistency within a school's management system.

PRACTICE ACTIVITIES

1. Identifying hierarchical relationships (p. 137)
   1.1 Identify hierarchical relationships. Build a circle diagram as you conduct the analysis to show the links between behavior classes and subclasses. Present examples for group discussion.
      a. Select a complex academic behavior in a content area that you have observed students working on in a classroom setting. Specify the behavior and the setting.
      b. List behavior subclasses of the behavior specified above. Ask "What component parts of the complex behavior class can be identified?" Try to identify subclasses that are exclusive of one another.
      c. Select one or more of the behavior subclasses above and repeat the subclassification procedure.
      d. Repeat the above for a complex social behavior class in the setting where you observed the academic behavior.
   1.2 Identify hierarchical structures in classroom settings. Build a circle diagram as you conduct the analysis to show the links between behavior classes and subclasses. Present examples for group discussion.
      a. Arrange to visit a classroom during instruction in the content area you chose in 1.1a. Select an academic behavior students are learning in the classroom.
      b. List behavior subclasses to identify a hierarchy. Repeat the subclassification procedure until you are satisfied that the behavior is well defined.
      c. List a complex social behavior in the chosen setting, focusing upon the student social behaviors necessary for instruction to occur. Use the teacher's classroom rules for identifying these social behaviors.
      d. List behavior subclasses of the social behavior to identify a hierarchy, then repeat the subclassification procedure until you are satisfied that the behavior is well defined.

2. Identifying historical relationships (p. 141)
   2.1 Identify behavior prerequisites. Present examples for group discussion.
      a. For the preceding academic behavior hierarchy, identify behavior prerequisite (class-subclass) relationships. Ask "Which behaviors must be learned prior to others?"
      b. For the above, specify a learning sequence in which the behaviors can be taught. Describe orally how student behavior would change across time in progressing through the sequence. In doing so, specifically reference the historical and hierarchical class-subclass relationships.
      c. Repeat example 2.1 for the social behavior hierarchy in 1.2d.
   2.2 Identify behavior prerequisites in classroom settings. Present examples for group discussion.
      For the academic and social behaviors identified in 1.1 and 1.2, iden-

tify all behavior prerequisite relationships. Consult with the teacher as necessary.

3. Analyzing curriculum content by generating examples for group discussion (p. 147)
   a. Obtain a curriculum manual or teacher guide showing objectives in a content area for twelve weeks of instruction or more.
   b. Informally apply the analysis routine for behavioral classification. In doing so, use circle diagrams to indicate hierarchical relationships in the content area. Within the hierarchical relationships, show which behavior subclasses are historically interdependent by identifying behavior prerequisites.
   c. Outline the steps you followed in applying the analysis routine to the specific content area selected.
   d. Obtain the cooperation of a teacher or classmate. Present the content objectives you used for your analysis. Then, guide your helper through the analysis by having him or her follow your steps. Modify the steps as required.

4. Describing behavior evolution
   4.1 Describe class refinement changes. Present examples for group discussion. (p. 145)
       a. List five examples of social behavior in a classroom setting. Specify one quantity attribute for each behavior.
       b. For each example, specify a class refinement objective with respect to a quantity attribute. Ask "How should the behavior class change on this attribute after the refinement is successful?"
       c. For each example, describe how the behavior would change across time during refinement. Ask "What quantitative changes should I see as the behavior changes within the setting?"
       d. List five examples of student social behavior in a classroom setting.
       e. For each example, state a class refinement objective in terms of a behavior attribute that would improve the learning effectiveness of the classroom.
   4.2 Describe class expansion changes. Present examples for group discussion. (p. 145)
       a. Select an example of an academic behavior class in a basic skills area (e.g., reading comprehension, writing a story, mathematics problem solving) that you can observe developmentally through grades 2, 4, 6, and 8.
       b. List how the behavior class would be expanded from younger to older students. Ask "In what ways would the behavior class become more complex?"
       c. Repeat the above procedure for a classroom social behavior.
       d. Visit a classroom and observe students engaging in academic behavior in grades 2, 4, 6, and 8. Describe how the behavior class is expanded across younger to older students.
       e. Compare your observations with the examples you generated above.

4.3 Describe class combination changes. Present examples for group discussion. (p. 146)

   a. Refer to example 4.2 for hierarchical and historical relationships.

   b. Refer to the academic behavior learning sequence you developed. Illustrate how complex behavior classes are developed by combining component subclasses as student learning progresses.

   c. At the same time, trace student learning of the behavior historical sequence (identified previously) through the circle diagram showing the hierarchical analysis. Describe how the student behavior would change through class combination as students acquire the hierarchically arranged skills.

   d. Repeat the procedure for the social behavior hierarchy and historical learning sequence.

   e. Follow the procedures above for the examples of student academic and social behavior that you have observed in school classrooms and analyzed in terms of hierarchical and historical relationships.

5. Establishing and analyzing behavior structure from specific observations (p. 152)

   a. Arrange to observe classroom instruction in a content area you are not familiar with. List the specific learning tasks in which you see students engaged. Observe relevant instruction and daily assignments for one to three days.

   b. Consider the specific learning tasks as behavior instances. Define behavior subclasses for each different type of behavior observed. Combine these subclasses into more inclusive subclasses until you have constructed a class-subclass hierarchy. Try to represent the hierarchy in a circle diagram.

   c. Review the teacher's curriculum outline or behavior objectives. Compare the hierarchy you have constructed and revise as necessary.

   d. Identify any prerequisite relationships among behavior subclasses in the hierarchy. Compare the learning sequence used by the classroom teacher to see if it is consistent.

   e. Illustrate how student learning can be referenced to other subclasses through the hierarchy. Specifically illustrate how the evolution (i.e., development) of student behavior can be interpreted as class expansion and/or class combination.

REFERENCES

The background for Chapter 7 begins where Chapter 2 left off and requires a closer examination of both the curriculum and its objectives. The analysis of hierarchical and historical relationships requires a perspective on the evolution of behavior, the sequencing of instruction, and task analysis. B. F. Skinner has provided the evolutionary perspective, and numerous instructional researchers have provided the rest.

Bergan, J. R. The structural analysis of behavior: An alternative to the learning hierarchy model. *Review of Educational Research*, 1980, *50*, 625–646.

Briggs, L. J., & Wager, W. *Handbook of Procedures for the Design of Instruction*, 2nd ed. Englewood Cliffs, N.J.: Educational Technology Publications, 1981.

Davis, R. H., Alexander, L. T., & Yelon, S. L. *Learning Systems Design*. New York: McGraw-Hill, 1974.

Dick, W., & Carey, L. *The Systematic Design of Instruction*. Glenview, Ill.: Scott, Foresman, 1978.

Gagné, R. M., & Briggs, L. J. *Principles of Instructional Design,* 2nd ed. New York: Holt, Rinehart and Winston, 1979.

Gibbons, A. S. *A Review of Content and Task Analysis Methodology*. Palo Alto, Calif.: Courseware, Inc., 1977. (ERIC Document Reproduction Service No. 143 696)

Romiszowski, A. J. *Designing Instructional Systems*. New York: Nichols Publishing Company, 1981.

Skinner, B. F. *The Technology of Teaching*. New York: Appleton-Century-Crofts, 1968.

Skinner, B. F. *Contingencies of Reinforcement: A Theoretical Analysis*. New York: Appleton-Century-Crofts, 1969.

CHAPTER EIGHT

ADVANCED STATEMENTS

B asic condition and reward statements describe classes of behavior
desired by teachers or performed by students. Such descriptions also
provide students with an isolated picture of their behavior. But, as Chapter 7 indicated, teachers can also reference the hierarchical and historical relationships through which student behavior evolves. These descriptions reveal which behavioral components make up complex behavior, or which components students have performed. As a result, the teacher can inform students about where they are going or where they have been. By adding these additional elements, the teacher can greatly expand the content of condition and reward statements. This chapter addresses the construction and delivery of these "advanced" statements.

ADVANCED CONDITION AND REWARD STATEMENTS

The first two forms of advanced statements are presented together to reemphasize the relationship between the descriptive elements of condition and reward statements.

The Function of Condition and Reward Statements The principles that describe the functioning of advanced condition and reward statements are the same as those for basic condition and reward statements (see Chapters 3 and 5). The difference is in the effectiveness of advanced descriptions to increase future behavior. Although advanced statements do not instruct the student how to perform the components of complex behavior, they tell the student what to perform or what has been performed. While this information will not directly change the behavior, it will facilitate the behavior's evolution (as Chapter 9 will show). For social behaviors, referencing "what to do" or "what has been done" is often enough to change the behavior directly. But for most complex academic behaviors, instructional management procedures are required (see Chapter 1).

The Description of Multiple Behaviors The only difference between basic and advanced statements is in their descriptions of behavior: Basic statements describe a single behavior, and advanced statements describe multiple related behaviors. Multiple behaviors reference the hierarchical and/or historical relationships that exist among classes and subclasses of social and/or academic behavior, as represented in Chapter 7. The following pairs of examples reference multiple behaviors, presenting first the condition statement and second the corresponding reward statement. The first pair describes social behavior:

> "Everyone, who can *cooperate* by *paying attention to your own workbook* and *letting others do their workbook?*"

> "Everyone, you have let me know you can *cooperate* by *paying attention to your own workbook* and *letting others do their workbook.*"

These descriptions indicate the hierarchical relationship among "cooperation" and "paying attention" and "letting others do their workbooks." Thus, cooperation is defined by the specified subclasses. If cooperation were persistently presented with its other subclasses, the student would gain an excellent picture of the "bounds" of cooperation and, also, be rewarded for behavior falling within the bounds. Thus, the statement would increase the probability of the behavior's occurrence.

> "I look forward to this group showing me that it can *write clearly* by *using correct verb forms* and *capitalizing according to the posted rules.*"

> "This group has shown me that it can *write clearly* by *using the verb forms correctly and capitalizing according to the posted rules.*"

The above descriptions are the academic equivalent of the social behavior examples. The class "clear writing" is defined by "capitalizing according to the rules" and "using the correct form of the verb." By performing these behaviors, the students have met at least two teacher requirements for clear writing.

> "Mary Ann, today I would like you to work on *constructing paragraphs* with a *clearly stated main idea.* This will help your *compositions.*

> "Mary Ann, your *compositions* have *clearly constructed paragraphs.* Notice how each of them has a *main idea and further elaboration on that idea.* You're mastering another element of written composition."

In this content-dependent historical relationship, the "composition" class is expanded by the teacher's requesting and rewarding the subclass "main idea." Again, the advanced statements do not show the student how to construct the elements of a paragraph; but if instruction is effective, the statements increase the probability of the behavior's performance.

> "Demian, I know you can not only *read without an error* but also *complete your workbook on time* and *correct it when asked.*"

> "Demian, I knew you could *read without an error, complete your workbook on time,* and *correct it when asked.*"

These statements identify a procedural historical relationship: the first step is "reading without an error"; the second, "completing one's workbook on time"; and, finally, "correcting it when asked." Since much student behavior is procedural, it is crucial that these steps be targeted clearly in reward statements and condition statements.

> "Bonita, with *diligent study,* you get a *perfect spelling paper.*"

> "Bonita, your *diligent study* has gotten you a *perfect spelling paper.*"

The above examples point out a historical performance dependency between social and academic behavior. The social behavior, "diligent study" (condition), is required for a "perfect spelling paper." In this case, "perfect spelling paper" functions not only as a description of behavior but also as a consequence element of each statement. This double function of description and consequence often occurs when the teacher is referencing social behaviors necessary for academic behavior.

Examples of Complete and Partial Advanced Statements Like basic statement descriptions, advanced descriptions can be combined with the other elements to form complete statements. Borrowing from the above multiple descriptions, the following complete statements can be constructed. Again, pairs are presented so that a condition statement precedes a corresponding reward statement.

> "I look forward to this group showing me that they can write clearly by using verb forms and capitalizing according to the posted rules. Who will give it a try?" (*Students reply.*)

> "This group has shown me that they can write clearly by using the verb forms correctly and capitalizing according to the posted rules. This is the first time everyone has done it. I am pleased as I hope you are."

The condition statement has consequence and motivation elements similar to those in Chapter 5; the reward statement consequence and change over time are, in turn, similar to those presented in Chapter 3.

Partial advanced statements are also like basic statements, with the description of behavior as the primary element. Because advanced statements describe multiple behaviors, even partial advanced statements will be quite long. The description of multiple behaviors in the section above provide examples, but such descriptions can be abbreviated by referring to posted content procedure steps or a procedure for which students know the parts.

> "Johnny, I would like you to concentrate on the third step in the capitalization chart."

> "Johnny, you got all of the third-step capitalization examples correct."

The third step could be capitalizing the first word in each sentence or capitalizing proper names. For exclusive hierarchical relationships of this type, posting may reference all the subclasses that make up the content-dependent class (i. e., capitalizing) that has evolved by class expansion instructional procedures. Once all the steps are learned, the teacher might say:

> "Johnny, let's see if you can follow all the steps in capitalizing."

> "Johnny, you have followed all seven steps in capitalizing."

Now the teacher is ready to deal with capitalization using the class refinement procedures described in Chapter 7. Since the student exhibits all the component classes of capitalization, the teacher can refine these to present more complex conditions (e.g., sentence types and vocabulary) under which the behavior occurs. Notice that these examples do not name all the steps, but only refer to a posted list to which the student has access. Thus, even complex content classes and procedures can be dealt with in a concise and quick manner, yet inform students of exactly what they need to do or have done. It must be stressed that the effective use of such statements depends on the instructional program covering the steps with the student (see Chapter 9). This means, in part, that teachers must post critically important content and procedural descriptions.

Using Advanced Condition and Reward Statements Advanced statements are used in the same way as basic statements (see Chapters 3 and 5), except for the former's potential application with older students. Although advanced statements can and should be used with younger students, their use can be stressed with older students. This is especially true with multiple descriptions which focus on the development of new, more complex academic and social behavior. Examples have been shown, and another pair follows:

"Mary Ann, can you have each paragraph contain a main idea sentence? (*Student replies*). "This will add another element to your mastering written composition."

"Mary Ann, notice how each paragraph has a main idea and further elaboration on that idea. You are mastering another element of written composition."

The class "main idea" is a description that has the possible future consequence of "mastering written composition." A few more reward statements provide further illustrations:

"Martha, mastering the use of the microscope has you one step closer to performing the analyses to be performed in this class."

"Class, learning how books are shelved and catalogued made it possible to find books in the library."

"Thaddeus, your finding contradictions and evidence statements means you are getting close to the complete analysis of arguments."

These examples can be easily converted to condition statements. The first example could be considered a basic statement, because only a single behavior is part of the descriptive element (e.g., "mastering the use of the microscope") even though the consequence, "the analyses to be performed in this class," points to a class of behavior for which the class described is a subclass. The other two examples contain two behaviors that are part of the class of behavior described in the consequence element.

Thus, the use of advanced statements is similar to the use of basic ones. The primary difference is advanced statements' application to older students who find the acquisition of complex academic behavior a reward. At the same time, advanced statements may help to promote younger students' enjoyment of learning for learning's sake.

COMBINATION STATEMENTS

This chapter and Chapters 3 and 5 have detailed the use of verbal reward and condition statements, which are distinct management tools. But often classroom events are moving quickly; there is a need to save time; or, for variety's sake, the statement's separate use can hinder effective management. For these reasons, the "combination statement," which sets conditions and rewards at one time, also has an important function in management. This section develops teacher skill in building and using combination statements.

The Function of Combination Statements Combination statements both reward past behavior and set the occasion for future behavior. Their function can be described by the five principles related to condition and reward statements (see Chapters 3 and 5), but combination statements apply these principles in a different order. Specifically, combination statements perform reward functions and then condition functions. The sequential rearrangement of principles is as follows:

1. The occurrence of an appropriate instance provides an opportunity for delivering a reward statement.
2. Delivering a reward statement increases the future probability that the class of behavior will occur.
3. Delivering a reward statement increases the future probability of condition statements setting the occasion for any instance of the class of behavior following it.
4. Condition statements precede and set the occasion for an instance of appropriate behavior.
5. Setting the occasion for an instance increases the probability of the behavior occurring in the future.

Chapters 3 and 5 indicate that condition statements precede, and reward statements follow, behavior. This emphasizes the relationships among the elements of an isolated contingency (i.e., one separated from other past, present, and future contingencies). The interaction of contingencies emphasized in combination statements can begin to be illustrated by changing Figure 1.1 to create the following.

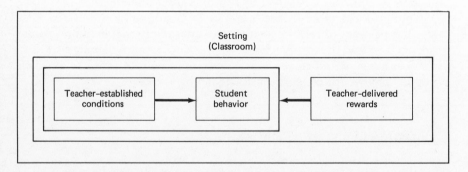

Adding a second box around teacher condition statements and student behavior depicts the link between teacher-delivered rewards, on one hand, and conditions and student behavior, on the other. The teacher's reward functions to simultaneously increase the probability of both the class of student behavior and the class of condition statements, as principles 2 and 3 indicate. Thus, the reward statement establishes a powerful "management unit" called a condition-behavior match.

In practice, student behavior is a continuing event into which teachers' statements are inserted. Figure 8.1 illustrates the function of condi-

FIGURE 8.1

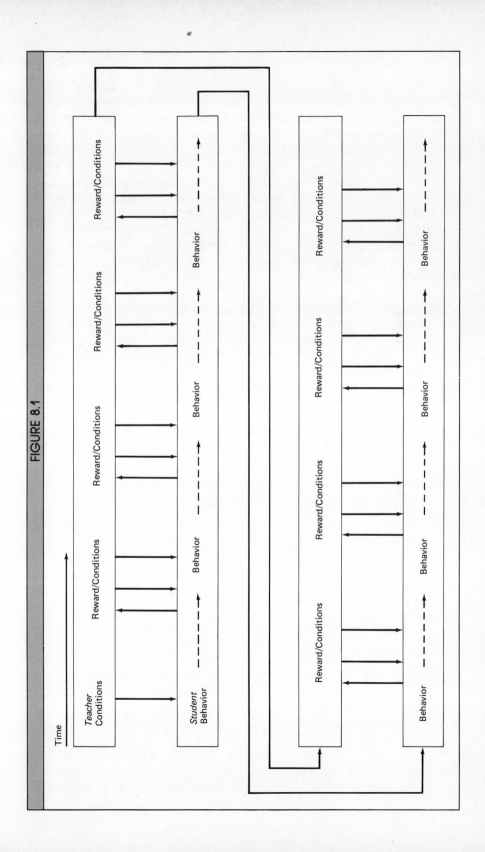

tions and rewards within such a behavior stream. In the ongoing stream, different classes of behavior occur. The teacher observes or catches instances of student behavior and describes them to students. A condition-behavior match cues the teacher (indicated in Figure 8.1 by the arrow from teacher conditions to student behavior) to present a reward statement and at the same time set the occasion for the recurrence of the behavior class. The resulting increased probability of appropriate student behavior is the reason that the reward element precedes the condition element in combination statements. Thus, the combination statement simultaneously rewards and sets the occasion for appropriate student behavior. Reciprocally, appropriate student behavior rewards the teacher's management and instructional behaviors and sets the occasion for their continued use.

Elements and Examples of Combination Statements The relationship between the elements of condition and reward statements provides a rationale for combination statements. Table 8.1 indicates this relationship. Each type of statement—condition and reward—includes an element relating to (1) a single behavior and/or multiple behavior description and (2) a consequence or consequences. The two remaining elements, the condition statement's motivational component and the reward statement's change-over-time component, are different. The overlap among these elements allows teachers to build combination statements which include: (1) the description of behavior, (2) the consequences of the behavior, (3) the behavior's change over time, and (4) the motivation component. In effect, the teacher's skills in building condition and reward statements provide the basis for constructing combination statements. For example:

> "Jennifer, you have obtained 24 of 25 items correct on your social studies worksheet; never before have you done so many correct. I think we are both proud of such a performance; can you do it tomorrow also?" (*Student replies.*) "I think you can."

TABLE 8.1   THE RELATIONSHIP BETWEEN CONDITION AND REWARD STATEMENTS

Condition Statement Elements	Reward Statement Elements
1. The needed behavior	1. The exhibited behavior
2. The possible consequence	2. The consequence
3. The motivational component	3. The behavior change over time

---

This combination statement has four elements: (1) twenty-four of twenty-five social studies items correct (behavior); (2) "never before have you done so many correct" (behavior change over time); (3) "I think we are both proud of such a performance" (consequence for student and others); and (4) "Can you do it tomorrow, also? I think you can" (motivation).

Elements 2 and 4 are especially important because they indicate a relationship among the behavior change over time, the motivational challenge component, and the future student behavior. In the preceding example, the challenge asks the student to repeat the behavior at the next opportunity. But the teacher could have asked for more of the behavior. The following examples show how the basic expressions of change over time (the first time, the xth time, the xth time in a row, and improving more each time) can be used to expand statement content. For convenience, behavior change over time is indicated by a dashed underline and the motivational element by a solid underline. For clarity, consequences have not been emphasized in the examples:

> "Martha, so far your best has been 20 out of 25 correct on your math problems. Today, do you think you can do 22 of 25?" (*Student replies.*) "I think you can make this the first time."

> "José, you have had all your story problems correct for four days in a row. Can you do it for a fifth day?" (*Student replies.*) "Give it a try. Another high grade is possible."

> "This group has had all members finish their worksheets on time three of four days this week. Can you make it four out of five?" (*Students reply.*) "I am looking forward to seeing the first four-out-of-five week!"

> "Melba, you have been improving each day this week on your fraction problems. Do you think you can get 90 percent today for the first time?" (*Student replies.*) "Great, I think so too and I know you have enjoyed improving."

Essentially, each statement either challenges or asks the student to go from one level of performance to another. In the first, the teacher challenges the student to achieve 22 correct for the first time. The second challenges the student to continue getting story problems correct for a fifth day, with the change-over-time element indicating prior student success for four days in a row. Example 3 challenges the group to go from three of four days to four of five days of finishing worksheets. The last example challenges Melba to continue to improve, so that a 90-percent correct level is achieved for the first time. Examples 3 and 4 indicate the challenge's range of application and ask for two changes in performance: Example 3 considers three of four times for the first time, while example 4 considers a first time for improved performance.

In each example, a key teacher decision is, "How much change can students make successfully?" In answering this question, the basic rule is, *When trying to build changes in behavior, do it in small steps.* In other words, the challenge (or any instructional presentation) should be planned so that the student is asked to change in relatively small ways across time. This helps ensure student success, which is amplified continually through teacher statements. Adding instructional challenges keyed to what the student has accomplished makes such sequential progress obvious. Although other types of motivational elements (related to condition statements, see Chapter 5) do not make behavior change explicit to the student, teachers must always be aware of the changes asked for by them or by the instructional program. If the change is too much for the student to accomplish, the student will not experience success even if the teacher has effectively set the occasion. Chapter 9 provides a broader look at changing behavior.

Dealing with Negative Replies to Combination Statements All of the preceding examples assume a positive student reply. The requirements for dealing with negative student replies are identical to those outlined in Chapter 5 for condition statements:

1. Emphasize that the student can do it. (e.g., "You did it yesterday, I know you can again today.")
2. Reward the appropriate behavior when it occurs and relate it to the challenge (e.g., "So far you have them correct, just keep it up and you will meet the challenge.")

If rule 2 is followed for positive and negative student replies, the chances of the student meeting and the challenge are improved. But when the challenge is not met, the teacher's response is important and requires a careful consideration of (1) what the student has done in relation to what the challenge asks for and (2) the related behaviors that make the asked-for behavior possible. The resulting statement should tell the student what he did and, with just a little more effort, what he can do to succeed. In effect, when the student tries to make the challenge, the teacher's statements serve as rewards; but when the student does not try, the statements function as a corrective statement.

> "John, you tried hard but you can't make a record everyday. One more problem and you would have had it. With such effort and practice, I know you will do it soon."

> "Class, you really paid attention to your work and almost made your goal. I know you will do it tomorrow. How many think you will?"

> "Clinton, to make your goal, you need to try hard and pay attention to your work. Can you do that tomorrow?" (_Student replies._) "OK."

> "This group needs to consider paying attention to their individual work if they are to make their objective of finishing their projects on time. I hope you can try next time. Can you?" (_Students reply._)

The first two examples are positive statements to students, even though the students failed to meet the challenge. The second two are more corrective, but ask the students to commit themselves to "do it next time."

A Variation of the Combination Statement While there is no real partial combination statement, since the elimination of one or two elements changes it into a condition or reward statement, an important variation is applicable to limited situations. Remember that the main task of combination statements is to simultaneously reward and set the occasion for an individual or group; the variation does both, but for two different individuals or groups. For example, the first group or individual is rewarded, while the conditions are set for the second group or individual:

> "Martha, errorless reading; Helen, keep it up!"
>
> "That's the correct answer, Mark. John, can you do the same?"
>
> "Harpo, you looked carefully and got it correct. Tim, can you do it for the next problem?"
>
> "You answered question 4 correctly, Rebecca. Marshall, can you do it for number 5?"

In each example, the first student's reward identifies the behavior for the next student, who is asked to do the same. This type of statement is particularly useful when instruction is fast paced and students are taking turns, as well as when the teacher is checking workbooks, answering questions, directing group reading, or leading classroom discussions.

When to Deliver Combination Statements The application of combination statements has three limitations. First, the repeated use of combination statements lacks variety. Repeated presentations of the challenge become tiresome, even if the behavioral classes are varied. Thus, the combination statement must be considered as only one part of a classroom management system.

Second, combination statements are limited to occasions in which the class of behavior is to be repeated. Each statement starts with a reward for past behavior and asks for the class again. But often, the teacher deals with new behavior classes or a particular behavior class may not be repeated for some time. Thus, the "repeat" time interval is an important consideration in using combination statements, with shorter intervals appearing more effective. The following statements indicate time interval differences:

> "John, I can see you already have 4 of the first 5 correct on these math problems. Yesterday you only had 2. Do you think you can make 9 out of 10 for the first time?" (*Student replies.*) "I know you can if you try, and it

"Gerry, you have just analyzed the chemicals within tolerance for the second time. Do you think you can do it for a third time next week?" (*Student replies.*) "I think you can, also. It would indicate you have mastered the analysis procedure."

"Susan, last week your composition got a score of 94 out of 100 points for the first time for an A. Do you think you can do it again this next week for another A?" (*Student replies.*) "OK, give it a try."

In the first example, the time interval is short and the conditions are being set for the same work period. The second example has an extended interval between the condition statement and the next opportunity for the behavior. The third example illustrates an even longer delay. Each example is effective in indicating when behavior is next required. In general, the use of combination statements for setting conditions over long-time intervals should not be overemphasized.

The third limitation of combination statement relates to the difficulty of describing a procedure with multiple behaviors. The addition of a series of behaviors or procedural steps may make combination statements too cumbersome. In such circumstances, it is more effective to set conditions first and to reward behavior later. However, once a procedure has been learned by students and can be described as a general class of behavior, combination statements can be used easily.

Combination statements have a special effectiveness when used to link one day's activity to the next, as the following examples illustrate:

(Day 1) "Class, all of you have finished your worksheet problems and there are five minutes left. This is a first! How many will finish their problems tomorrow?" (*Students reply.*) "I think you can, so let's remember our goal for tomorrow! With the time, let's play a little Guess-The-Word. That is enjoyable."

(Day 2) "Class, remember your pledge to finish your worksheets again today?" (*Students reply.*) "How many think they can still do it?" (*Students reply.*) "I still think you can and would like to see you do it for the second time."

The first day sets the challenge as the behavior is being performed and rewarded. The second day's statement ensures that students remember the behavior and the challenge and commit themselves to the new level of performance. As before, repeated use of this type of combination statement can be overdone. But its use when the class or group needs a motivational boost, such as before vacation, can have a dramatic effect.

PROCEDURES FOR BUILDING AND DELIVERING ADVANCED STATEMENTS

The building procedures for advanced statements combine those for condition and reward statements, and add the element of multiple behaviors. They are presented here to summarize a combined set of questions related to building any statement type. The delivery procedures combine the checklists from Chapters 3 and 5 with a few modifications.

Combination Statement Building Routine To clearly distinguish reward, condition, and combination statements, teachers should compare the differences in the three routines. A helpful practice device is to use the same activity and behavior, social or academic, and build one statement of each type. All of the following questions must be asked to construct combination statements. Reward statements do not require the use of steps 6a and b. Condition statements do not require steps 4a through c. To help the user consider multiple behaviors and the construction of future statements, steps 3c and 3d have been added.

1. *What activity is of immediate interest?* The answer gives the teacher part of the context in which to frame questions 3 through 5.
2. *To what individual or group should the statement be directed?* The answer provides the rest of the context in which to build statements. After building a number of statements, the teacher needs to see if there is a bias towards or away from some portion of the students.
3. *What class of behavior does the student perform that matches the conditions?* The teacher should examine the instances remembered. Further considerations include:
    a. *Is the behavior social or academic?*
    b. *What qualitive and quantitative attributes of the class are evidenced by the instances?* This question facilitates thorough description.
    c. *Does the class of behavior represent a procedure (multiple, related subclasses)?* If the answer is yes and the class is newly learned, it is important to describe each behavior of the procedure.
    d. *What are some related classes of behavior?* The answer will indicate what other behaviors can possibly be used to construct future statements or to determine how a procedure has been evolving (more subclasses can be performed).
4. *How has the class of behavior changed over time?* Considerations should include the following:
    a. *Have there been any qualitative changes in behavior?*
    b. *Have there been any quantitative changes in behavior?*
    c. *How often has the change occurred?* Is it the first, *x*th, *x*th time in a row, more than ever, etc. that the change has occurred.

5. *What consequences could occur?* Considerations should include the following:
   a. *Are the consequences of the social or academic behavior related to emotional changes, access to activities, or a restructured world.*
   b. *Are the consequences related to the student or others?*
   c. *Are the consequences in the immediate future or distant future?* This answer has implications for the statements' use with older and younger students.
6. *What can be said to get the student motivated to perform the behavior?* This becomes two questions:
   a. *What can be said to have the student acknowledge that he or she can do it?* The commitment is the form explored to get student acknowledgment. There may be others.
   b. *What can be said to acknowledge that the teacher believes the student can do it?* These are short portions of the condition statement such as "I agree," "I know you can," or "It's up to you."
7. *What can be said to a negative acknowledgment by the student?* Instead of dwelling on the negative behavior, teachers should emphasize that the student can do it.

Advanced Statement Delivery Checklist The delivery checklist for advanced statements is the same as the checklists for basic condition and reward statements in Chapters 3 and 5:

1. *Does the behavior match the conditions?* The reward statement is delivered contingent on a condition-behavior match.
2. *Does the statement or the teacher's presence unambiguously reference the group or individual the statement is intended for?*
3. *When would the statement be most effectively used?* Consider the following facets:
   a. *Is the behavior new or a problem?* If the answer is yes, the complete reward statement is appropriate.
   b. *Do the students have extensive social or academic skill deficits?* If the answer is yes, deliver reward statements at a high rate.
   c. *Is the statement to be presented at the start or the end of an activity?* If the answer is yes, the complete reward statement is appropriate.
   d. *Is the aim of the statement to keep setting the occasion*

throughout the activity? If the answer is yes, then the partial statement is appropriate.

4. *How would the statement be most effectively presented?* Again, many facets are present:

   a. *Is sincerity present?* Believing that the behaviors and consequences are important is essential.

   b. *Is the smile present?* Again, believing that the behaviors and consequences are important is essential.

   c. *Does the voice have enough volume and tonal qualities (nonmonotone)?* If so, the teacher has a higher chance of keeping student attention.

   d. *Is eye contact made during the statement's presentation?* This will ensure that the student attends to the statement's presentation.

   e. *Is the statement delivered quickly without redundancy or repetition of content?* If the answer is yes, there will be little interruption of instruction.

PRACTICE ACTIVITIES

1. Building statements for multiple behaviors
   1.1 Construct condition statements with multiple behavior descriptions. Present examples for group discussion. (p. 160)
      a. List five different class-subclass relationships that could be used to illustrate multiple academic behaviors. Each example should consist of one general behavior class and from three to four subclasses:

      Class name: _____
      Subclass names: _____
                           _____
                           _____
                           _____

      As appropriate, use the analyses of hierarchical and historical relationships prepared in the Practice Activities for Chapter 7.
      b. For each example, construct a behavioral description of a multiple behavior for use in a condition statement using the following format: "I would like to see you *CLASS NAME* by *SUBCLASS 1* and *SUBCLASS 2.*"
         If necessary, write the multiple behavior description for each of the five examples.
      c. Now practice presenting each multiple behavior description aloud in a relaxed fashion. (These descriptions would be considered partial condition statements.)
      d. Practicing aloud, repeat the examples again, varying the subclass names associated with each class name (refer to the list of subclass names generated for each).
      e. Use each description of multiple behavior in a complete condition statement including the following elements:
         (1) Multiple behavior description
         (2) Future consequences
         (3) Motivational challenge
      f. Repeat exercise 1.1 with five social behavior examples.
   1.2 Construct reward statements with multiple behavior descriptions. Present examples for group discussion. (p. 160)
      a. Using the five examples of multiple academic behaviors from 1.1, construct a behavioral description of a multiple behavior for use in a reward statement with the following format: "I see you can *CLASS NAME* because you have *SUBCLASS 1* and *SUBCLASS 2.*"
         If necessary, write each multiple behavior description for each of the five examples.
      b. Now practice presenting each multiple behavior description aloud in a relaxed fashion (these descriptions would be considered partial reward statements).
      c. Use each of the five descriptions of multiple behaviors in a complete reward statement including the following elements:

  (1) Multiple behavior description
  (2) Change in behavior (referencing the class name)
  (3) Consequences of the behavior
  d. Repeat exercise 1.2 with the five social behavior examples used in exercise 1.1.

1.3 Construct paired condition and reward statements with multiple behavior descriptions. Present examples for goup critique and discussion. (p. 160)

  a. Using the ten examples (five academic and five social) from exercise 1.1, write each of the class names on cards. Sort the cards in random order.

  b. For each card in order, generate aloud a complete condition statement and then a complete reward statement for the class name. If necessary, refer to the behavior subclass names associated with each class name. However, use the same subclass names for each condition statement—reward statement pair for a given class name.

  c. Generate the examples in a relaxed fashion, maintaining positive delivery skills (e. g., eye contact, enthusiasm). Then reshuffle the cards and repeat until you are able to work in a relaxed fashion through the ten examples in three minutes or less.

2. Delivering condition and reward statements with multiple behaviors in a classroom context (p. 170)

  2.1 Simulate the delivery of condition and reward statements that reference multiple behavior descriptions.

  a. Arrange to return to the classrooms observed for the Practice Activities of Chapter 7. Refer to the analyses of hierarchical and historical relationships prepared in Chapter 7, as appropriate. Observe the classroom academic and social behaviors, identifying examples of multiple behaviors which could be used in condition and reward statements. List examples of five academic multiple behaviors and five social multiple behaviors.

  b. Imagine that you are the classroom teacher. Simulate the presentation of condition and/or reward statements referencing multiple behavior descriptions, as appropriate. Try to achieve a rate of three statements per minute for five minutes. In generating the multiple behavior descriptions, reference the previous examples and analyses of the classroom, as needed. In addition, try to use one of the following procedures to identify the class name and subclass names:

  (1) Identify two or more specific behavior classes. Then identify a class name that includes them.

  (2) Identify a class name. Then identify specific subclass names that students exhibit.

  Continue the simulated delivery of multiple behavior descriptions until confident.

  2.2 Present condition and reward statements referencing multiple behavior within a regular classroom setting. Have a classmate observe and critique your statement delivery. (p. 179)

   a. Arrange to substitute for the teacher or to work with a small instructional group in the classroom you have observed. Deliver condition, reward, and correction statements referencing simple behaviors as described in preceding chapters.

   b. Also deliver condition and reward statements referencing multiple behavior descriptions with one or more individual students, or with the group as a whole, through the duration of the activity.

3. Building combination statements referencing simple behavior classes

   3.1 Identify elements for delivery practice. Present examples for group discussion. (p. 163)

      a. Select two examples of a complete reward statement from the text in Chapter 3, one for social behavior and one for academic behavior. Use each as a starting point in listing all of the following elements of reward and condition statements for academic and social behavior (modify the examples as necessary):

         (1) Reward statement: behavioral description (simple behavior), change in behavior, consequence to student, consequence to others.

         (2) Condition statement: desired behavior (simple behavior), possible consequences to student, possible consequences to others, motivational challenge.

      b. Using the elements above, list an example of a shortened combination statement for a social and for an academic behavior including, in order, the behavioral description from the reward statement and the motivational challenge for the behavior/behavior change from the condition statement. Write this out in the form that you would say.

      c. Using the combination statements you just generated, expand each statement to include the following elements: change in behavior, consequence to student, consequence to others. Insert these, in order, between the behavior and motivational challenge. Write each combination statement in a form you would say it.

   3.2 Practice delivery of combination statements. Present examples for group discussion.

      a. Practice effective delivery of the shortened combination statements, until you can present each quickly in a relaxed fashion. Use classmates and/or media aids as required.

      b. Follow the same procedure for practicing effective delivery of expanded combination statements. Repeat until you achieve quick relaxed delivery of each element.

   3.3 Generate combination statements. Present examples for group critique and discussion. (p. 163) (For each combination statement, first generate reward statement elements and then add a motivational challenge.)

    a. List ten student behaviors in a classroom setting—five social and five academic. Try to make the behaviors as different as possible.

    b. Read through each behavior on the list, identifying an example of each element of a combination statement in the following order: behavior, change in behavior, consequence to student, consequence to others, motivational component. In doing so, think "Reward statement first, then motivational challenge." This time, do not write any elements.

    c. Next, for each behavior on the list, generate a combination statement that includes an example of each of the elements in 3.3b. Practice delivering the ten statements effectively and unhurriedly.

    d. Work through the list faster and faster until all ten statements can be delivered effectively within 75 seconds. Don't worry about remembering each specific element; just try to produce an example in a standard order.

4. Delivering combination statements referencing simple behavior

  4.1 Identify social behaviors for combination statements. (p. 171)

    a. Observe the scheduled activities in the same regular classroom observed for Chapter 7's activities. Imagine you are a teacher. Within the structure of the activities, present combination statements, to yourself, consisting of reward statements and an added motivational challenge. Try to present one to four statements per minute. If possible, use a tape recorder in the rear of the room or behind a one-way glass.

    b. Within the structure of activities, list a plan for delivering condition and reward statements to students. In the plan, note when condition statements (including rules) should be presented. Specify a time schedule for presenting descriptive reward statements (at a rate of three or four per minute), as appropriate. Be certain that at least one activity, including the transition at the beginning and end, is included. Specify, in advance, which reward statements will be changed into combination statements with the addition of a motivational challenge. Review the activities and your plan for delivery of condition, reward, and combination statements to determine the reasonableness of your strategy.

    c. Next, observe the classroom and, to yourself, present the condition, reward, and combination statements in the manner you have planned. In doing so, repeatedly scan student behavior so that all statements are distributed across all members of the class and presented in a contingent fashion. Remember to note inappropriate student social behavior, and simulate the presentation of effective correction procedures, as appropriate.

  4.2 Deliver combination statements in controlled classroom context. Have another individual observe and rate your behavior. (p. 172)

    a. Arrange to work as a monitor in a regular classroom. Use the classroom you have observed previously. Use the plan you practiced in exercise 4.1 or build a new plan. Identify, in advance, activities and appropriate student social and academic behaviors desired.

b. Present condition, reward, and combination statements in a contingent fashion to the class. Try to address as many students (or student groups) as possible. Maintain a rate of descriptive reward statements of one to four per minute, and condition statements as appropriate. Present combination statements at a rate of one per minute, by adding the motivational challenge to reward statements. Use correction procedures as appropriate.

c. Try to keep the present and future structure of the activities and academic curriculum in referencing student academic and social behavior, present and desired.

5. Building combination statements referencing advanced behaviors (p. 170)

5.1 Link one day's activity to another day's simple behavior descriptions. Present examples for group discussion.

a. List five examples of combination statements for linking one day's academic behavior to another using the following elements:

(1) Present-future: simple behavior description (present), change in behavior, consequence of the behavior, motivational challenge (for same behavior tomorrow).

(2) Past-present: simple behavior description (recall past), change in behavior, consequence of behavior, motivational challenge (for same behavior today).

Refer to examples in the text as necessary. Practice presenting the examples aloud, until relaxed delivery of past-present and present-future formats is achieved.

b. Repeat the above exercise with five social behaviors.

5.2 Link one day's activity to another day's multiple behavior descriptions. Present examples for group discussion.

a. Refer to examples in the preceding activity in which condition and reward statements were paired using multiple behavior descriptions. Select five academic multiple behaviors and five social multiple behaviors. For each example, both the class name and associated subclass names should be included.

b. Using the academic multiple behaviors, provide the elements for present-future and past-present combination statements by substituting multiple behavior descriptions for the simple behavior description. In doing so, use the format for multiple behavior descriptions for reward statements presented in the preceding activities: "I see you can *CLASS NAME* because you can *SUBCLASS 1* and *SUBCLASS 2*." (Change the tense of the statement from present to past for the past-present statement.)

c. Repeat the preceding activity using the five social multiple behaviors.

REFERENCES

The theoretical background of Chapter 8 is identical to that of Chapter 7. The technology for advanced condition and reward statements evolved from the interaction of the theoretical underpinnings in Chapters 3 and 5. In contrast, the combination statement was designed to operate as a "double function" stimulus in an ongoing "chain" of behavior, in which the consequences of one instance of behavior both reward and set the occasion for another instance of behavior. B. F. Skinner was the first to recognize the double function of stimuli in a behavioral chain. None of the work on chaining has related it to classroom management procedures, but chaining has been discussed in terms of practical, everyday behavior, as examination of the following references will indicate.

Catania, A. C. *Learning.* Englewood Cliffs, N.J.: Prentice-Hall, 1982.

Ferster, C. R., & Culbertson, S. *Behavior Principles,* 3rd ed. Englewood Cliffs, N.J.: Prentice-Hall, 1982.

Millenson, J. R., & Leslie, J. C. *Principles of Behavior Analysis,* 2nd ed. New York: Macmillan, 1979.

Skinner, B. F. *Science and Human Behavior.* New York: Free Press, 1953.

CHAPTER NINE

THE EVOLUTION OF BEHAVIOR

For the emergence and refinement of behavior, contingencies must be constructed and implemented around an ongoing stream of behavior. The engineering and construction of conditions for the emergence of new behavior are far more complex than those for the refinement of existing behavior. So far, this text has taught the analysis skills required to identify important behaviors and their relationships. It has also taught the application of basic and advanced procedures (e.g., statements and corrections) for increasing or decreasing the probability of behavior classes. But it has not described procedures that utilize basic and advanced statements that dynamically change behavior over time. This chapter shows how the sequencing of condition and reward statements over time can facilitate the refinement, expansion, or combination of a class of behavior illustrated is Chapter 7. In doing so, Chapter 9 approaches the gray area between classroom management and instructional management.

CLASS REFINEMENT PROCEDURES

The refinement of an existing behavior class is indicated by a change in a quantitative attribute, usually the frequency (rate) or length (duration), of class instances relative to some past occurrence. For example, a student may "attend to instruction" for only half the time one week and full-time the next week. This indicates a change in duration or length of "attending." An example of a change in frequency or rate would be an increase in the number of correct addition problems from an average of 10 one week to 14 the next (the total number of problems to be worked being held constant). The refinement of a behavior class does not require consideration of historical relationships. Thus, the applications required are far simpler than for the construction of behavior through class expansion and combination procedures.

Duration and Rate Behaviors The *duration* of behavior is defined as *the time needed for an instance of behavior to be performed.* Some behaviors take very little time or a goal may require that an instance's performance take a very short time. Examples include (1) solving an addition fact, (2) writing a single word, (3) finding the conclusion to a deduction, (4) opening a textbook.

Other behaviors take a great deal of time, or the goal may be to have an instance's performance take a very long time. Often when these behaviors are not exhibited, students are said to have short attention spans, be behavior problems, or be hyperactive. Examples include (1) listening to others during a group reading, (2) sitting during a lecture, (3) cooperating during mathematics, and (4) attending to the class announcements.

The *rate* of behavior is defined as *the number of times an instance of a class of behavior is performed in a period of time.* Some behaviors are performed at a fast rate, or the goal may be to have instances performed many times during an activity. There is a practical advantage to a fast rate: More practice occurs in a fixed time and assignments are completed. Examples include (1) identifying words, (2) spelling words, (3) answering a comprehension question, and (4) writing.

Other behaviors are performed at a slow rate, or the goal may be to have instances performed only once during an activity. Examples include (1) cooperating with others, (2) following a rule, (3) accepting the mistakes of others, and (4) helping others.

There is an important relationship between rate and duration behaviors for social and academic classes. In general, the classes of behaviors that the teacher wants to increase in duration are social behaviors, and the classes that the teacher wants to increase in rate are academic behaviors. At the same time, the social behaviors being increased in duration are also low in rate, and the academic behaviors being increased in rate are short in duration. Table 9.1 illustrates these logical relationships.

All the examples given above fit this classification. But there are exceptions. For example, putting away a book, lining up at the door, or sharpening a pencil are social behaviors that should take a short time. Academic behaviors that are concerned with long duration include handstands or other physical education skill classes. But such exceptions are few; and, in all cases, the definition of the class of behavior as defined by the behavioral objective should include rate or duration specifications. Social behavior exceptions are handled by giving condition and reward statements which clarify the rate of behavior. Academic exceptions involve instructional design procedures not covered in this text.

TABLE 9.1 MATRIX OF BEHAVIORAL DIMENSIONS FOR APPROPRIATE BEHAVIOR		
	Duration	**Rate**
Academic behavior	Short	High
Social behavior	Long	Low

In changing the rate or duration of behavior, the relationships expressed in Table 9.1 indicate that procedures to increase the duration of a class typically are applied to social behaviors and procedures to increase the rate of a class typically are applied to academic behaviors. Moreover, the relationship between rate and duration indicates that whenever a high rate is achieved in a fixed time frame, the duration is decreased. The outcome is that only one procedure is needed to alter social behavior along the desired dimensions, and only one procedure is needed to alter academic behavior as desired.

A Procedure to Increase Long-Duration Social Behaviors   The procedure to increase long duration is applicable to all the long-duration social behaviors of an activity which are necessary for academic behavior to occur. These are primarily the social behaviors covered by the general and specific sets of activity rules outlined in Chapter 4 and apply to individuals and groups. The teacher's goal is to have an instance of the class take place over the entire activity.

The procedure and the placement of its steps can be illustrated by an activity time line.

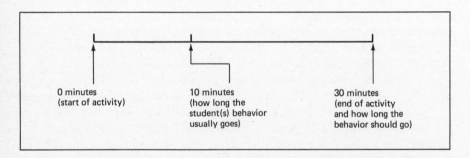

0 minutes
(start of activity)

10 minutes
(how long the
student(s) behavior
usually goes)

30 minutes
(end of activity
and how long the
behavior should go)

The following time line illustrates the placement of statements across the length of the activity. The crucial part of the procedure is the random presentation of combination statements while the behavior is being exhibited, not only before or after the behavior. For example, if the social behavior is "staying in seat," the teacher takes the following steps:

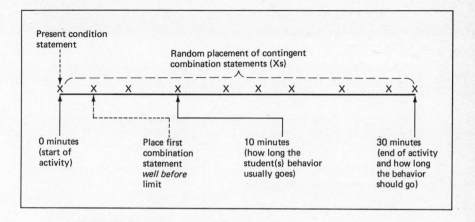

1. At the start of the activity, present a condition statement.

> (*Goes over rules for activity.*) "Today, how many think they can stay in their seats for the full worksheet activity?" (*Students reply.*) "John, can you do it? Mary, what about you?" (*Students reply.*) "Remember, if you can, it will help you get a higher grade for the activity."

2. After a short time and before the student is inappropriate, give a combination statement.

> (*After a few minutes.*) "I am glad to see that you all are staying in your seats and finishing your work. John, and everyone, keep it up. Can you do it?" (*Students reply.*) "I agree."

3. For the rest of the activity, randomly give combination statements for appropriate behavior.

> "Class, you are working hard and staying in your seats. Can you keep it up?" (*Students reply.*) "I think you can and I know it will help you understand your worksheets."

> "Class, look at John. He has been in his seat for 20 minutes. Let's give him a hand so that he will keep it up." (*Students reply.*)

> "John, what is it I like that you are doing?" (*Student replies.*) "Yes, sitting and working hard. Can you keep it up?" (*Student replies.*)

4. At the end of the activity, reward students if the behavior has been present longer than on previous occasions.

(*Day 1*) "John, I am happy you stayed so long in your seat during the lesson—much longer than usual. Can you do it again tomorrow?"

(*Day 3*) "John, I am proud of you! Staying in your seat for almost the full activity is an accomplishment. You have not done it before. Keep it up."

(*Day 7*) "John, you have done it. The full 30 minutes of the activity you stayed in your seat. This is a great first."

5. If inappropriate behavior occurs, correct it with the appropriate correction procedure.

"John, this is a warning. You should be sitting in your seat working, not walking around bothering others." (*Student sits down.*)

(*After student has sat appropriately for a short time.*) "John, do you think you can continue to sit and work for the rest of the period as you are now doing?" (*Student replies.*) "Excellent, and I know you will enjoy the work."

Step 1 sets the occasion for appropriate behavior by emphasizing the importance of the behavior. The combination statement in step 2 is crucial because it occurs in the context of ongoing appropriate behavior. Step 3 statements can be given variety by using reward statements and relating the behavior of interest to other social and academic behavior classes. This strategy also provides students with a broader view of their behavior (see Chapter 8). Step 4 is the most difficult. Because the teacher cannot time the students' duration behavior, there is no exact measure of how long the behavior occurred during the activity. Even so, the teacher who is carefully attending to the behavior often senses that a change has occurred. But even when there is some uncertainty, a qualified statement is possible. For example, "John, it appears that you were sitting in your seat longer than you have in the past" may accurately express what the teacher knows. This statement should be followed up by asking the student to commit to more of the behavior on the next occasion. Step 5 follows the correction forms detailed in Chapter 6.

Many variations of this procedure can be used. The teacher can direct it to an individual student, on a one-to-one level, by asking before class if the student could try to follow the behavior of interest for the duration of the class or activity, and then following the above procedure by delivering the statements privately to the student. The procedure must be used for several days before the behavior increases and a long duration is maintained. The section in this chapter on the course of change outlines how the patterns of behavior change from short duration to long duration.

A Procedure to Increase High-Rate Academic Behaviors   Unlike the procedure to increase the duration of social behaviors, the procedure for high-rate academic behavior is restricted to independent work activities. During a teacher presentation or workcheck activities, students are not engaged in the academic activities in an unrestricted manner. This is an advantage in that the teacher can more conveniently focus on increasing the rate of the academic behavior and provide individual instruction or remediation. The goal of the procedure is to have as many instances of academic behavior take place as possible, or reach the limit of practice items over a specified time. The procedure's main element is the presentation of reward or combination statements only when random checks of the behavior reveal increased numbers of problems completed.

Again, the procedure can be illustrated by an activity time line.

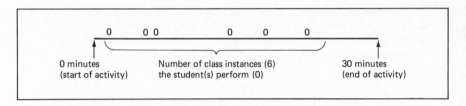

The number of class instances performed refers to the items done on a worksheet or from a textbook. The number of division problems done correctly, the number of sentences punctuated correctly, the number of arguments correctly analyzed, the number of sentences written in a story, the number of additional lines or elements added to a painting, and the number of notes added to a musical score are all examples. The last three examples show that often a class of academic behavior can be broken into smaller units in order to apply the increase-in-rate procedure. This relates back to the class-subclass relations discussed in Chapters 2 and 7. The main point is that careful examination of the academic behavior will reveal some aspect that can have the rate procedure applied to it. The next time line illustrates at what rate the teacher would like the student to be performing; this rate is the goal of the procedure.

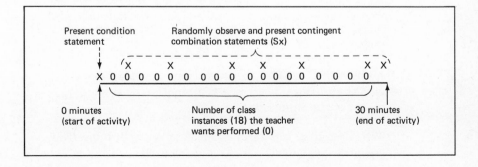

The first time line indicates a rate of six instances or items completed during the activity. The second time line shows that the goal is eighteen. In order to achieve the desired rate, the following steps must be taken by the teacher:

1. At the start of the activity present a condition statement.

> "Ernestine, do you think that you can do ten problems on your worksheet today?" (*Student replies.*) "I would appreciate it. So, give it a try; it will be a first."

> "Today, I would like to see you all finish your worksheets by the end of the activity. Who will do it?" (*Students reply.*) "That is great! We are starting off on the right foot towards a new record."

2. Randomly observe the number of instances the student has performed. If the number is greater than the last observation, present a combination or reward statement for working at a high rate.

> "Ernestine, you already have three done in only ten minutes. If you keep up this pace, you will do more problems than ever before. I hope you can do it."

> "This group has set to work. Everyone has three or more problems done in the first six minutes. You're cruising for a record."

3. Randomly observe the number of instances the student has performed. If the number is not greater, but most of the problems done are correct, deliver a reward-correction statement.

> "Ernestine, these problems are all correct and I think that is very important, but I would like to see you do the problems faster. Can you do it?" (*Student replies.*) "I know you can do it too."

> "This group is getting their problems correct and we all know that is important, but we need to do more problems during the independent study activity. Can you do it?" (*Students reply.*) "OK, let's see if everyone can do 3 more problems in the next 5 minutes."

4. At the end of the activity, if the student has done more problems than before, present a combination or reward statement for the high rate.

> "Well, Ernestine, you did it again. Another record day. That must make you proud. It does me. Keep it up."

"This class had everyone do more problems than before. This has only happened once before. Who think they can finish all the problems next time?" (*Students reply.*)

The presentation of combination and reward statements is easier for the rate procedure than for the duration procedure. The teacher has a record of previous rates of items completed by the student and can easily remember the rate for the activity; with larger groups, the teacher can simply mark the student's work to indicate the point completed on the last observation. It is important to recognize that rate is tied to the correctness of the behavior. If the work is not correct, the behavior of interest is not being performed and the academic correction (presented in Chapter 6) or instructional procedures should be followed. The examples given for each step indicate that the rate-increase procedure can be used with groups. When the procedure is applied to groups, a contingency error may be made (see Chapter 1). An error exists if one or more of the individuals in the group are not exhibiting behavior which matches the condition. This error can be avoided by presenting only individual statements, but the teacher should try to deliver accurate group level statements.

SOCIAL BEHAVIOR CLASS EXPANSION PROCEDURES

Because of the hierarchical nature of social behavior, class expansion can occur in two ways: First, the limits of the initially referenced class can be broadened; second, the conditions under which the behavior is performed can be widened. The first is inclusive class expansion and the second exclusive subclass expansion.

Inclusive Social Behavior Expansion Chapter 8 showed how an isolated statement would affect the inclusive expansion of a class. The point is to describe a class instance the student has performed and then indicate what more inclusive class it is an example of. But the teacher also needs know how to expand classes over time. At some point the teacher should not have to always reference the less inclusive class but rather the more inclusive classes. (The less inclusive class should be described occasionally in order to help students recall the limits of the more inclusive referenced class.) The following examples indicate how statements change over time. The examples indicate time change, with the first statement of the pair being the earliest.

Example 1

(*Condition statement.*) "Class, the rules for independent reading are, Do your own work, let others do their own work, and raise your hand if you have a question. Raise your hand if you think you can follow these rules." (*Students reply.*) "I have explained your assignment to you. I think you can do it, so go to it and get an A for your effort."

(*Reward statement.*) "Verbena, thank you for doing your own work today. It was a pretty sight. I hope you can do it tomorrow."

Example 2

(*Condition statement.*) "Verbena, can you do your own work today?" (*Student replies.*) "Great, I will look forward to it."

(*Reward statement.*) "Verbena, you did exactly what you said. You did your own work. That is certainly a flower in your hat."

Example 3

(*Condition statement.*) "Verbena, can you do your own work today?" (*Student replies.*) "Great, that will show me you can follow directions. It will help you get an A for today."

(*Reward statement.*) "You did follow directions as indicated by doing your own work, Verbena. I look forward to it again tomorrow. Can you do it?" (*Student replies.*)

Example 4

(*Condition statement.*) "Verbena, can you follow directions today?" (*Student replies.*) "That will make me happy. Thank you."

(*Reward statement.*) "Well Verbena, you certainly are showing me that you can follow directions."

Example 5

(*Condition statement.*) "Verbena, are you going to follow directions again today?" (*Student replies.*) "Excellent, that is a big step in learning to cooperate with others."

(*Reward statement.*) "You demonstrated cooperation with others by following directions, Verbena. I think everyone appreciates it. Keep up the good work!"

Example 6

(*Condition statement.*) "Verbena, can you demonstrate cooperating with others today?" (*Student replies.*) "I would appreciate it; I know it will help you to hold a job in the future."

(*Reward statement.*) "Verbena, thank you for cooperating with others. You have followed instructions and worked on your own for seven days in a row. That is a first."

Example 1 sets out the rules for the classroom Verbena is in. This represents the social behavior context that is repeated on the days of the other examples. Example 2 gives the rule "do your own work" and rewards the class of interest. Example 3 links "do your own work" with "following directions." The class of interest is now "following directions." In terms of the classification of behavior, "doing your own work" is considered a subclass of "following directions." The reward element reemphasizes this relationship. Example 4 illustrates setting conditions only for the class "following directions." The conditions for the instances of this behavior will have to be set repeatedly before the general activity context reliably sets the occasion for the onset of class instances. Example 5 makes the transition between "following directions" and "cooperating with others." Example 6 focuses on "cooperating with others" as the class of interest. Transitioning from "doing your own work" to "following directions" to "cooperating with others" presents the student with a partial picture of what her social behavior is and what its consequences are. In this series of examples, the descriptions begin with the smallest and most clearly defined subclass and gradually expand to the larger class. In the examples presented in Chapter 8, the single statement presents both the class with multiple subclasses indicating the limits of the class. The reward statement in example 6 does the same thing, with some variation.

Exclusive Social Behavior Expansion   As indicated, inclusive expansion presents only a partial picture for defining the limits of social behavior. Exclusive expansion completes the picture by showing the student the variety of conditions under which a class applies. Consider the following examples:

Example 1

(*Condition statement.*) "Everyone, you all know how to move quietly from activity to activity. Can you also do it on the way to the lunch room?" (*Students reply.*) "I look forward to it."

(*Reward statement.*) "Well, everyone walked quietly to the lunchroom. Thank you. Now we can eat without delay. No one had to be corrected."

Example 2

(*Condition statement.*) "I am very proud that you can all follow instructions in biology lab. I would like to think the same thing can happen on the field trip to the biological research labs. Who thinks they can?" (*Students reply.*) "We will find out in only two days!"

(*Reward statement.*) "Thank you for following instructions on the field trip. It made the trip a very pleasant experience for me, as I hope it did for you."

Example 3

(*Condition statement.*) "Bayard, you have often helped me with tasks around the classroom; could you help Mr. Barcroft the same way?"

(*Student replies.*) "Excellent. Then go to his classroom after lunch."

(*Reward Statement.*) "Bayard, Mr. Barcroft tells me you did the tasks he asked most effectively. We both appreciate it."

All of these examples indicate to the student that the class of behavior is being performed in one location and the teacher desires it to be performed in a different location where the conditions are similar. In the first example, the students are to "move quietly" on the way to the lunchroom as well as in the classroom. In the second, the student is to "follow instructions" on the field trip in the same way as in the biology lab. In the third, "helping with tasks" is to be performed for another teacher as well as for the regular teacher.

These examples differ in one important area: Some of the conditions in which the behavior is requested to be performed seldom happen, as in examples 2 and 3. In such cases, conditions must be set several times before the behavior is to be performed; that is, condition statements like those in examples 2 and 3 must be repeated over several days before the activity. But if the behavior is performed often, as in the lunchroom example, the use of such statements depends on the time it takes for students to master the behavior. The section on the course of behavior change will indicate what the teacher can expect as far as the attainment of mastery is concerned. After mastery has been obtained, the teacher can occasionally reference the behavior more directly.

By referencing inclusive and exclusive classes, students are given a complete picture of their social behavior. Referencing by the condition statement sets the occasion for the desired class. Referencing by the reward statement increases the probability of the desired class occurring and also increases the class of conditions and condition statements setting the occasion (see Chapters 3 and 5).

ACADEMIC BEHAVIOR CLASS EXPANSION AND COMBINATION PROCEDURES

Condition and consequence statements tell students what to perform and what they have performed. Class expansion and combination procedures bring the elements of behavior together and provide for the emergence of behavior. Together they provide the necessary and sufficient conditions for the emergence, mastery, and maintenance of behavior.

The use of condition and reward statements to facilitate the expansion and combination of behaviors is dependent on the time frame of the instructional sequence. To this extent, examples such as those in Chapter 7 must be sequenced in conjunction with the instructional sequence. Depending on the skills of the student and the complexity of the behavior desired, this sequence may take days, weeks, or months.

When expanding a behavior class, statements reference the added qualitative attribute(s) of the behavior and possible consequences resulting from the added attribute. If the behavior has been in the students' repertoires for a while, the teacher would also indicate the changed behaviors class over time. At this point the procedures of class refinement are used. The following examples illustrate the use of statements in the evolution of an expanding class. Again, each example indicates a time change, with the first the earliest.

Example 1

"Mary Ann, I would like you to add a main idea to each of your paragraphs. Do you think this is possible?" (*Student replies.*) "So do I. It will indicate you are mastering an important element of paragraph writing."

"Well you did it, each paragraph has a clearly written main idea. This is a first; keep it up."

Example 2

"Mary Ann, could you make a special effort to make sure that the sentences in your paragraphs elaborate on this idea?" (*Student replies.*) "Excellent."

"Mary Ann, I very much liked the way your paragraphs presented clear main ideas, and also the way each sentence elaborated on them. Can you do this two days in a row by doing it tomorrow?" (*Student replies.*) "I will be watching."

Example 3

"Mary Ann, today I would like you to try to include a transition sentence in the paragraphs you are about to write. It will be the last important element of paragraph writing we will learn. Can you do it?" (*Student replies.*) "That's the spirit."

"You did it, Mary Ann. You have not only included transitional sentences but also remembered the main ideas and elaborated on those ideas. You are a complete paragraph writer. Keep up your fine work."

After the teacher's instruction on one of the qualitative attributes of paragraph writing (main idea, idea elaboration, and transition sentences), condition and reward statements can increase the probability of the subclasses and, ultimately, the mastery and maintenance of the larger class of paragraph writing.

When combining behavior classes, statements follow the evolution of each class by referencing the class just taught, the classes to be taught, and/or the more inclusive class of which the others are members. This approach applies to both content and procedural dependencies. In all cases, the class just taught and the more inclusive class could be referenced. Examples in Chapter 8 partially illustrate the temporal sequence of statements for a content dependency. The following examples expand on those in Chapter 8 by fully illustrating the temporal sequence. In this set of examples, the teacher has determined that four capitalization steps need to be learned before "capitalizing" can be mastered. Thus, the teacher is defining a content dependency, relative to instruction. Each example contains a condition and reward statement, with each occurring later in a temporal sequence.

Example 1

"Marilyn, can you capitalize the months of the year and days of the week on your worksheet?" (*Student replies.*) "If you can, it will be a step toward being a clear writer."

"I see that you capitalized all the months and days of the week. Let's see if you can do it two days in a row tomorrow."

Example 2

"Marilyn, you can capitalize all your months and days. Can you do it for people and languages of a country?" (*Student replies.*) "If you can, you will have learned half of what is required to master capitalization this year."

"Marilyn, you capitalized the names of people and languages of a country in each example."

Example 3

"Marilyn, now it is time to show that you can capitalize places, streets, and avenues. Can you do it?" (*Student replies.*) "I know you will try hard."

"Fantastic, Marilyn! You have capitalized places, streets, and avenues correctly. You also used the other elements of capitalization we have learned and practiced."

Example 4

"Marilyn, I would like to see you succeed on the last element of capitalization to be stressed this year: geographical locations. Do you think you can?" (*Student replies.*)

"Marilyn, you not only capitalized all the geographical locations but all the other elements of capitalization taught this year. Fantastic! You have mastered capitalization."

In these examples the teacher has gradually taught the component elements of capitalization within the given instructional time frame. Not all content dependencies are so arbitrarily defined, but they all use statements that follow the above pattern: In each example a new element of the class of behavior is asked for and rewarded when performed.

An examination of the expansion and combination examples reveals the similarity of statement forms. This is because both types of statements ask for part of a whole or describe the parts performed. As a result of this similarity, the management procedures for the expansion of a class and the combination of classes are essentially the same. The critical element is the timing of statements so that day-to-day practice leads to the efficient development of mastery. Each attempt at the behavior cannot be expected to be successful. The behavior will go through a changing pattern of performance over time, before the majority of attempts are successful and mastery is achieved. The next section examines this course of change.

THE COURSE OF BEHAVIOR CHANGE

It is important to understand the course of change from the emergence to the mastery of a class of behavior for two reasons. First, the teacher has a benchmark to determine if instruction (in the form of learning activities) and management procedures (in the form of conditions, rewards, and corrections) are bringing students to mastery. Second, teachers will also better manage their own behavior in terms of persistence and consistency because of their perspective on the course of student change.

Once a behavior has emerged and is in a student's repertoire, mastery of the behavior is approached in terms of class refinement. The rate or duration of the behavior relative to some standard of performance establishes mastery for the present purposes. Whether students are identifying conclusions as part of argument analysis, finding geographical locations as part of map reading, or using commas as part of punctuating, these behaviors must be mastered or approaching mastery before they can be used in other, more inclusive classes. The question is, "Given the emergence of a behavior class, what patterns of behavior performance can be expected prior to and during mastery?" Because the alteration of behavior primarily involves duration and rate, the performance patterns necessarily follow these two dimensions.

If knowledge of hierarchical and historical relationships were extensive, instruction designed flawlessly, and implementation rigorously delivered, the evolution of behavior from one class to another and the refinements in performance would be smooth and continuous. This, of course, is not the case. Knowledge, design, and classroom delivery are always flawed to some degree. Otherwise, the teacher would be able to plan every detail of classroom practice to a fine degree. But even without smooth and continuous changes in behavior, patterns can be found and described.

To illustrate these performance patterns, graphs and timelines will be used. Only through these illustrations can a perspective on change be given. In the classroom, the teacher is not expected to graph classroom behavior to see change. Only the chapter's practice activities involve graphing. Figure 9.1 shows a standard graph form. The horizontal axis, called the abscissa, represents the successive occurrences for an activity. Each mark indicates an activity. The unit of time has two features: (1) the amount of time is uniform from unit to unit and (2) the general conditions of the tasks students perform remain consistent. In practice, most classroom activities structured following the procedures presented in Chapter 4 meet these two requirements. For example, a daily independent worksheet activity will involve a consistent length of time with tasks of a similar nature. Without consistency of time and conditions, the changes are not comparable. The consecutive units of the abscissa indicate that the observations are made as often as the activity occurs and that the time between the activities is similar in length. The vertical axis, called the ordinate, represents the amount of behavior performed during the fixed unit of time.

Figure 9.1A illustrates an ordinate describing an alteration in the rate of behavior. The rate is described as the number of behavior class instances exhibited during an activity. Since rate is associated with academic behavior, this form is used when dealing with academic behavior change. The class represented could be any academic behavior that takes place during the activity of interest. Figure 9.1B presents an ordinate for duration behavior, with "duration" described as the total time the behavior instances were exhibited during an activity. Because duration is associated with social behavior, this form is used when dealing with social behavior. The class represented could be any social class that takes place during the activity of interest. When rate or duration are plotted on their respective graphs, they give a picture of the change in behavior from activity to activity. In both parts of Figure 9.1, the first four activities have been filled in. Figure 9.1A shows that 10, 4, 18, and 13 instances are exhibited for activities 1 through 4, respectively. Figure 9.1B shows that the total time the class instances were exhibited is 18, 22, 14, and 18

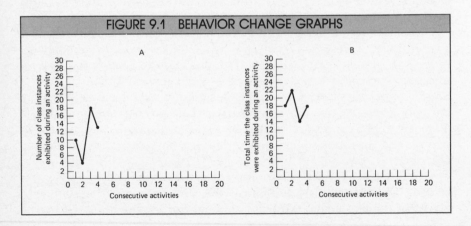

FIGURE 9.1   BEHAVIOR CHANGE GRAPHS

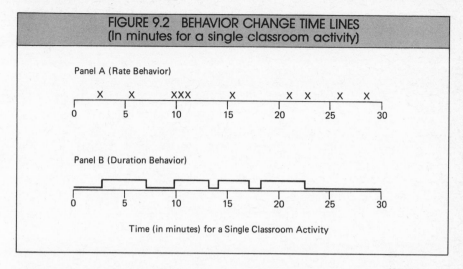

FIGURE 9.2   BEHAVIOR CHANGE TIME LINES
(In minutes for a single classroom activity)

Panel A (Rate Behavior)

Panel B (Duration Behavior)

Time (in minutes) for a Single Classroom Activity

minutes for activities 1 through 4, respectively. Thus, the teacher can see that both the rate and duration behaviors changed from activity to activity.

Figure 9.2A illustrates the rate and Figure 9.2B the duration timelines which describe behavior change during a single activity session. The abscissa represents the minutes of an activity, which again should be held constant for the comparison of different activity sessions on other timelines. For rate (Figure 9.2A), each instance of the behavior is indicated by an X. For duration (Figure 9.2B), the time during which the behavior occurs is indicated by a line raised above the abscissa. In Figure 9.2A, the rate is 10 instances for the activity, with the behavioral instances spread across the length of the 30-minute activity. In Figure 9.2B, the four instances of a behavior are performed for a total of about 15 minutes, with most of the behavior performed in the middle of the activity. The elements of change can be described within the context of these graphs and timelines. The next three sections describe the course of behavior change: variability, trend, and stability.

Variability   *Variability* is a property of all behavior. The term describes the degree to which the instances of a class are present or absent across repeated time intervals. The extent of the presence or absence of instances refers to the amount (rate or duration) of behavior performed. Consistent time intervals are required to interpret change. (If the time interval is not consistent, the data may be transformed into measures such as percentages, but interpretation will remain somewhat problematic.) The emergence of new behavior or behavior existing in the context of inconsistent contingencies has extensive variability.

Figure 9.3 illustrates several patterns of variability, which can be described in terms of range and oscillation. *Range* is defined as the minu-

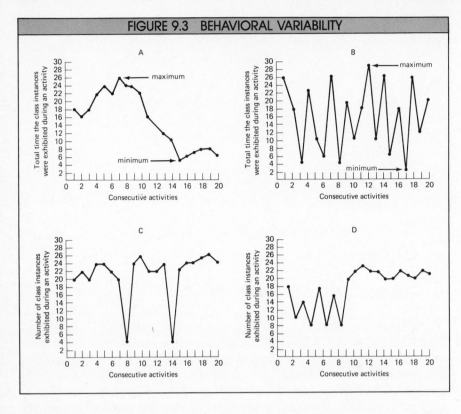

FIGURE 9.3 BEHAVIORAL VARIABILITY

mum and maximum amount of behavior found over a set of time intervals. *Oscillation* is defined as the number of times a behavior shifts in the direction of minimums and maximums (range) over a set of time intervals. Figure 9.3A shows fairly extensive variability, with a range from 26 minutes of behavior (duration) performed during activity session 7, and 5 minutes during session 15; the variability also oscillates slowly; without dramatic activity-to-activity shifts. Figure 9.3B shows an extreme range, from 29 minutes on activity session 12 to 2 minutes on session 17, and rapid oscillation. Figure 9.3C (rate) also shows extensive range, but very slow oscillation; the two points at which the behavior is at or near its minimum range, just after being near its maximum and then returning, are called behavioral spikes. These are usually caused by an extensive but temporary change in the student's contingencies at home or school. Figure 9.3D displays variability characterized by a small range and fast oscillation for the first 9 activities, and then slow oscillation and reduced range for activities 10 through 20. Figure 9.3B and the first half of Figure 9.3D best describe the pattern of variability found for newly acquired behavior or for behavior that has been in the context of inconsistent contingencies. With the careful construction and implementation of conditions and consequences, these forms of variability undergo modification.

Trend As any behavior comes under consistent and persistent conditions and consequences, its rate or duration take on direction, which is called a *trend*. A trend can be increasing or decreasing, depending on the direction of behavior change. For example, if a teacher is interested in having a student do more problems during a mathematics period, the teacher would look for an increasing trend after consistent and persistent conditions and consequences have been started. Trends are usually accompanied by a decrease in the oscillation of behavior. Figure 9.4 illustrates types of trends and the accompanying changes in oscillation. The first 7 activities of Figure 9.4A indicate the behavior before trends begin. The arrow indicates the point at which contingencies change, causing the trend to begin. Note that the oscillation between activities is also reduced. From activity 2 to 3, the amount of behavior changes 12 units; the maximum change after activity 7 is 8 units, from activity 10 to 11. Figure 9.4B also shows an increasing trend, but with continually slowing oscillation. Figure 9.4C shows a rapidly decreasing trend, with an accompanying absence of oscillation. Figure 9.4D also shows a decreasing trend, but with one extreme oscillation, a behavioral spike, at activity 15.

For acquisition of appropriate behavior under consistent and persistent contingencies, the trend is increasing, with reduced oscillation (Fig-

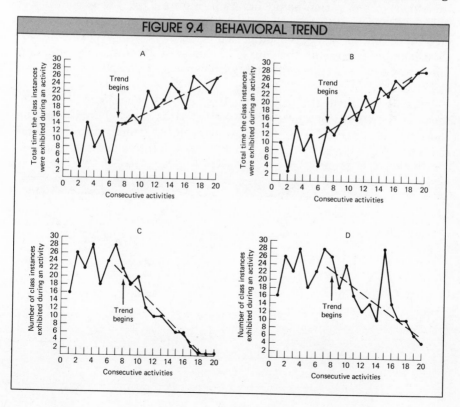

FIGURE 9.4 BEHAVIORAL TREND

ures 9.4A and B). For inappropriate behavior that is consistently and persistently corrected, the trend is decreasing, with reduced oscillation (Figures 9.4C and D). The rate of increase or decrease is dependent on the appropriateness of the contingencies established, teachers' consistent and persistent application, and the competing contingencies that exist in the classroom (see Chapter 10). If a trend does not begin to show itself or the oscillation and range do not decrease, a problem exists, and the procedures presented in Chapter 12 are required.

Stability *Stability* is the final phase of performance that exhibits relatively little variation (a relatively small range and little oscillation) and no trend in the amount of behavior. When this occurs for some time, the behavior is said to be in a stable state. When behavior becomes stable, it is said to be "mastered." Figure 9.5 illustrates the evolution through variable, trend, and stability phases of a rate behavior and a duration behavior. Figure 9.5A illustrates a rate behavior which begins to enter a stable state at activity 14, after a rapidly increasing trend was preceded by several days of extreme variability. The relative range and oscillation are greatly reduced, with the stable behavior being performed near the maximum rate required (as indicated by the ordinate). Figure 9.5B presents the stages of a duration behavior. As in Figure 9.5A, the variability is reduced throughout the trend, with stability in behavior beginning about day 14. Except for the extended period of variability in Figure 9.5A, either example represents the course of change in performance which an appropriate behavior goes through with consistent and persistent use of contingencies.

Figure 9.6 illustrates three time lines for rate behavior. These cross-sections show how instances of a behavior class could change over the course of the three behavioral phases (variability, trend, stability). Figure 9.6A shows the early phase, in which variability is present. The pat-

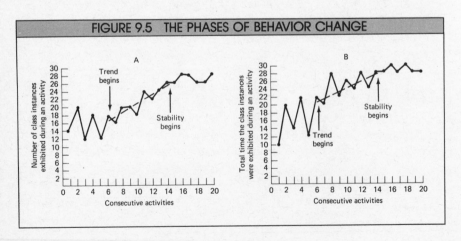

FIGURE 9.5   THE PHASES OF BEHAVIOR CHANGE

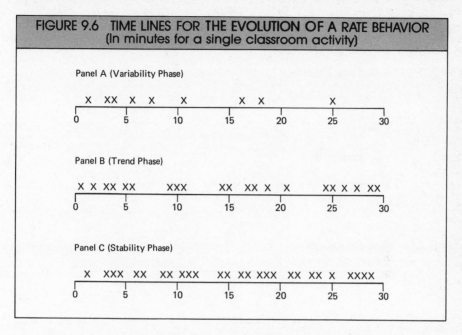

FIGURE 9.6 TIME LINES FOR THE EVOLUTION OF A RATE BEHAVIOR
(In minutes for a single classroom activity)

tern of behavior indicates extensive time between instances of behavior. The early part of the activity contains a large portion of the instances. For most new academic behavior, the performance is hard work and the student quite expectedly slows up after a time. Figure 9.6B shows that the rate is increasing during the trend phase, with only a few pauses in performing. The beginning and end of the activity have similar amounts of behavior. The student is benefiting from a history of reward and, as learning progresses, the work is less difficult. Figure 9.6C indicates performance of a stable skill, in which there are few pauses during the activity. Ultimately, the efficient delivery of conditions and consequences brings about a stable state, or mastered skill.

Figure 9.7 illustrates three timelines for duration behavior. Figure 9.7A shows a number of long and short durations of the behavior occurring across a single activity. Ten instances of the class of behavior are shown. If the goal is to have the behavior performed throughout the activity, the performance must undergo extensive change. Figure 9.7B shows an increase in the duration of the instances; the number of instances has gone from 10 to 5. Figure 9.7C shows the behavior in its desired form. The student's total duration in performing the behavior exceeds 90 percent of the activity. If the social behavior of interest were attending to academic work, having a student perform at the 90-percent level or better would support the practice of any academic skill and, thus, facilitate academic learning. Figure 9.7 illustrates the value of teachers constructing and implementing the contingencies related to classroom management as effectively as possible.

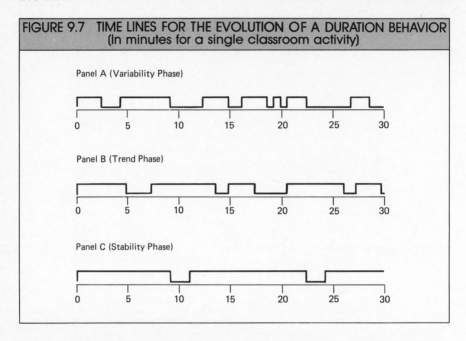

FIGURE 9.7 TIME LINES FOR THE EVOLUTION OF A DURATION BEHAVIOR
(In minutes for a single classroom activity)

Panel A (Variability Phase)

Panel B (Trend Phase)

Panel C (Stability Phase)

ROUTINES FOR CHANGING BEHAVIOR OVER TIME AND GUIDING EXPECTATIONS DURING CHANGE

This chapter has presented procedures, within the scope of management practices, for evolving and refining behavior over time. It has illustrated the patterns associated with such change. The following two sections highlight these two areas.

Changing Behavior Routine   The following questions help utilize the procedures for changing behavior over time.

1. *What type of behavior change is of interest?* Consider the following:
   a. *Is rate or duration the primary interest?* If the answer is yes, use class refinement procedures.
   b. *Are qualitative elements to be added to an existing class, thus, increasing its complexity?* If the answer is yes, use class expansion procedures.
   c. *Are classes of behavior to be combined to evolve new classes of behavior?* If the answer is yes, use class combination procedures.
2. If class refinement procedures are to be used, ask the following questions and perform the related procedures.

    a. *Is the class of interest a long-duration social behavior?* If the answer is yes, implement the following steps:
- **(1)** At the start of an activity, present a condition statement.
- **(2)** After a short time and before the student behaves inappropriately, give a combination statement.
- **(3)** For the rest of the activity, randomly give combination and reward statements for appropriate behavior.
- **(4)** At the end of the activity, reward the student if the behavior has been present longer than on previous occasions.
- **(5)** If inappropriate behavior occurs, correct it with the appropriate correction procedure.

    a. *Is the behavior of interest a high-rate academic behavior?* If the answer is yes, implement the following steps:
- **(1)** At the start of the activity, present a condition statement.
- **(2)** Randomly observe the number of instances performed and present a reward or combination statement if the number completed is higher than on previous observations.
- **(3)** Randomly observe the number of instances performed and present a reward-correction statement if the number is not higher than previous observations but most instances are correct.
- **(4)** At the end of an activity, when the student has done more problems than before, present a reward or combination statement for the higher rate.

3. If the behavior change of interest is related to the class expansion of social behavior, ask the following questions and perform the related procedures.

    a. *Is the expansion related to more inclusive classes?* If the answer is yes, implement the following procedures:
- **(1)** Start with condition and reward statements that describe the smallest and most clearly defined subclass and gradually expand to the larger class over a number of days.
- **(2)** When expanding to a more inclusive class, the condition and reward statements should contain a description of both the less inclusive and the more inclusive classes.

    b. *Is the expansion of interest related to exclusive classes?* If the answer is yes, implement the following procedures:

     (1) In the condition statements, indicate where the behavior has been performed appropriately and where it could also be performed appropriately.

     (2) If the location where the behavior is to be performed is seldom encountered, establish conditions as in (1) several times before the event.

     (3) In the new location, present combination statements as the appropriate behavior is being performed.

     (4) After the performance of the behavior in the new location, give a complete reward statement.

4. If the interest is in the class expansion and class combination of academic behavior, the following procedures need to be considered. (Remember that these procedures are not sufficient in themselves to evolve behavior.)

    a. If the interest is in the expansion of an academic class, the condition and reward statements should describe the class, the added qualitative attribute, and any resulting consequences.

    b. If the interest is in the combination of academic classes, the advanced condition and reward statements should as often as possible describe the classes taught, the classes to be taught, and/or the more inclusive class of which the others are members.

Teachers who can make the required decisions using the above questions and follow the procedures for sequencing advanced condition and reward statements are ready to evolve behavior within the limits of classroom management practices.

Changing Behavior Expectations As teachers seek to establish the conditions and consequences necessary to change social and academic behavior, they will be better able to succeed if they know what to expect. These changing behavior expectations are as follows:

1. No matter how "powerful" the instructional and management procedures used, expect mastery of the behavior to take time (often a great deal of time).
2. Once behavior has emerged, expect extensive variability.
3. Once behavior has started a trend, expect variability, in the form of oscillation and range, to decrease (often slowly).
4. Even after behavior has stabilized, expect an occasional occurrence of inappropriate behavior, academic or social.

5. Even after behavior has stabilized, expect to present conditions and consequences related to the behavior on a regular basis (fairly often mostly).
6. Because so many related behaviors are being evolved and refined in the classroom at one time, expect to have to describe these relationships to students.
7. If the expected behavior change does not occur, use the procedures of Chapter 12.

Teachers who know what to expect are more likely to be patient during the course of change and remain composed in the face of day-to-day fluctuations (oscillations) in student behavior. Teachers' awareness of the course of change and the procedures to change behavior will allow them to enjoy their students' growth both socially and academically.

PRACTICE ACTIVITIES

1. Practicing procedures for changing behavior duration and rate
   1.1 Generate examples, practice, and discuss procedures for changing behavior duration. Remember that "duration" refers to how much time a behavior occurs, and "rate" refers to how often a behavior occurs. (Social behaviors are typically long duration, low rate; academic behaviors are typically high rate, short duration.) (p. 181)
      a. Refer to an example in the text of a long-duration social behavior. List five new examples of different long-duration behaviors. Make the examples as different as possible.
      b. Choose one long-duration social behavior. Assume that the student typically engages in the behavior for the first 25 percent of the activity and then stops. Describe the contingent procedure you would follow to increase the duration of the behavior. Include specific examples of the verbal statements in each of the steps below: (p. 182)
         (1) Initial condition statement
         (2) First combination statement
         (3) Random combination/reward statements
         (4) Activity-ending reward statement
         (5) Warning correction
      c. Briefly describe how you would predict the daily student behavior duration to change across a three-week period in terms of the following three phases: (p. 193)
         (1) Behavior variability
         (2) Improved trend
         (3) Behavior stability
   1.2 Generate examples, practice, and discuss procedures for changing behavior rate. (p. 185)
      a. Refer to an example in the text of a high-rate academic behavior. List five new examples of different high-rate academic behaviors. Make the examples as different as possible.
      b. Choose one high-rate academic behavior. Assume that the student typically engages in the behavior for the first 25 percent of the activity and then stops. Describe the contingent procedures you would follow to increase the rate of the student behavior. Include specific examples of the verbal statements in each of the following steps: (p. 185)
         (1) Initial condition statement
         (2) First combination statement
         (3) Random combination/reward statement
         (4) Activity-ending reward statement
         (5) Warning correction
      c. Briefly describe how you would predict the daily student behavior rate to change across a three-week period in terms of the following three phases: (p. 193)
         (1) Behavior variability

        (2) Improved trend

        (3) Behavior stability

1.3 Refine procedures for changing rate and duration behaviors. Present examples for group discussion.

    a. Combine the five long-duration and five high-rate behaviors into a list of ten randomly sequenced examples (write each on a card, mix the cards).

    b. Next, read each of the behaviors in a relaxed fashion as you imagine its occurrence in a typical classroom setting. For each behavior, in turn, do the following:

        (1) State whether the behavior should be addressed in terms of duration or rate.

        (2) Present verbal statements to illustrate the five-step procedure for changing rate or duration behavior: initial condition statement, initial combination statement, random combination/reward statement, ending reward statement, and warning correction statement.

    c. Next, mix the list of behaviors (or obtain a similar list from a classmate) and follow the above procedure again, presenting each behavior example at 15–20-second intervals.

2. Graphing and interpreting duration and rate behavior (p. 193)

    2.1 Graph and interpret duration behavior trends. Present examples for group discussion.

        a. Assume that you are observing whether a student is sitting in his seat during a thirty-minute period. Assume further that the student is "in seat" for ten minutes of the thirty-minute period. Make a different timeline graph to illustrate each of the following:

            (1) Most of the student's time "in seat" occurs during the first fifteen minutes of the activity.

            (2) Most of the student's time "in seat" occurs during the last fifteen minutes of the activity.

            (3) The student's "in-seat" time is distributed equally across the thirty-minute activity.

        b. Assume further, that you have observed the number of minutes of the student's "in-seat" behavior during the thirty-minute period for the following 15 successive days:

Day	Minutes	Day	Minutes
1	10	9	18
2	11	10	17
3	10	11	19
4	9	12	18
5	12	13	20
6	8	14	19
7	14	15	20
8	16		

Construct a graph showing the number of in-seat minutes across the fifteen-day observation period. Assume that on day 4, the classroom teacher began a procedure to increase the duration of student in-seat behavior. Describe the student improvement trend across the fifteen-day interval.

2.2 Graph and interpret rate behavior trends. Present examples for group discussion.

   a. Assume that you are observing the number of arithmetic problems completed by a student working independently during a thirty-minute period. Assume further that the student completes twenty problems during the thirty-minute activity. Make a different timeline graph to illustrate each of the following:

   (1) Most of the problems are completed during the first fifteen minutes of the activity.

   (2) Most of the problems are completed during the last fifteen minutes of the activity.

   (3) The problems are completed equally across the activity.

   b. Assume further that you have observed the number of problems completed during the thirty-minute period for the following fifteen successive days:

Day	Problems Completed	Day	Problems Completed
1	20	9	28
2	19	10	27
3	20	11	29
4	21	12	30
5	22	13	29
6	20	14	31
7	25	15	30
8	22		

Construct a graph showing the number of problems completed across the fifteen-day observation period. Assume that on day 5, the classroom teacher began a procedure to increase the number of problems completed. Describe the student improvement trend across the fifteen-day interval.

3. Implementing behavior change procedures for rate or duration in regular classrooms

   3.1 Observe and graph student behavior. Present descriptions for group discussion. (p. 193)

   a. Consult with a regular classroom teacher to identify one or more problem students in the classroom you observed in preceding chapters. Determine whether the behavior to be targeted for improvement is an academic or social behavior. Specify whether behavior duration or rate will be focused on. Specify the classroom activity during which the behavior will occur.

   b. Observe the behavior for three to five days. Graph the student behavior targeted on a timeline for each day. Make a graph showing the occurrence (duration or rate) of the behavior across days.

3.2 Plan and practice a behavior change program. (p. 200)

    a. Beginning with day 5, outline the steps you would follow to increase the duration or rate of the behavior if you were the teacher. Next, imagine you are the teacher implementing the five-step behavior change procedure during the activity; present the condition, combination, reward, and correction statements across the activity. If possible, use a tape recorder in the rear of the room or behind a one-way glass. Repeat for two successive days, if possible. Continue graphing student behavior on a timeline each day. Continue adding to the graph summary student behavior across days. Note on your timeline when you presented statements to the target students.

    b. Next, continue to plan and simulate implementation of the change program for the targeted student while you observe. In addition, also present condition, reward, and correction statements to other students as appropriate. Again, use a tape recorder in the rear of the room or behind a one-way screen. Continue construction of the timelines and graphs as before. Repeat for two successive days, if possible. Note on the timeline when you made statements to the target student.

    c. Review your timeline and graphs with a classmate or with the classroom teacher. Describe your procedures in relation to the student behavior each day. Predict how the student behavior might have changed if the treatment had been implemented, referring to your graphs of the student behavior across days.

3.3 Plan, implement, and discuss behavioral change in a regular classroom. Have an observer critique your behavior change program. (p. 200)

    a. Arrange to work as a monitor or teacher in the classroom you observed. (If a new classroom or student is selected, follow the procedures in the example above until three days of student behavior have been observed.) Arrange also to have a classmate or the teacher observe your behavior and the student's behavior on a timeline graph.

    b. Implement your planned change procedure for the targeted student for six to twelve days. While doing so, be sure to maintain the delivery of condition, reward, and correction statements for all students in the class during the activity. Review the timeline data each day and continue graphing the occurrence of student duration or rate behavior each day. Write a short paragraph explaining the graphs and procedures you followed or discuss them with another student and the teacher.

REFERENCES

Selecting references for Chapter 9 involves the same problems encountered in Chapter 8: The theoretical background is clear (it is identical to Chapters 2 and

7), but the accompanying research and technology are sometimes difficult to identify. The research findings seem clearest for rate and duration behavior change. The procedures in Chapter 9 expand on recent research and technology by relating rate and duration; social and academic behaviors; and the application of condition, reward, and combination statements within a time frame. A summary of the research and technology can be found in texts on the principles of behavior and/or their application to the classroom. The following are clear presentations.

Ferster, C. R., & Culbertson, S. *Behavior Principles,* 3rd ed. Englewood Cliffs, N.J.: Prentice-Hall, 1982.

Millenson, J. R., & Leslie, J. C. *Principles of Behavior Analysis,* 2nd ed. New York: Macmillan, 1979.

Reese, E. P. *Human Behavior: Analysis and Application.* Dubuque, Iowa: William C. Brown Company, 1978.

Sulzar-Azaroff, B., & Mayer, G. R. *Applying Behavior-Analysis Procedures with Children and Youth.* New York: Holt, Rinehart and Winston, 1977.

Like the development of advanced condition and reward statements, the technology of class expansion and class combination procedures appears to be an outgrowth of the interaction between the theory and technology of verbal statements. Each time problems were encountered, the application of theory and the technology developed has led to further procedures. Part of this theory relates to the evolutionary course of behavior change. Thus, the last part of Chapter 9 covers the perspective on the course of change required to use the procedures effectively. Murray Sidman has given the most thorough and accurate picture of the course of behavior change and its evaluation from the viewpoint of examining an individual subject. Recently, James Johnston and H. S. Pennypacker have focused the single-subject perspective on applied research settings such as the classroom.

Johnston, J. M., & Pennypacker, H. S. *Strategies and Tactics of Human Behavioral Research.* Hillsdale, N.J.: Lawrence Erlbaum, 1980.

Sidman, M. *Tactics of Scientific Research: Evaluating Experimental Data in Psychology.* New York: Basic Books, 1960.

CHAPTER TEN

ESTABLISHING COMPATIBLE CONTINGENCIES

T he preceding chapters have provided procedures for establishing key aspects of effective classroom contingencies. But "effectiveness" is a relative term and contingencies effective for one teacher with a particular set of students may not be effective for another with different students. The first teacher may have students who exhibit some self-control and independence when given an academic task, while the second may have remedial students with a history of inadequate self-control. For effective management, the second teacher will need more powerful contingencies. If both teachers use the procedures and skills introduced in previous chapters, the second teacher may still experience some failure in managing the classroom. Fortunately, there are several procedures for establishing very powerful contingencies designed to eliminate established inappropriate social behavior and to motivate academic behavior. This chapter considers procedures for increasing contingency power.

ESTABLISHING COMPATIBLE CONTINGENCIES

Each individual in the classroom establishes a set of contingencies by setting conditions for and rewarding particular behaviors of others. Teachers do this explicitly when they follow the procedures presented in this text. Students usually do so implicitly or without awareness. The problem is that the contingencies of teachers and students often are not compatible. Compatible contingencies within a setting facilitate (set the conditions for and reward or correct) the same classes of behavior. To have all students establish contingencies that facilitate the teacher's contingencies, the teacher must reward only the appropriate classroom behavior and correct only inappropriate behavior. An extensive increase in appropriate and a substantial decrease in inappropriate behavior should result. This chapter discusses four procedures for arranging compatible contingencies: (1) establishing compatible contingencies student by student, (2) using group contingencies to establish compatible contingencies, (3) establishing compatible contingencies through students helping students, (4) establishing compatible contingencies in the home and school. These procedures should be used together in order to maximize the chance of success.

Establishing Compatible Contingencies Student by Student   The student-by-student procedure first determines which students are establishing compatible contingencies. Through their modeling (demonstration), these students are setting conditions for and rewarding appropriate behavior for other students. Second, the teacher needs to reward students for such behavior and continue to set conditions and consequences individually for inappropriate students. As each student begins to exhibit appropriate behavior, one less set of contingencies will facilitate the inappropriate behavior of others and one more will facilitate appropriate behavior. Once a student starts to become enthusiastic about the academic tasks, via being reinforced through success and reward statements, the teacher can shift the focus to another student, not forgetting to set conditions and deliver rewards to the students already contributing to compatible contingencies. As with shifting reward from one class of behavior to another (see Chapters 3, 5, and 8), teachers shift emphasis from one student to another while maintaining the delivery of conditions and rewards to those who are a part of the compatible contingency system.

The following statements establish compatible contingencies student by student. They stress cooperation and the consequences for other students.

"Kerry, once again you have followed the rules and displayed cooperation. That helps the other students do their work by showing them what to do and, also, by not distracting them from their assignments. I hope you can continue doing it."

"Beatrice, your hard work on the assignments is a fine model for what other students should be doing. I hope you enjoy the work and can continue showing others how it should be done."

"Siegfried, you have demonstrated to yourself and others how to participate in class. I especially like to see your classroom assignments completed as fast as they are. Can you keep it up?" (*Student replies.*) "I think so, too."

"Renée, you have really changed and are now an example for others to follow. Do you find that enjoyable?" (*Student replies.*) "I would, too."

Each of these examples relates the student's behavior to what it does for others by modeling the appropriate behavior others should be exhibiting. The last two examples involve a student response. Example 3 seeks the student's commitment to keep demonstrating the behavior, and example 4 seeks confirmation of the positive emotion to which the teacher has referred. Repeating reward statements in this form increases the probability of compatible contingencies. At times such statements need to be given privately. This is especially true in the middle grades or when starting to use such statements.

Using Group Contingencies to Establish Compatible Contingencies Although planning and delivering conditions and consequences student by student will, under many circumstances, establish compatible contingencies throughout the classroom, group contingencies can be used to accelerate the process. Whenever teachers deliver condition and consequence statements at a group level, they are using a group contingency. This section discusses three types, each of which fosters compatible contingencies by providing a reward for all, contingent (dependent) on the behavior of the group or some part of it.

Interdependent Group Contingencies. When conditions are set so that the desired behavior is requested of all group members, and a group consequence is delivered only if all members of the group perform the behavior, teachers are using an interdependent group contingency. For example, if the group is requested to finish worksheets for an extra bonus point (a supplementary reward), the points can only be given if every member of the group finishes his or her worksheet. The group members increase the probability of receiving the reward by aiding each other. They also feel that they are working for a reward not only for themselves but also for their peers. Because upper elementary and secondary students are involved in a continual socialization process and because social rewards dramatically increase the behavior they are contingent on, the interdependent group contingency is a powerful management tool. The following statements illustrate how the teacher can set conditions and deliver consequences for interdependent group-contingencies.

Example 1

(*Statement to set conditions.*) "I think that today can be a day when everyone tries hard. If everyone can do that so no warnings are given to anyone, I will play some of your music selections for the last ten mintues of independent work."

(*Statement during the activity.*) "Everyone certainly is working toward the music. No one has been warned, and this shows that you all are gaining self-control. Let's see if you can keep it up."

(*Statement at the conclusion of the activity.*) "Guess what? You did it. No warning given and the hard work I saw made me proud of your self-control. Let's see if you can keep it up during the music time."

Example 2

(*Statement to set the conditions.*) "Everyone, this is the second day in a row that everybody has been here. That makes me happy enough to say that for each day that everyone is here and on time, I will award everyone an extra point that goes toward your social behavior award letter. How would everyone like that?" (*Students reply.*) "Very good, I will start today by giving everyone a first point. You can earn up to 5 points toward your weekly letter."

(*Statement during the contingency.*) "It is Thursday and you have earned 3 out of 4 extra points toward your letters. This is tremendous, and your attendance has improved so much. I hope you can keep it up. Can you?" (*Students reply.*) "I will look forward to it."

(*Statement at the conclusion of the award time interval.*) "As I hand out these awards, I would like to say that not only did everyone in the class earn an award, but this also is the first week that everyone has been here everyday. I can't believe it, it is wonderful. Give yourselves a great big hand." (*Students clap.*) "You must really enjoy the work we do here."

The nature of the interdependent group contingency requires a public statement to set the conditions. The conditions established in example 1 apply only to a single activity, but example 2 describes behavior continuing across activities, with rewards given daily and weekly (e.g., award activity time). For the latter type of contingency to continue to be effective, the statements and awards must be varied and presented with enthusiasm. The statements given during the contingency for example 1 relate the contingency behavior to the class of self-control skills and ask the students to "keep it up." The use of a negative class (calling attention to the nonuse of the warning procedure) to help define the positive class ("try hard") clarifies the broad positive class and helps objectify (through an example of inappropriate behavior) its evaluation for the teacher and students. The conclusion statement of the first example points again to self-control and to maintaining it during music time, which indicates that class rules will be operating. Example 2 relates the social behavior of attending school to the students' liking of academic work. It is important to always link the social with the academic; this linking fosters the students' learning being rewarded by academic activities.

Dependent Group Contingencies. When conditions are set so that the desired behavior is requested of all group members, but a group consequence is delivered to all students if only one member (or some selected portion) of the group performs the specified behavior, teachers are using a dependent group contingency. For example, a group may be asked to follow classroom rule 4, and if Leonard and Tom do so, the group receives a consequence of a few minutes' extra recess or an extra point toward their grade (see Chapter 11). Here the group members can increase the probability of receiving reward by facilitating (setting conditions for and rewarding or correcting) the members Leonard and Tom, on whose behavior the group's reward is dependent. In turn, the members on whom the reward depends are influenced by the chance to impress or reward their friends and those they would like to become friends with. Such contingencies are especially powerful for students in the middle elementary grades through high school, where the socialization process is at its most formative stage. The following examples show how the teacher might set conditions for, and deliver consequences related to, dependent group contingencies.

Example 1

(*Statement to set conditions.*)"I would like to see everyone follow the rules today. Who think they can do it? I am glad to see that Carmen and Celeste think they can. If they can, I will give everyone two minutes of extra free time during Friday's activity time. Is that okay with you two?" (*Two students reply.*) "So, let's begin."

(*Statement during the activity.*) "I think that Carmen and Celeste are showing everyone how to do it. They are splendid models and so are the rest of you. I sure want to give a little extra time on Friday."

(*Statement at the conclusion of the activity.*) "That's it, time to stop working and hand in your papers. Please do so now. Also consider that Celeste and Carmen followed the rules and earned everyone extra points. Class, give Carmen and Celeste and yourselves a hand for following the rules."

Example 2

(*Statement to set conditions—privately presented.*) "Dennis, you have been rapidly improving on getting along with others and trying hard. If you can do it again today, I would enjoy giving the class some music to work by for the last few minutes of independent work. Is that okay with you?" (*Student replies.*) "I know you can, too, so give it a try."

(*Statement during the activity—privately presented.*) "Dennis, keep trying hard and cooperating with others. The extra music is just around the corner. You're doing a fantastic job."

(*Statement at the end of the activity.*) "Class, I am impressed with how most of you have been working today, and especially with Dennis. Because he has cooperated and tried so hard today, I have decided to give you a little music to work by for the last five minutes of class. Thank Dennis for that." (*Teacher starts to clap and students join in.*)

Statements which set the conditions for the dependent group contingency usually follow a review of the relevant rules. In the first example the statement is given to the class, and in the second it is given privately. The advantage of the first is that peers can influence the dependent students; this is not so in the second example. Both examples provide the dependent students with a chance to win a reward for their friends. Statements during the activity can also be given publicly or privately. The advantage of the first example is that everyone is rewarded. Both examples' concluding statements are given to the class, indicate whether the consequence has or has not been obtained, and point out to other students what the dependent students have done for them. This last point is very important when other students do not follow the behaviors specified, but the dependent students do. If the reason for the consequence is not made clear to the inappropriate students, the teacher could accidentally reward these students for some inappropriate behavior.

Independent Group Contingencies. When conditions are set so that the desired behavior is different for each member of the group and a group consequence is delivered only if all members of the group perform their behavior, teachers are using an independent group contingency. For example, each member of the class may be required to do different amounts and/or different math problems, and only if all members do their assigned problems will the group receive the rewarding consequence of talking to their neighbors for the last few minutes of class. The major advantage of the independent group contingency is that the behavior specification can be tailored to the needs of the individual student. In contrast, use of the interdependent group contingency with a diverse group requires the teacher to specify behavior criteria that the lowest performer can achieve. The dependent group contingency can be adjusted to individuals, but only for a small portion of the group. Therefore, only a small portion of the group is influenced by a dependent group contingency. As a result, the independent group contingency is the most appropriate for academic behavior assignments. The following examples show how the teacher can establish conditions and consequences for independent group contingencies.

Example 1

(*Statement to set conditions.*) "Yesterday, most of you did more correct problems on your worksheets than usual. Today, I would like everyone to do it. So I have a goal for each of you to meet today. If everyone can do it, we will all take the last 10 minutes of class to practice for our program skit. Would you like that?" (*Students reply.*) "I knew it. I will give you your assignments as I walk around, so let's go."

(*Statement during the activity.*) "Delia, you are ahead of your assignment goal. Your answers look correct also. Keep it up and you will do your part in helping others receive the extra practice time."

(*Statement at the conclusion of the activity.*) "The way that everyone worked must have been a labor of love. You all did it. You completed your individual assignments. That is only the second time that has happened and because of it, you will get your extra practice time on the program skit. I think that such things will happen more in the future."

Example 2

(*Statement to set conditions.*) "I liked the way that everyone came in and started right to work. If everyone can keep it up by doing the assignment written on the top of his worksheet, everyone will get three bonus points toward his academic grade for the week. Can each of you do it?" (*Students reply.*) "It will be hard, but I know you can do it if you try. So let's help each other improve your grades."

(*Statement during an activity.*) "I like the way each of you is helping the other. If everyone keeps trying, you will make it. The extra points are almost yours!"

(*Statement at the conclusion.*) "It looks to me like you all did your assignments. Because of the long announcement by the principal, we will not have time to correct them now. But I will tell you at the beginning of class tomorrow if you all earned your extra points. How many think you did?" (*Students reply.*) "We will find out tomorrow. Have a good day."

The statements at the beginning of examples 1 and 2 differ in the method the teacher uses to give the individual assignments. Any statement that gives the students the assignment as fast as possible is appropriate. The second example's beginning statement is useful when in-class time is short, but does require more teacher preparation. The statements during the activity indicate that either group or individual statements are appropriate. In both examples, the element of students helping each other is included. The first example's conclusion statement does two important things: It relates academic tasks to enjoyable emotional events, and it tells students they will be doing such behavior more often in the future. The latter point indicates that the teacher sees and is telling the students about the evolution of their behavior. The second example's conclusion shows how the teacher adapts to an interruption, something that often happens in the classroom.

Precautions and Considerations in Using Group Contingencies. Three main precautions and considerations apply to using group contingencies. The first is the possibility that a particular individual or individuals cannot perform the class of behavior desired. This concern is applicable to all types of group contingencies. As mentioned above, the interdependent group contingency must be adjusted to the lowest performer, and the dependent and independent contingencies to the dependent students and each class member, respectively. An error in judgment can easily be made. This precaution is most applicable to academic behavior which is newly emerged in the students' repertoire. To be conservative, the teacher should restrict the use of group contingencies to behavior that students can perform with some proficiency. The other alternative is to set the behavioral requirement at an achievable level.

The second precaution is to prepare for students who fail to make the group contingency. Chapter 5 has indicated that failure statements specify what has been done appropriately, how close it came to the criteria for reward, and provide a motivational component to set the occasion for the next performance of the behavior. This information makes failure less harsh, so that students may see their performance as adequate, but not extra special. Students are helped to see that not every day can be a "first," and each class activity performance has at least some positive aspect.

The third precaution deals with the possibility that one or two individuals may subvert the contingencies or beat the system. Subversion goes beyond testing the rules. As discussed in Chapter 4, the rule-testing student seeks to obtain rewards by not following the rules. The subverter is rewarded for disrupting the system. Such disruption is rare, but teachers have some procedures to use. If the inappropriate behavior is social, correction procedures can be used. If the inappropriate behavior takes an academic form, then the teacher can use a dependent contingency with a consequence the subverter finds more rewarding than the inappropriate behavior of subverting. For example, the student's earning extra free time for others to engage in activities is an effective reward. These activities should include something that each student wants to do more than anything else. Between the reward of this activity and the elements of reward associated with the group contingency, the student subverter will stop the inappropriate behavior in a short time. (The section "Rewards in the Classroom" explores some possible rewards.)

There are two considerations in using group contingencies: (1) How to use them involves all the points made in the chapters on reward and condition statements. Thus, the teacher must be sincere, descriptive, and truthful. (2) When to use them depends on the time the students need to change. Variety is essential and group contingencies are another way to vary the conditions and consequences. Group contingencies can be used to special advantage just before a holiday or vacation time. Their power to keep student learning is often needed during these periods.

Establishing Compatible Contingencies through Students Helping Students Group contingencies allow students to set conditions for and give rewards to other students. The teacher's statements associated with the use of group contingencies identify these events. But there is another side to having students help each other: by providing students with procedures to reward and correct each other within the classroom. Such procedures should be usable in or out of the context of teacher-established group contingencies.

Procedures for Students Rewarding Students. Many teacher-delivered rewards can involve students. For example, during the presentation of awards (see Chapter 11), the teacher can ask the students to clap for, or shake hands with, those who meet the award criteria. After some time, the students will start to do this without the teacher's request. At the end of an activity, the teacher can ask the students to shake their neighbor's hand for a job well done (if, in fact, it was). If students tutor each other, the tutor and tutored can deliver statements to each other on the appropriateness of academic and social behavior. Chapter 6, on corrections, has identified procedures for using students as tutors and the correction procedures (containing a reward element) these students should use. The goal of all these examples is to have each student realize that the other students would like him or her to be appropriate, as defined by the classroom contingencies.

But one of the most effective ways for students to directly reward their peers is through their chance to affect the grade of another student. This can most easily be done in the context of a point system, as described in Chapter 11. The student can award another student with 0, 1, or 2 points for social behavior during the week. The teacher must stress to the students the importance of what they are doing for the other student. If the awarding student gives the maximum number of points and the awarded student has not earned them (as determined by the number of times the awarded student has lost points during the week), the awarding student is facilitating the awarded student's inappropriate behavior. In order for the student reward procedure to be used effectively, the teacher must specify what is required for 0, 1, or 2 points. For 2 points, for example, the student should have a week without the loss of more than 1 or 2 points for social behavior, and no warnings or separations. On the other hand, the loss of points and a separation could be considered grounds for a zero. The teacher must work these criteria out very carefully. The presentation of the procedure to students must cover all details and, like the introduction of rules (Chapter 4), must be reviewed numerous times for the students to see and feel the extent to which they must evaluate their peers. The student evaluation assignments should be on a rotating list, so that over the year, a student can award points to each of the other students in the class. During the introduction of the procedure, the teacher needs to inform the students that the procedure can be eliminated if she feels the students are not fairly assessing their peers. After the students have been under such a system for some time or have been a part of classrooms with the rules and procedures described in this text, the students can elect a group who decide the grading criteria, with or without the teacher. This is "participatory" management.

Procedures for Students Correcting Students. Chapter 6 has shown how student tutors should correct inappropriate academic behavior. Social behavior correction procedures for students follow directly from the rules of the classroom or activity in session. The student part involves a signal to the inappropriate student which indicates that he or she is not following the rules. Two good signals are the "open hand" gesture used by police to stop traffic, and a small red card placed on each student's desk. If a student is bothering another, the other may simply pick up the card or use the signal to tell the student to stop the inappropriate behavior. Other students can join in with the same signal. If these peer signals bring the inappropriate behavior to the attention of the teacher, the teacher should wait to see if the student correction is effective before using one of the social corrections outlined in Chapter 6. If it is effective, the students who used the procedure should be discreetly rewarded then or at a later time. This correction procedure should not be introduced until the students are familiar with the teacher's posted social correction procedures. The student procedure should also be posted at its introduction. In introducing the procedure, the teacher needs to review the signal and indicate that more than one student can use the signal at one time. It is useful to role-play with the students over several days until the procedure becomes familiar. If a student starts to use inappropriate signals or gestures, a warning should be given. It is useful to cover this point in the procedure's introduction. This is another participation management procedure. It can be even more participatory if the students are involved in establishing classroom rules.

Establishing Compatible Contingencies in the Home and School

In Chapters 3 and 6, procedures for informing the school and home of the reward and correction procedures were presented as a first step in establishing compatible contingencies outside the classroom. This section presents a few more techniques.

Establishing Compatible Contingencies in the School. In school, two important steps can be taken: The first is to *establish a set of school level rules* or revise those that exist so that they follow the specifications in Chapter 4. The major difficulty is that school rules are often adopted by a committee of school personnel with limited training in procedures like those in this text. In these cases, the effective procedure is to work slowly to win these individuals over by rewarding their correct statements about rules and expanding on each point they make by adding another element of effective rules. Volunteering to do the brunt of the work in establishing the rules also helps and may be the most critical factor. Above all, tact, graciousness, and calmness are absolutely necessary. Without them, all the procedures learned in this text will fail to be realized at the school level. Finally, the teacher needs to find others whose contingencies are compatible and join their efforts in establishing effective rules and school procedures.

The second step, which can begin before or during the establishment of school rules, is to *set up school level rewards*. This includes both awards and statements for performance of school level social behavior. Some questions to consider are, What happens to students who enter the school quietly, await their turn in the lunch line, walk in the hall, or help pick up some trash in the hall? Do they get a bonus slip from the staff member who sees these things happen or a statement relating the specific behavior to the school rules and larger classes of behavior? If the answer is no, the above procedures for establishing school rules are also necessary for establishing rewards. The section on establishing rewards in the classroom provides a fuller account of what can be used for school rewards.

Establishing Compatible Contingencies in the Home. Letters to parents describing the school's reward and correction procedures are a beginning step in establishing compatible contingencies in the home (see Chapter 11). Another approach is to have a parent conference, either in person or by phone, to cover three areas. First, the teacher needs to find out what social and academic behaviors the parents would like from their child. This information will help the teacher direct the student's social behavior in the classroom and provide a basis for recontacting the parents at a later date. If the parents do not know what they want, which is often the case, the teacher should restate his academic and social behavior objectives and ask for parent agreement. This will also establish a basis for recontact. Second, the teacher needs to summarize the reward and correction procedures with the parents, and ask for their agreement with them. Again agreement and familiarity are essential. Third, the parents should be asked if they will pay attention to and ask the student what specific awards, points, and grades the student achieved each week (the next section and Chapter 11 clarify their use). The extent to which the parents ask about the student's grades, points, or awards can be assessed by simply asking students if their parents have asked about these things. The assessment should be done multiple times to provide the teacher with a picture of what is happening at home in terms of parental interest in the student and the extent to which the student is rewarded by the parents.

The last approach to increase the chances that the home will reinforce appropriate school behavior is to tell the student to ask his or her parents what they think about the student's awards, grades, and points. Here the child must be shown how to facilitate parental reward. When this step is combined with the assessment of rewards given in the home, the following examples of such teacher-student interaction might occur:

Example 1

(*Day 1*) "Everyone, you have put in a lot of hard work this week and your grades show it. Also, I would be very proud of your awards. These are things you need to show your parents and ask them what they think about them. Who is going to show and ask about these things?" (*Students reply.*) "Please do because I am interested in what your parents say about them."

(*Day 2*) "Class, how many of you asked your parents about what they thought about your grades and awards?" (*Students reply.*) "I am glad to see that over half remembered to do this. Of those who asked, how many found that their parents liked what they had achieved?" (*Students reply.*) "OK, you can see what asking can do for you. I hope the rest of you will remember to show your parents tonight."

Example 2

(*Day 1*) "Nathan, this is the first week you achieved the Try-Hard Award and also got an A. Your parents should be proud. You should show them your achievements and ask them what they think about them. Will you do so?" (*Student replies.*) "I will be very interested in what they think of such fine work."

(*Day 2*) "Nathan, what did your parents say about your award?" (*Student replies.*) "That is great! I can tell they appreciate your hard work and are very proud of you. Thank you for asking them."

The first example provides statements being presented to a group. This group approach is an effective initial step. Many of the students will initially forget to ask, but later will come to do so. Some students need to see their peers ask and receive a reward for it. But if a student continually fails to ask, the teacher can use a phone call to prompt the parents to ask. If the teacher has set conditions at both ends, student and parents, the probability of a positive student-parent interaction is increased. The teacher needs to follow up the next day with inquiry statements to the student (see example 2, day 2). Example 2 indicates what a one-to-one interaction may look like. Many teachers find it difficult to present these types of statements, especially the group statements, to high school students. Students who are newcomers to a rewarding classroom will initially find such statements a little strange. The newcomers' reaction will change after they have been in a classroom containing the management elements detailed in this text, and the statements will no longer seem strange. The teacher who practices and builds these type of statements over and over, before entering the classroom, will find them easy to use. If a teacher has trouble presenting them, the best place to start is with individual students who are already exhibiting compatible behavior.

REWARDS IN THE CLASSROOM

Besides the above procedures to establish compatible contingencies, powerful teacher-delivered rewards can be used. Thus far, rewards have consisted of teacher statements referencing three types of possible consequences for the student: emotional reactions, a newly structured world, and/or access to events or activities (see Chapter 3). This section examines these types of rewards in order to show how many of them can be found and used in the classroom to promote appropriate behavior, and thus facilitate the construction of compatible contingencies.

Grades A grade represents how the student has changed, how the student has been working, and what is expected of the student in the future. Grades are extremely powerful consequences if used properly. In order for grades to be effective, the teacher should do the following:

1. Make grades a composite of each major academic activity.
2. Make grades dependent on established criteria.
3. If necessary, give grades for social behavior related to the classroom rules.
4. Amplify the importance of grades within condition and reward statements.
5. Award grades daily (if possible).
6. Have a weekly or biweekly grade award presentation.

Items 1 and 2 stress that the teacher needs to consider the percentage that each activity contributes to the overall grade, and determine criteria for the grade (e.g., the number of answers earning an A, B, C, or D for each activity). By keeping the criteria consistent day to day, the teacher can post the criteria, allowing students to determine their standing on a daily basis. Item 3 considers activities where student work cannot be easily evaluated, as in a teacher lecture on new material or a gym class game activity. For these activities, grades should be awarded for the demonstration of appropriate social behavior. If the first items are covered, the fourth, fifth, and sixth follow easily. The statements by the teacher should refer to grades as often as possible:

> (*Condition statement.*) "Everyone, turn to your comprehension questions. You have 15 minutes to complete them. I know if you all work hard you can get the 9 or 10 correct for an A. Can you do it?" (*Students reply.*) "Then go to it."

> (*Condition statement.*) "Jerry, I would like to see you get an A today. Will you try hard?" (*Student replies.*) "I know you can and will."

> (*Reward statement.*) "Bonnie, you got another A. That is four days so far this week. If you can do it one more day, you will have an A for the week. Gosh, I hope you do it."

> (*Reward statement.*) "This is a first! Everyone in the group got an A today! That is what I like to see. Let's give ourselves a hand." (*Students clap.*) "I would love to see it tomorrow."

In the typical classroom, grades are not mentioned daily in this way. Generally, there is a long delay between the student's academic performance and the grade. Statements make the importance of the grade a daily affair. The weekly award ceremony for the weekly grade indicates that the students have accomplished an important goal: They have changed and the importance of their change is acknowledged to others. The award ceremony should be quickly done, but with the necessary fanfare, such as music, congratulations, and a handshake. The awards must be frequent; a letter to the parents or a filled-in printed certificate often suffice. The statements that are part of the ceremony should indicate students' past, present, and future behavior—as do the following:

> "John (*student comes forward*), you had an A for the first four weeks of this grading period. That shows continued hard work and means that if you can do it for two more weeks your report card will for sure have an A on it. Class, do you think John can do it?" (*Students reply.*) "I agree."

> "Marva, I would like to shake your hand. This is the first time you have made an A. I knew you could do it if you came to school every day for a week. Can you try hard to be here all next week so you have the chance for another A?" (*Student replies.*) "I will look forward to it."

The first example not only references the past, present, and future state of the behavior, but also asks the class to give its support to the student in the future. The teacher sets the conditions so that students support other students, helping to create compatible contingencies in the classroom. The second example stresses to the class the importance of attending in order to attain a high grade. This approach is important with students who exhibit a great deal of inappropriate behavior.

The activities of a high school class do not always enable the teacher to give students grades immediately. There is often a day's delay for the grading of papers. Also, the activities of many classes are not repeated daily, but are cycled in some form. This means that the grades are delayed and their makeup differs from day to day and week to week. (Specific procedures for this situation are covered in Chapter 11.) By following the six steps provided, the teacher shows students how they have been working, how they have changed, and gives them future direction.

Activities What happens after the student has completed an assignment or at the end of the week when the student has received an A for hard work and appropriate social behavior? A grade is given, but what else? Access to activities is one answer. In order for access to activities to be effective, the teacher must:

1. Make activities contingent on appropriate social or academic behavior.

    2. Clearly set conditions for the beginning, duration, and end of the activity.

    3. Amplify activities' importance within condition and reward statements.

Activities such as field trips or weekly free time require students to work for a period of time before they gain access to them. On the other hand, activities such as working on an individual project or going to the library can occur during an activity after the student has finished assigned work. Both types of activities require specified amounts of behavior before they can be engaged in. These criteria must be presented to the students so that they know when they can engage in the extra activity. Students must also know the limits of the social behaviors that accompany the activity. If other students are working, it will be necessary for the activity conditions to be quiet. The field trip will require different conditions. The students will have to behave a certain way while traveling on the bus, another way while being guided, and a different way during any breaks that occur. For all forms of activities, it is necessary to practice appropriate social activity behaviors. During the performance of an activity, the teacher must reward appropriate social behaviors with descriptive statements. The condition and reward statements used for the learning activity which wins access to the reward activity must clearly indicate how the reward becomes available.

> (*Condition statement.*) "Remember, if you finish early and have your work from yesterday corrected, you can work on your individual projects. How many would like to do that?" (*Students reply.*) "You all can if you work hard. So go to it."

> (*Reward statement.*) "Etta, because you got all your problems correct yesterday, you do not have any to correct today and, thus, have time to work on your own project. Your careful work pays again."

> (*Condition statement.*) "Wilda, you have all questions correct, so you can go to the activity area. Please read the activity rules before starting. I know you can follow them and still have an enjoyable time. Thank you for working hard."

> (*Reward statement.*) "Wilda, you certainly are following the rule about being quiet while others are working. This lets them work so that they may have a chance to get some activity time too."

If the conditions are set and rewards given, the activities will operate smoothly.

    Many activities are available to the teacher at the elementary, middle, and high school levels. The following gives just some of the possibilities available to the individual teacher. Special conditions may eliminate some of these possibilities or suggest others.

Activities for Individuals

Working on special projects

Collecting or passing out workbooks and worksheets

Grading papers for the teacher

Being first in line for lunch or other class or school activities

Sitting in a special place to read a book

Skipping an assignment

Reading a library book

Putting together puzzles

Being exempt from a test

Helping tutor students in another room

Passing out pencils

Feeding classroom pets

Writing stories about any topic

Helping keep the classroom neat and clean (clean blackboards, erasers, etc.)

Working on a hobby

Running teacher's errands

Listening to recorded stories and music with headphones

Decorating the classroom

Being the leader of a group (e.g., reading, math)

Putting away teacher or classroom materials

Answering questions for other students

Being a member of the classroom decision-making group

Activities for Groups

Free time

Games

Puzzles

Visitors

Field trips

Listening to music

Movies

Outdoor lessons

Dancing

Parties

Talent shows

Making signs and displays for the school

Recognition Most rewards are a form of recognition. Teachers' reward statements are a good example. But recognition rewards dramatically acknowledge that students have mastered some skill or met some criteria. Such mastery by the student is recognized in the form of a letter to parents, a certificate, a mark on a chart, or even a note from the principal. Like the other reward forms, recognition consequences are dependent on specific criteria and amplified by condition and reward statements. Some sample statements follow:

(*Condition statement.*) "It is only Tuesday, but if everyone works like yesterday, everyone will earn a note from the principal for hard work this week. I know you can all do it, so get started and enjoy yourselves."

(*Reward statement.*) "Doreen, your work today is bringing you closer to the letter to your parents. You had only 1 wrong out of 25 problems on your math worksheet. Can you keep it up?" (*Student replies.*) "I agree."

Recognition statements are similar to those for activity rewards. The former statements indicate the extent to which the student is working toward the distant reward of recognition.

Recognition awards can be given for almost any social or academic behavior that takes place in the school, from attendance to specific academic areas. As with activity rewards, what the teacher can use as a reward depends on the conditions and objectives of the classroom, and what student and parents show an interest in. Often recognition takes the form of a "Certificate of award" or certificates for "outstanding achievement," or "scholastic accomplishment." These are the more formal awards, which are given for some large achievement such as mastering the course objectives or getting an A for a grading period. There are also short-term (i.e., weekly or biweekly) "letters to parents," "fuzzy grams," or "working hard awards," which indicate to the students how they are progressing toward the larger award. Finally, there are awards for mastering specific important objectives such as math facts, vocabulary words, or scientific classification. These are often related to students' remembering specific information on which later learning is dependent. "Super Summer," "Word Master," or "Classy Classifier" are the type of names often used for these awards, which all indicate a specific behavior performed by the student.

A ROUTINE FOR ESTABLISHING COMPATIBLE CONTINGENCIES

The following questions will help guide the teacher in constructing compatible contingencies. They will prove especially useful in the early stage of learning to establish such contingencies.

1. *Which students are already helping to establish compatible contingencies?* These are the students who are behaving according to the teacher's established contingencies.
2. *Which individual students are the least inappropriate?* With these students identified, the teacher can start to deliver condition and reward statements to emphasize their part in making the group work together.
3. *Which individual students are the most inappropriate?* Group contingencies can be used effectively here, and the dependent group contingency is the most powerful.

4. *What behaviors would the teacher like to require of all students?* Again, this is a place for group contingencies. Often the social behaviors of finishing worksheets and homework are critical.
5. *What can be done to make the school and home contingencies compatible with the classroom?* Establishing school rules and rewards are important, as are getting parents to pay attention to what their child does.
6. *What can be done to get students to reward and correct other students?* Several procedures have been mentioned and illustrated. Others also exist.
7. *What rewards can be added to the classroom?* These additions will increase appropriate behavior and give the group contingencies added support.

Once teachers become proficient in the analysis of behavior, the use of condition and reward statements, the implementation of correction procedures, the establishing of compatible contingencies, and can patiently deal with the slow course of change, they are well on their way to effective management. Chapter 11 will further facilitate effective management by outlining a management system that puts all these elements together.

PRACTICE ACTIVITIES

1. Generating examples of compatible contingency procedures for group discussion
    1.1 Student by student: Describe a small group classroom setting in which student-by-student compatible contingencies could be established. Outline steps you might follow in terms of condition, combination, and reward statements. Present an example to illustrate each form of statement in the beginning, during, and after the procedure. Predict how student behaviors would change if the procedure were effective. (p. 210)
    1.2 Group contingencies: Repeat example 1.1 for each of the following:
        a. Interdependent group contingencies (p. 211)
        b. Dependent group contingencies (p. 212)
        c. Independent group contingencies (p. 214)
    1.3 Students helping students. Repeat example 1.1 to illustrate one possible procedure for each of the following: (p. 216)
        a. Students rewarding students in a group setting.
        b. Students correcting students in a group setting.
    1.4 School and home contingencies: Repeat example 1.1 to illustrate one possible procedure for each of the following: (p. 218)
        a. School-level rules, rewards.
        b. Establishing parent interest.

2. Generating examples using classroom rewards for discussion
    2.1 Grades: Describe a classroom setting in which grades are assigned for academic performance. Outline the steps you might follow in assigning grades to students and managing the grading system. (p. 221)
    2.2 Activities: Describe a classroom setting in which activities are used to reward student behavior. Outline a procedure you might follow in using activities as rewards and managing the reward system. (p. 222)
    2.3 Recognition: Describe a classroom setting in which recognition is used to reward student behavior. Outline a procedure you might follow in using recognition as a reward and managing the reward system. (p. 224)

3. Implementing procedures for establishing compatible contingencies and using rewards in the classroom (p. 225)
    3.1 Establish compatible contingencies and reward systems at the classroom level. Try to work with an instructional group of ten to twelve students for this activity.
        a. Observe student behavior within a specific small group or regular classroom setting across two or more successive activities. Follow steps 1–4, 6–7, in the building routine to design classroom procedures for building compatible contingencies and adding rewards to the classroom. Draw upon alternative procedures within the text, as appropriate.

    b. Review the plan with the classroom teacher to assess its workability. Modify the plan if required.

    c. Implement the plan for a period of five days within a specific activity. Arrange to substitute for the teacher or to observe the teacher while the plan is being implemented.

    d. Informally evaluate the success of the plan in terms of improved student behavior. Discuss the results with the classroom teacher.

3.2 Establish compatible school and home contingencies.

    a. Identify school-level rules and rewards that would support the classroom behavior targeted in exercise 3.1. Outline a plan for establishing the school rules and rewards you identify. If possible, try to have the rules and rewards adopted by the school. Review the plan with the school principal and a sample of teachers to determine workability and support. Modify as required.

    b. Follow the guidelines in the text and outline a plan for involving parents in establishing compatible contingencies. Review the plan with the principal and a sample of teachers. Modify the plan as required. If possible, implement the plan and informally determine its effect.

REFERENCES

Chapter 10 draws upon many diverse areas of research and practice. Establishing compatible contingency procedures has the objective of producing cooperative learning within the classroom. Recent reviews in the cooperative learning area by Slavin, Sharon, and Johnson and colleagues have all agreed that cooperative group practices foster better school attitudes, self-concepts, and greater academic achievement than many consolidated classroom organizations. Don Hake and Dennis Olvera give an excellent picture of the research problems involved in studying cooperation and competition. As education turns to small group, peer-tutoring, and individualized instructional formats, management practices will have to promote cooperation and be as flexible as possible. Thus, Chapter 10 points out how the basic procedures of previous chapters can be combined with others to facilitate cooperation in the classroom.

Aronson, E., Bridgeman, D. L., & Geffner, R. The effects of a cooperative classroom structure on student behavior and attitudes. In D. Bar-Tal & L. Saxe (Eds.), *Social Psychology of Education: Theory and Practice*. New York: Halsted Press, 1978.

Hake, D. F., & Olvera, D. Cooperation, competition, and related social phenonmena. In A. C. Catania & T. A. Brigham (Eds.), *Handbook of Applied Behavior Analysis: Social and Instructional Processes*. New York: Irvington, 1978.

Johnson, W., Skon, L., & Johnson, R. Effects of cooperative, competitive, and individualistic conditions on children's problem-solving performance. *American Educational Research Journal*, 1980, *17:* 83–93.

Sharon, S. Cooperative learning in small groups: Recent methods and effects on achievement, attitudes, and ethnic relations. *Review of Educational Research,* 1980, *50,* 241–271.

Slavin, R. E. Cooperative learning. *Review of Educational Research,* 1980, *50,* 315–342.

The procedures used to establish compatible contingencies student by student emphasize student modeling and imitation, aided by teacher-delivered consequences. Albert Bandura has pioneered modern research on modeling and imitation. Vicarious reinforcement, the increase in appropriate behavior by one peer when a second peer receives reward statements by the teacher, is related to modeling and imitation. Alen Kazdin's research has increased our understanding of this area. These two areas give extensive support to the procedures presented. A recent review by Grover Whitehurst on observational learning provides a detailed view of the nature and complexity of this learning form.

Bandura, A. *Social Learning Theory.* Englewood Cliffs, N.J.: Prentice-Hall, 1977.

Kazdin, A. E. Vicarious reinforcement and direction of behavior change in the classroom. *Behavior Therapy,* 1977, *8,* 57–63.

Whitehurst, G. J. Observational Learning. In A. C. Catania & T. A. Brigham (Eds.), *Handbook of Applied Behavior Analysis: Social and Instructional Processes.* New York: Irvington, 1978. Pp. 142–178.

The second procedure to establish compatible contingencies uses group contingencies; this approach has been researched and practiced in the Soviet Union and the United States. Although cautions must be followed, group contingencies in the classroom have clearly positive effects. Urie Bronfenbrenner has detailed the Soviet Union's use of group contingencies. In the United States, the use of group contingencies is not as widespread, but numerous researchers have shown the effectiveness of these methods in the classroom.

Axelrod, S. Comparison of individual and group contingencies in two special classes. *Behavior Therapy,* 1973, *4,* 83–90.

Barrish, H. H., Saunder, M., & Wolf, M. M. Good behavior game: Effects of individual contingencies for group consequences on disruptive behavior in a classroom. *Journal of Applied Behavior Analysis,* 1969, *2,* 119–124.

Bronfenbrenner, U. *Two Worlds of Childhood: U.S. and U.S.S.R.* New York: Russell Sage, 1970.

Brown, D., Reschly, D., & Sabers, D. Using group contingencies with punishment and postive reinforcement to modify aggressive behaviors in a Head Start classroom. *Psychological Record,* 1974, *24,* 491–496.

Bushell, D., Jr. The design of classroom contingencies. In F. S. Keller & E. Ribes-Inesta (Eds.), *Behavior Modification: Applications to Education.* New York: Academic Press, 1974.

Bushnell, D., Wrobel, P. A., & Michaelis, M. L. Applying "group" contingencies to the classroom study behavior of preschool children. *Journal of Applied Behavior Analysis,* 1968, *1,* 55–61.

Greenwood, C. R. Hops, H., Delquadri, J., & Guild, J. Group contingencies for group consequences in classroom management: A further analysis. *Journal of Applied Behavior Analysis,* 1974, *7,* 413–425.

Hamblin, R. L., Hathaway, C., & Wodarski, J. Group contingencies, peer tutoring, and accelerating academic achievement. In R. Ulrick, T. Stachnik, & J. Mabry (Eds.), *Control of Human Behavior,* Vol. 3. Glenview, Ill.: Scott, Foresman, 1974.

Harris, V. W., & Sherman, J. A. Use and analysis of the "good behavior game" to reduce disruptive classroom behavior. *Journal of Applied Behavior Analysis,* 1973, *6,* 405–417.

Kazdin, A. E., & Forsberg, S. Effects of group reinforcement and punishment on classroom behavior of retarded children. *Education and Training of the Mentally Retarded,* 1974, *9,* 50–55.

Packard, R. G. The control of "classroom attention": A group contingency for complex behavior. *Journal of Applied Behavior Analysis,* 1970, *3,* 13–28.

Schmidt, G. W., & Ulrick, R. E. Effects of group contingent events upon classroom noise. *Journal of Applied Behavior Analysis,* 1969, *2,* 171–179.

Switzer, E. B., Deal, T. E., & Bailey, J. S. The reduction of stealing in second graders using a group contingency. *Journal of Applied Behavior Analysis,* 1977, *10,* 267–272.

Wodarski, J. S., Hamblin, R. L., Buckholdt, D. R., & Ferritor, D. C. The effects of different reinforcement contingencies on cooperative behaviors exhibited by fifth graders. In R. D. Rubin, J. D. Brady, & J. D. Henderson (Eds.), *Advances in Behavior Therapy,* Vol. 4. New York: Academic Press, 1973.

Establishing compatible contingencies through students helping students draws on two areas of research: students as change agents and peer tutoring. The research on students as agents of change focuses on the extent to which peers can successfully change their fellow students through the use of consequences. This work has been going on sporadically since the late 1960s, but the results clearly show that peers can change their classmates.

Abrams, L., Hines, D., Pollack, D., Ross, M., Stubbs, D. A., & Polyot, C. J. Transferable tokens: Increasing social interaction in a token economy. *Psychological Reports,* 1974, *35,* 447–452.

Axelrod, S., Hall, R. V., & Maxwell, A. Use of peer attention to increase study behavior. *Behavior Therapy,* 1972, *3,* 349–351.

Graubdard, P. S., Rosenberg, H., & Miller, M. B. Student applications of behavior modification to teachers and environments or ecological approaches to social deviancy. In R. Ulrich, T. Stachnik, & J. Mabry (Eds.), *Control of Human Behavior,* Vol. 3. Glenview, Ill.: Scott, Foresman, 1974.

Greenwood, C. R., Sloane, H. N., & Baskin, A. Training elementary aged peer-behavior managers to control small group programmed mathematics. *Journal of Applied Behavior Analysis,* 1974, *7,* 103–104.

Sanders, M. R., & Glynn, T. Functional analysis of a program for training high and low performance peers to modify disruptive classroom behavior. *Journal of Applied Behavior Analysis,* 1977, *10,* 503–504.

Solomon, R. T., & Wahler, R. G. Peer reinforcement control of classroom problem behavior. *Journal of Applied Behavior Analysis,* 1973, *6,* 49–56.

Willis, J. W., Morris, B., & Crowder, J. A remedial reading technique for disabled readers that employs students as behavioral engineers. *Psychology in the Schools,* 1972, *9,* 67–70.

Peer-tutoring research has a very lengthy history. The most recent work points out the necessity of training students in the tutoring process and of using structured materials if the tutorial process is to be effective. The references on tutoring bring together theory, research, principles, and/or applications of tutoring.

Allen, V. L. (Ed.) *Children as Teachers: Theory and Research on Tutoring.* New York: Academic Press, 1976.

Blumfeld, S. L. *How to Tutor.* Milford, Mich.: Mott Media, 1977.

Bramley, W. *Group Tutoring: Concepts and Case Studies.* New York: Nichols Publishing Company, 1979.

Ehly, S. W., & Larsen, S. C. *Peer Tutoring for Individual Instruction.* Boston: Allyn and Bacon, 1980.

Ellson, D. G. Tutoring. In N. L. Gage (Ed.), *The Psychology of Teaching Methods: Seventy-Fifth Yearbook of the National Society for the Study of Education.* Chicago: University of Chicago Press, 1976.

Endsley, W. R. *Peer Tutorial Instruction.* Englewood Cliffs, N. J.: Educational Technology Publications, 1980.

Harrison, G. V., & Guyman, R. E. *Structured Tutoring.* Englewood Cliffs, N. J.: Educational Technology Publications, 1980.

Melaragno, R. J. *Tutoring with Students: A Handbook for Establishing Tutorial Programs in Schools.* Englewood Cliffs, N.J.: Educational Technology Publications, 1976.

Thiagarajan, S. *Tutoraids.* Englewood Cliffs, N.J.: Educational Technology Publications, 1978.

The fourth set of procedures, establishing compatible contingencies in the home and school, are important for two reasons. First, because the classroom is not a closed system, what happens outside it has an impact on it. Second, the positive behavior changes that occur in the classroom should generalize to the rest of the student's world. As Stokes and Baer, and Marholin and Siegel, have shown, generalization cannot be expected to happen; procedures must be established to facilitate it. The recommendations of this chapter are but a first step.

Copeland, R. E., Brown, R. E., & Hall, R. V. The effects of principle-implemented techniques on the behavior of pupils. *Journal of Applied Behavior Analysis,* 1974, *7,* 77–86.

Marholin, D., & Siegel, L. J. Beyond the law of effect: Programming for the maintenance of behavior change. In D. Marholin, II (Ed.), *Child Behavior Therapy*. New York: Gardner Press, 1978. Pp. 397–415.

Schumaker, J. B., Hovell, N. F., & Sherman, J. A. An analysis of daily report cards and parent-managed privileges in the improvement of adolescents' classroom performance. *Journal of Applied Behavior Analysis,* 1977, *10,* 449–464.

Stokes, T. F., & Baer, D. M. An implicit technology of generalization. *Journal of Applied Behavior Analysis, 1977, 10,* 349–367.

Finally, the types and variety of rewards used in the classroom can be seen by examining almost any research journal connected with educational problems. The journals in this and other chapter reference sections are exemplars. Of special interest is the use of free-time activities and special academic activities to reinforce academic behavior. The following references present the considerations for using these activities successfully.

O'Leary, S. G., & O'Leary, K. D. Behavior modification in the school. In H. Leitenberg (Ed.), *Handbook of Behavior Modification and Behavior Therapy*. Englewood Cliffs, N.J.: Prentice-Hall, 1977.

Taffel, S. J., & O'Leary, K. D. Reinforcing math with more math: Choosing special academic activities as a reward for academic performance. *Journal of Educational Psychology, 1976, 68,* 579–587.

CHAPTER ELEVEN

THE CLASSROOM MANAGEMENT SYSTEM

The preceding chapters have delineated the essential elements of classroom management. If the teacher were to stop here, the skills gained would prove highly valuable in managing any classroom. But a system that integrates these management elements into a classroom management system provides teachers with even greater classroom effectiveness. Chapter 11 begins by describing the functions of such a system and then outlines the considerations in establishing it. Although the details of any system depend on the setting in which the system exists, there are many commonalities. This chapter covers both setting idiosyncrasies and the commonalities relevant to the day-to-day operation of the management system.

THE FUNCTION OF A MANAGEMENT SYSTEM

The value of any management system depends upon its effectiveness in increasing the time allotted to instruction. Such effectiveness can only be achieved when all the elements of the system are maximally utilized and coordinated. This means the system must have the following functional characteristics:

1. Facilitates the application of teacher condition and reward statements.
2. Provides procedures which account for and document academic achievement.

3. Provides procedures which account for and document social achievement.
4. Provides procedures to account for corrections.
5. Provides procedures for delivering rewards.
6. Provides system procedures which are practical.

The first function stresses the importance of the system's elements that set the conditions for, and add content to, the teacher's statements. The second and third functions relate to procedures that enable the teacher to know at any time each student's standing in terms of social and academic performance. Also, students continually need to know their performance in relation to reward criteria such as grades and activities. Thus, the delivery system must have accounting procedures for both teachers and students. The fourth function stresses the need to document the use of correction procedures for all concerned parties (e.g., parents). This involves specifying the time, type, and student to whom correction procedures are applied. In solving individual problems, accounting procedures are critical (see Chapter 12). The fifth function is important because many rewards given in the classroom are often delayed for days or weeks. Teachers must know continually how the students are progressing toward rewards. Such knowledge will facilitate the delivery of condition and reward statements over time (function 1). Many of these rewards require a special presentation procedure for effective delivery. This is especially true of awards. Finally, the sixth function emphasizes the importance of a practical management system. Can the teacher use the system simply and quickly? If all the procedures are easy to use and take very little time to implement, then the system is simple, efficient, and maximizes instructional time.

The following section outlines general procedures for setting up a management system, but the idiosyncrasies of the individual classroom require teachers to make modifications. To evaluate these modifications, teachers must ask if each allows the functions of a management system to occur. If the answer is yes, the modification is appropriate.

SETTING UP A MANAGEMENT SYSTEM

The most difficult aspect of establishing the elements of a management system is determining how to adjust them for differences across classroom settings. The settings in which a system is used vary along two dimensions. The first is the age of the student, and the second is the classroom activity structure (see Chapter 4). The age of the student is important because it reflects the social and academic skills with which the student enters the system. Older students are more able to contribute to managing the system. Younger students, especially those in the primary grades, require very simple systems that are almost totally managed by the teacher, so that maximal time can be devoted to instruction.

Classrooms generally fall into two types: (1) self-contained, which normally occur in grades kindergarten through 6; and (2) subject-specific, used from grades 7 through 12. One exception occurs in grades 4 through 6, where the language arts teacher may have students two to three hours of the day; for the rest of the time the students are in one-hour subject-specific classes such as art, science, and physical education. The procedures used by the language arts teacher in this situation are a mixture of those of primary grade and subject-specific teachers. The following description of the basic management system's elements encompasses this range of setting differences. Three continuing examples are used to illustrate possible applications. They include a first-grade classroom, a sixth-grade language arts classroom, and an eleventh-grade science classroom.

Chapter 4 has presented the initial five steps in setting up a management system:

1. Determine the activities for each class.
2. Determine the necessary social behaviors for each activity.
3. Make a set of general activity rules.
4. Determine which activities need a list of rules.
5. Make a set of rules for the selected activities.

Teachers who have completed these first five required steps in formulating rules are ready to complete the nine additional steps in setting up a management system. The following discussion begins with step 6.

Determine the Pattern of Activities   Given a list of activities that comprise the regular classroom cycle and the special activities that are inserted at regular or irregular intervals, teachers are ready to determine the pattern of activities (step 6). The pattern of activities deals with the flow of events in the classroom. This flow can be seen from the perspectives of the teacher and the student. For example, while the teacher is delivering instruction to one group of students, another group may be doing independent work. When listing the flow of activities, teachers should indicate if portions of the class are involved in different activities.

The four considerations in determining the classroom activity pattern are (1) the number of instructional groups, (2) activity cycle (fixed or variable), (3) activity repetition (equal or unequal), and (4) activity time (fixed or variable).

The use of instructional groups requires teachers to consider how they and students will move from group to group and what groups should be given instruction first. Often the lower performing students need initial help in starting an assignment and, therefore, require the teacher early in the flow of activities. The number of groups determines the length and type of assignment the students receive.

Activity cycle refers to *the time needed to perform (complete) all the instructional activities of a classroom.* There are two types of cycles: fixed and variable. Fixed activity cycles usually occur in elementary classrooms and have a cycle length of one day. Within this one-day cycle each class activity is usually performed once. This cycle length is usually repeated day after day, so that the term "fixed" is applied. Variable activity cycles often occur in secondary classes because activities cannot always be adjusted in length. Some science "units" and art "projects," with all their associated activities, take one class session while others may take two or three or more. This changing activity cycle length prompts the term "variable" cycle.

Activity repetition refers to *the number of times an activity is repeated relative to others within a cycle.* There are two types of activity repetition: equal and unequal. Equal activity repetitions occur when activities are repeated the same number of times per activity cycle. In the elementary classroom, each activity usually occurs once within an activity cycle. Unequal activity repetitions occur when activities are not repeated an equal number of times per activity cycle. Science and art classes provide two examples. In a science class, lectures may be followed by short worksheets two or three times before students do a related laboratory experiment. In art, two or three projects may be done for each teacher presentation.

Activity time refers to *the time students spend in an activity from activity cycle to activity cycle.* The two types of activity time are fixed and variable. Fixed activity time occurs when the duration of the activity remains constant from activity cycle to activity cycle. Elementary classrooms usually use fixed activity times for most activities. Variable activity time occurs when the duration of the activities changes from activity cycle to activity cycle. Many upper level classrooms incorporate variable activity time because the activities of "units" and "projects" vary in complexity and detail. For example, one science experiment may take one hour while another may take two or three. The same is true of projects in art or composition.

The determination of activity time requires teachers to apply their knowledge of the subject area and instructional methods. This determination is critical for teachers using one-day fixed cycle patterns. Teachers must consider how long their presentations of new and review material should take each day. For independent work, the number of items or the length of an assignment must allow all other activities to be completed. The length of the independent or practice activity will depend, in part, on the time allotted to the workcheck and if the teacher is working with multiple groups. Even if there is no workcheck and homework involves finishing assignments not completed during independent activities, time needs to be established for these activities. Also, if the teacher is working with small groups and the independent work activity is long, students will finish at different times during the activity. The teacher must prepare for this by having extra-credit work or reward activities available. (This is further discussed in step 13.) Another aspect of activity time allotment is identifying the time needed to transition from activity to activity. The time allotted each activity should take transitions into account.

These four elements—activity cycle, activity repetition, activity time, and the number of instructional groups used—provide the teacher with a language to talk about and plan the pattern of classroom activities. Having a clear pattern will facilitate the successful completion of the remaining steps in designing a classroom management system. In turn, completion of the remaining steps may require some modification of the initial pattern.

Table 11.1 shows the activity cycle for a first-grade classroom. In general, this class has a fixed activity repetition, fixed activity time, and a fixed one-day cycle time. The only deviations occur in activities 16 and 17, where art and physical education, science and social studies, alternate. All teacher presentations of basic skills instruction occur in the morning before lunch. The morning meeting (activity 1) starts the day with the teacher covering the rules and activities for the day. Then the teacher's ten-minute penmanship presentation is followed by a fifteen-minute student assignment. The first teacher-directed reading presentation is next, with the second group working on their penmanship. If they finish, the second group will engage in an extra-credit work or a reward activity. When the teacher begins the second reading presentation, the first group starts to work on spelling and reading assignments. With the completion of reading, the teacher gives the first language presentation and assignment. During this time, the second group is working on language or what remains of their penmanship assignment. Recess follows, with most of the students having about ten minutes of assignments to complete. After recess, the teacher spends twenty minutes checking student work and remediating problems. This time may not allow all the work to be checked, but a large portion should be checked and marked in the grade book. When the checking time is completed, the spelling presentation is given, along with a fifteen-minute assignment. Now the teacher gives the first mathematics presentation (activity 10) and assignment. During this time, the second group does the spelling assignment. The second mathematics presentation (activity 11) follows. Activity 12 is another workcheck and remediation period for the teacher. Again, this checking is done while the students finish their assignments from math or any other activity. After lunch (activity 13), the teacher presents supplementary work (activity 14) to the entire class, with this work being related to the instructional problems of the class or groups. The assignment related to this work allows the teacher another fifteen minutes to check work and remediate (activity 15). At the end of this time, the teacher must be certain that all student work has been collected or filed according to a standard procedure. Thus, student work throughout the day has been continuous, except for those who finish early and engage in reward or extra-credit events within an activity.

The final part of the day begins with art or physical education (activity 16). Unlike the morning activities, these are variable activities. Art may occur on Tuesday and Thursdays, and physical education on Mon-

TABLE 11.1 FIRST-GRADE ACTIVITY CYCLE	
Activities	**Activity Time**
1. Morning meeting	15 minutes
2. Penmanship presentation (15-minute assignment)	10 rninutes
3. First reading presentation (20-minute assignment)	20 minutes
4. Second reading presentation (20-minute assignment)	20 minutes
(Cumulative activity time)	(1 hour 5 minutes)
5. First language presentation (15-minute assignment)	15 minutes
6. Second language presentation (15-minute assignment)	15 minutes
7. Recess	15 minutes
8. Checking and remediating independent work	20 minutes
(Cumulative activity time)	(2 hours 10 minutes)
9. Spelling presentation (15-minute assignment)	15 minutes
10. First math presentation (20-minute assignment)	20 minutes
11. Second math presentation (20-minute assignment)	20 minutes
12. Checking and remediating independent work	15 minutes
(Cumulative activity time)	(3 hours 20 minutes)
13. Lunch	40 minutes
14. Presentation of supplementary work	15 minutes
15. Checking and remediating independent work	15 minutes
(Cumulative activity time)	(4 hours 30 minutes)
16. Art/physical education	30 minutes
17. Science/social studies	30 minutes
18. Recess	15 minutes
19. Afternoon meeting	15 minutes
(Total cumulative activity time)	(6 hours)

TABLE 11.2 SIXTH-GRADE LANGUAGE ARTS ACTIVITY CYCLE	
Regular Activities	**Activity Time**
1. Language presentation (20-minute assignment)	15 minutes
2. Spelling presentation (10-minute assignment)	10 minutes
3. First reading presentation (20-minute assignment)	10 minutes
4. Second reading presentation (20-minute assignment)	10 minutes
5. Third reading presentation (20-minute assignment)	10 minutes
6. Teacher observation/remediation of student independent work	30 minutes
7. Student workcheck/awarding points	25 minutes
8. Cleanup	10 minutes
(Total Activity Time)	(2 hours)
Special Activities	
9. Homework (given each day for one subject)	—
10. Spelling test (once per week)	—
11. Award time (once per week)	—

day, Wednesday, and Friday. Generally, the time for art activity is hard to control because of the use of materials and cleanup. Science and social studies (activity 17), like art and physical education, are full classroom activities which introduce the students to the world around them. Next is recess (activity 18), and then the final activity of the day, afternoon meeting (activity 19), where the teacher rewards those who have worked hard and sets the conditions for the next day. This system of activities is not unusual for a first-grade classroom. Over the six-hour class day, the teacher will have directed twenty-four activities, with independent work and teacher presentations occurring simultaneously. The management of this many activities for twenty-five to thirty students, not yet as self-managed as adults, provides the teacher with a challenge that few corporate executives could meet. Thus, it is easy to see that without a well-practiced set of management procedures, teachers cannot meet with success, managerially or instructionally.

Table 11.2 shows the activity cycle for a two-hour sixth-grade language arts class. Like the first grade, this sixth grade has a one-day fixed cycle time pattern, with equal activity repetition and fixed activity time. The first two activities are teacher presentations which provide the students with independent assignments while the teacher engages in presentations to the three reading groups. The time allotments indicate that the students working independently have ten minutes less planned assignment time than the teacher has presentation time (i.e., the students have fifty minutes of independent work including language, spelling, and reading and the teacher has sixty minutes of reading presentations or observation/remediation of independent work). During this unplanned time, students engage in extra-credit or reward activities. Following the reading presentations, the teacher observes and remediates independent work problems. It is also an excellent time to precheck student work so that when students check their work, the teacher knows something about their checking accuracy. The teacher awards points at the end of work-check, and ten minutes of cleanup end the class. This final activity helps students see a set of completed tasks and enables the teacher to set conditions for the next day. Putting papers, books, desks, and folders in order following a set of tasks provides students with some basic skills of self-management. The teacher in this example would manage nine activities during the two hours, and if the teacher had two language groups, there would be eleven activities. The special activities in Table 11.2 also must be fit into the total cycle time; thus, their presentation requires shortening the regular activities. Again, the teacher is faced with a complex management task.

Table 11.3 shows the activity cycle for a one-hour high school science class (e.g., biology, chemistry, or physics). Most of these have the same variable cycle time pattern, with unequal activity repetition and, generally, fixed activity time. The variable time cycle is a result of organizing material into sets of related concepts or "units." All science textbooks structure material this way, and most give estimates of how long each unit should take to complete. Only five class activities (there may be

TABLE 11.3 ELEVENTH-GRADE SCIENCE ACTIVITY CYCLE	
Regular Activities	**Activity Time and Cycle**
1. Teacher presentation	35 minutes per presentation
2. Independent worksheet (covers material related to present unit of study)	10 minutes following each presentation
3. Workcheck (check independent work)	5 minutes following worksheet
4. Laboratory	1 or 2 days following unit presentation
5. Unit test	1 per unit, full class period
Special Activities	
6. Reading assignment	On any particular presentation or laboratory day
7. Homework problems	On any particular presentation or laboratory day
8. Award activity	Biweekly or once per grading period
(Total cycle time)	(Variable)

homework) span multiple days. The first activity is the teacher presentation, which lasts about thirty-five minutes (fixed activity time), followed by a ten-minute worksheet to cover the new unit's presented material. This worksheet provides the teacher with a view of what the students remember and understand of the last teacher presentation. Only the highlights are covered. The workcheck follows and helps the teacher evaluate the latest presentation and decide where to adjust the next lecture's content. The workcheck also is an excellent time to give points and deliver reward statements. This fixed repetition of presentation, independent work, and workcheck may be repeated for two, three, or four classes before a laboratory activity is required. The actual timing depends on the number of days (presentations) required to cover some subset of unit material related to a laboratory activity. The cycle of presentations, independent work activities, workchecks, and a laboratory activity may be repeated two or three times before a unit is completed and the unit test is given to complete the activity cycle. The unit test is included as the last activity because it takes a full class period and marks the end of a major task. (For the lower grades, a test is considered a special activity.) The next teacher presentation would be spent discussing test results.

Any of the above classrooms could have different activity patterns for the same classes of activities (e.g., teacher presentations, workchecks, laboratories). For example, in the first grade, the number of groups could change for any of the subject areas, and the placement of the activities could be altered. In the sixth grade, the language presentation could be given to two groups. This would shorten the observation and remediation activity or the activity of each reading group. Another change would be to insert five minutes of teacher observation and remediation between each of the reading groups. This would give the teacher a chance to adjust any difficulties that might occur. One of the major options for the science class would be the use of "block experiments," where all the experiments for a unit are done at the end of the teacher presentations on the unit materials. Whatever the structure of the activities, the major requirement is that they help achieve the functions of a management system and facilitate learning.

Determine the Number of Grading Areas for a Class Step 7 requires the teacher to examine the larger grading system of the school. Student report cards tell teachers how many academic areas are related to each class. For example, the self-contained first-grade classroom covers numerous subjects, from arithmetic to spelling, which usually are graded in terms of excellent (E), satisfactory (S), and needs improvement (N). The sixth-grade language arts classes usually have separate grades for reading, language arts, spelling, and penmanship. They generally use an A, B, C, D, F grading system. The single-subject class, in contrast, has just one grading area for academic behavior.

Most report cards, from kindergarten to twelfth grade, mention social behavior. Usually, the first-grade report card grades students on their social behavior, again with an E, S, or N. For the sixth grade A, B, C, D, or F grades are usually used. But, from the seventh grade up, teachers only comment on the extent to which the student needs to improve or is improving. It is recommended that teachers supplement the comments with a separate social grade for the upper level students. When doing this, step 13 needs to be considered, as does a latter section on informing the school and parents of the management system.

Determine the Number of Products for a Grading Area Step 8 determines the number of products for a grading area. Depending on the type of class, the number of academic products that make up a grade vary widely. For the self-contained primary class with several grading areas, there is usually only one product per grade, generally done in an independent workbook activity. For the single-subject class, two to four products usually make up a grade. These include independent in-class work, homework, papers, and/or tests.

Self-contained classroom products are directly linked with an in-class activity, but the single-subject late elementary and secondary classroom products often result from out-of-classroom activity. In high school, many of the products, except for tests, are completed outside the classroom. It is recommended that students complete some academic product in class each day. This allows the teacher a continuing opportunity to assess student progress. A simple and effective procedure for this assessment is to grade some portion of independent student work. If the students are starting an assignment in class and finishing it as homework, the assignment can be divided into two parts, one for in-class grading and another for homework. By adding a student workcheck, the teacher can gain a great deal of knowledge about student progress with little effort. One of the most important reasons for regularly assessing student progress is that this provides an excellent opportunity to establish conditions and deliver reward statements that reflect the student's progress or change over time.

For the social behavior grading area, each activity also has a product. If the students follow all the rules for an activity, the product is satisfactory. Teachers must determine if all or some portion of the activities should receive a social behavior grade. If students are relatively mature, one grade is often enough, especially if reward statements for social behavior occur with regular frequency. But if students are remedial and exhibit social behavior problems, more than one social grading point is often required. Activities without an academic product are the best place to put social grades. The problem with delivering multiple social grades is the amount of time required. However, it is necessary to take some time if the future conduct of these problem students is to become appropriate. (Chapters 9 and 12 provide specific procedures for dealing with these problems.) Simplifying a grading system should the students have greater self-control than expected is easier than strengthening the system so that it can handle the inappropriate behaviors students enter with. Thus, initial management decisions by teachers are often very important.

Determine the Importance Each Product Has to a Grading Area
In step 9 "importance" is defined as the relative weight each academic or social product contributes to a grading area. How to weigh in-class and homework assignments, for example, is decided in relation to the time needed to complete such assignments, the degree to which the teacher can be sure the students did their own work, and the importance of the material to the class objectives. The weight of tests depends on how often they are given, how much class material they cover (e.g., a week's, month's, or semester's material), and the extent to which classwork and homework have confirmed for the teacher the mastery of the material by the students. For example, independent classwork may count two-fifths, homework one-fifth, and two tests given during the grading period may each count one-fifth. Thus, a high grade can only be given if the student does well in all areas.

The weight given to any particular social product depends on the problems that the teacher expects from an activity. The inappropriate social behaviors for each activity (determined in Chapter 6) need to be reexamined to remind the teacher of potential problems. Also, the length and complexity of the activity may affect the weighing.

Determine the Points to Be Given Each Product of a Grading Area Traditionally, grades are tabulated from the points earned for the academic products ranging from daily independent work to tests. The management system presented here continues this tradition but in step 10 makes some minor modifications to strengthen the management system's functions of facilitating condition and reward statements, and of accounting for and documenting academic and social behavior. Thus, points are given for both types of behavior.

The goal in assigning points to a grading area is to consider the following:

1. The weight each product contributes should be clear.
2. Students should be able at any time to determine where they stand in relation to a grade.
3. The teacher should be able to account for and document achievement quickly and accurately.

In item 1, the number of points reflects the weight of the product (social or academic); item 2 keeps the number of points comprehensible for students. Item 3 helps make the management system practical.

Often, points are awarded by teachers on a scale of 0 to 100, without a concern for the weight of different products in the makeup of a grade. Homework and test scores might both be worth up to 100 points, for example, although the test may be given more weight. This approach does not show students what is most important and where they stand. The numbers of points being earned becomes impossible to comprehend after a day or two, causing students to lose sight of where they stand and giving teachers a difficult management task. Assigning points is a difficult problem because it is hard to design a system that satisfies all three of the above criteria (weight, student standing, and documentation practicality). Thus, determining social and academic points is discussed later, after step 12, when all elements of grading have been covered and displayed in Tables 11.4, 11.5, and 11.6.

Determine Criteria for Academic Success Two questions must be answered in step 11 to quantify academic success. The first, "What are the cutoff points for student grades?" is concerned with the demarcations of As, Bs, Cs, etc., for academic behavior. Is 90-percent accuracy acceptable for an A, or should 92 percent differentiate A from B students? This is, in part, a question of "mastery" or "firmness," which have thus far escaped rigorous theoretical description and technological applications. Establishing cutoffs is mostly guesswork and, as such, should be treated with reservation and caution. But decisions must be made, if only because a grade provides students with a reward and a picture of themselves. Thus, the grade does not compare the student with other students, but with established criteria. A student who performs at some percent of the criteria gets a grade related to that percent. For grades made up of multiple products, it is not necessary to determine a grade for each product. Each product is awarded points on the basis of the number correct (or from the negative perspective of number wrong, which is often easier for both the teacher and student to tabulate), and the grade is calculated by summing all the products' points. Since the weighing was done previously, the only task remaining is to decide how many points equal each letter grade. Grades derived from a single product are not totaled—just assigned a letter grade. One important thing to remember is to have a point spread between letter grades; this allows students to see differences in grades and facilitates the teacher's condition and reward statements (see the section "Using the Management System" below).

The second question is, "At what level does each student work?" The answer to this question qualifies the first. Grading needs to be considered from the student's incoming skill level. For example, if the student enters a sixth-grade class performing fourth-grade objectives, the teacher should not teach sixth-grade objectives, but objectives that follow from the student's entry point and grade the student according to the entry level. This student may function appropriately on fourth-grade level objectives, but fail on the sixth level. Such students should still be told that they are performing their work successfully. The qualification regarding the level of performance should be communicated to the parents and to the students, but not daily or publicly. Setting the qualification aside and rewarding students from their entry point in the manner outlined in this text is the procedure recommended.

Determine Criteria for Social Success What inappropriate behaviors would cause students to make less than the total social points and to what extent would each of these subtract from the total? (The types of behavior that require the application of correction procedures have been covered in Chapter 6.) The extent to which the individual class of inappropriate behavior subtracts from the total is dependent on the severity of the behavior. Behavior that causes the separation procedure to be used would cause students to lose more points than a behavior that only required a warning procedure. The number of points subtracted also depends on the number of activities that have specific numbers of social points assigned to them (are given a social grade). If specific points are given for an activity, then the inappropriate behavior during that time should only subtract from the activity's social points. No matter how many activities are graded for social points, the student separated from a group by a correction procedure should not be able to make an A for the day and/or week. Assigning grades to social and academic behaviors can be clarified by a review of the three management examples.

Table 11.4 presents the grading areas, grading area products, product weights, and success criteria for the first-grade classroom. In this example, nine academic areas and one social area receive a grade. Each of the academic grading areas has one product, which contributes 100 percent of the academic grade. Each of these areas are given 0 to 3 points, with 3 indicating excellent, 2 satisfactory, and 0 to 1, needs improvement. The social behavior grade covers all class activities. To show the importance of this grading area, 10 points are assigned. The success criteria in points is indicated. The points lost could be 3 for a separation, 2 for a warning, and 1 for ignore-reward behavior. The numbers in parentheses under "Points Assigned" indicate the total possible points for a five-day school week.

Table 11.5 presents the grading areas and related categories for a sixth-grade classroom. The grading areas include language, reading, spelling, and social behavior. Each is considered to have two products. The academic products come from daily classwork and from a homework

		TABLE 11.4 FIRST-GRADE ASSIGNMENT OF GRADES		
Graded Activities	Products	Product Weight (Percent)	Points Assigned	Criteria for Success (Weekly)
1. Penmanship	Worksheet	100	0–3 (15)	13–15 = E 10–12 = S 8–9 = N
2. Reading	Workbook	100	0–3 (15)	13–15 = E 10–12 = S 8–9 = N
3. Language arts	Workbook	100	0–3 (15)	13–15 = E 10–12 = S 8–9 = N
4. Mathematics	Workbook	100	0–3 (15)	13–15 = E 10–12 = S 8–9 = N
5. Spelling	Workbook	100	0–3 (15)	13–15 = E 10–12 = S 8–9 = N
6. Science	Teacher observation	100	0–3 (15)	13–15 = E 10–12 = S 8–9 = N
7. Social studies	Teacher observation	100	0–3 (15)	13–15 = E 10–12 = S 8–9 = N
8. Art	Teacher observation	100	0–3 (15)	13–15 = E 10–12 = S 8–9 = N
9. Physical education	Teacher observation	100	0–3 (15)	13–15 = E 10–12 = S 8–9 = N
10. Social behavior	Teacher observation	100	0–10 (50)	45–50 = E 38–44 = S 0–37 = N

or a spelling test given once a week. In all grading areas, the points from the two products are summed. Although the teacher may begin the year with one homework assignment per week (studying for the spelling test included) per academic area, later in the year this may be increased as each student begins to turn homework in on a regular basis (and is, hopefully, rewarded for it). Notice that for language and reading, students cannot make an A unless they have done some of the homework assignment correctly. Even if academic bonus points are given, the teacher may have to specify that an A can only be achieved if the homework is handed in. The social behavior grade depends on two products: independent work

TABLE 11.5 SIXTH-GRADE ASSIGNMENT OF GRADES				
Graded Activities	Products	Product Weight	Points Assigned	Criteria for Success (Weekly)
1. Language	1. In-class workbook	5/6	0–5 (25)	27–30 = A 24–26 = B
	2. Homework (once per week)	1/6	0–5 (5)	21–23 = C
2. Reading	1. In-class workbook	5/6	0–5 (25)	27–30 = A 24–26 = B
	2. Homework (once per week)	1/6	0–5 (5)	21–23 = C
3. Spelling	1. In-class workbook (once per week)	3/5	0–3 (15)	22–25 = A 19–21 = B 17–18 = C
	2. Spelling Test (once per week)	2/5	0–10 (10)	
4. Social behavior	1. Independent work	50%	0–5 (25)	45–50 = A 40–44 = B 33–39 = C
	2. Teacher presentation	50%	0–5 (25)	

and teacher presentations. These products need to be considered separately only if the teacher expects problems with either one or both activity types. Notice that even for a C, the student cannot lose more than 1 or 2 points per day. The criteria for success are specified for the week for all graded activities.

Table 11.6 presents the grading system for an eleventh-grade science (e.g., chemistry, physics, biology) class. Only one academic grade and one social grade are given. The academic grade is composed of three product types. The worksheets are given twelve times per six-week grading period, the laboratories are given eight times, and there are four unit tests (one about every five to ten days). The points represent what can be earned each time the activity occurs, and the total points possible (shown in parentheses under "Points Assigned") are cumulative for the six-week grading period. The social behavior is engaged in each day and is given 10 points per day, or 300 for the thirty days of a six-week grading period. The criteria for losing social points could be minus 5 for separation, minus 3 for a warning, and minus 1 for a reward-ignore statement. Thus, by the criteria for success, a student who is separated from the group once a week and loses no other social points, will not be able to achieve an A.

TABLE 11.6	ELEVENTH-GRADE SCIENCE CLASS GRADING SYSTEM			
Graded Activities	Products	Product Weight	Points Assigned	Criteria for Success
1. Academic	1. Worksheets (12)	1/6	10 (120)	720–800 = A
	2. Laboratories (8)	1/3	35 (280)	640–719 = B
	3. Unit tests (4)	1/2	100 (400)	560–639 = C
2. Social behavior	All activities (30)	100 percent	10 (300)	270–300 = A
				240–269 = B
				210–239 = C

Determine the Rewards for Appropriate Academic and Social Behavior   Chapter 10 has discussed and illustrated some potential rewards available in the classroom. At this point, teachers must decide what rewards they would like to use and the degree of student success needed to obtain them. Three main types are recommended. First are the awards to be presented for academic and/or social behavior. Perhaps any student with a B or an A should get a letter or a certificate to take home. This could be done weekly for primary and elementary students and every other week for secondary students (or weekly if the secondary students have extremely inappropriate academic or social behavior). The second type involves classroom jobs that help the teacher (e.g., tutoring other classmates or students in the lower grades). Tutoring is a very strong reward; most students will work very hard for it. Third are the activities that a student can do after completion of academic work. This area includes working on special projects, solving a puzzle, or even doing an extra-credit worksheet. These extra activities are especially important because students work at different speeds, so that teachers who are teaching multiple groups must have alternate activities for students whose academic assignments have been completed. Every aspect of when and where the rewards are to be given by the teacher or assessed by students must be worked out. Only the individual teacher knows his or her space and time limitations. While these limits can always be revised, the first step is their establishment. For the first-grade classroom, the use of a reward area where students can engage in rewarding activities following the completion of their work is very important. If this area cannot be provided, in-seat reward activities can be selected. Weekly awards for academic and social behavior are almost a necessity, since first graders are just learning to behave academically and socially. Strengthening desired behavior requires numerous rewards quickly following the behavior. Reward statements are the main procedures, but supplementary rewards should also follow the appropriate behavior. The weekly awards can be presented during the afternoon.

For the sixth-grade classroom, the same types of rewards as for the first grade are appropriate. But different activities must be chosen to reward sixth graders. For example, the time for awards can come from the cleanup time as well as an academic activity.

For the eleventh-grade chemistry class, rewards depend to a great extent on the type of students. If the students are academically advanced, as in an honors class, the rewards should be related to time off from some class work or exemption from a test. For example, exemption from a unit test could be given if all the students' worksheets or labs were at an "A" level. Awards are important only for academic behavior. Generally, when most rewards relate to special academic activities, students find academics rewarding. If the students are having academic problems, the rewards can be related to social behavior also. With high school students, reward statements are a major tool and sometimes the only tool of management.

Make Point Charts for Teachers and Students The teacher's point chart is a grade book. It lists the daily points earned by each of the students for each grading area. If the three grading areas for a certain math class include in-class work and social behavior, this makeup would be reflected in the chart. Figures 11.1, 11.2, and 11.3 show the teacher's grading charts. The first grade (Figure 11.1) and sixth grade (Figure 11.2) are set up by the week, and the eleventh grade (Figure 11.3) for the six-week grading period, which consists of two parts. Besides providing space for each grading area, the chart or grade book must be easy to refer to and mark accurately. Also, if the number of tests, papers, worksheets to be completed vary because of holidays, assemblies, and instructional delays, it is best to plan for the maximum number possible. In Figure 11.3, Part A, there is a place for a worksheet each day, although the eleventh-grade plan presented in Table 11.6 only calls for twelve worksheets. Thus, there are extra spaces for adapting to new needs. In Figure 11.3, Part B, ten laboratory spaces are presented, although the grading period covered in Table 11.6 calls for eight. Another grading period may require the space provided. Thus, the point chart should be flexible for a highly variable class.

The students' grade sheets allow them to have continual access to their academic and social success. The primary problem in their makeup is simplicity. This is especially true for the younger students. Figures 11.4 and 11.5 show the student grade sheets for the sixth-grade language arts class and the eleventh-grade science class. Because of their skill level, first graders would normally not have an individual point chart. However, a wall chart showing progress on one or two grading areas could be used. Generally, student grade sheets can be used in the third

FIGURE 11.1   FIRST-GRADE WEEKLY TEACHER GRADE SHEET

Week of ————————————— Class ————————————— Teacher —————————————

Student Name	Day 1				Day 2	Day 3	Day 4	Day 5	Total
1.	R L	M S	P B	SS PE					
2.	R L	M S	P B	SS PE					
3.	R L	M S	P B	SS PE					
4.	R L	M S	P B	SS PE					
5.	R L	M S	P B	SS PE					
6.	R L	M S	P B	SS PE					
7.	R L	M S	P B	SS PE					
8.	R L	M S	P B	SS PE					
9.	R L	M S	P B	SS PE					
10.	R L	M S	P B	SS PE					
11.	R L	M S	P B	SS PE					
12.	R L	M S	P B	SS PE					
13.	R L	M S	P B	SS PE					
14.	R L	M S	P B	SS PE					
15.	R L	M S	P B	SS PE					
16.	R L	M S	P B	SS PE					
17.	R L	M S	P B	SS PE					
18.	R L	M S	P B	SS PE					
19.	R L	M S	P B	SS PE					
20.	R L	M S	P B	SS PE					
21.	R L	M S	P B	SS PE					
22.	R L	M S	P B	SS PE					
23.	R L	M S	P B	SS PE					
24.	R L	M S	P B	SS PE					
25.	R L	M S	P B	SS PE					

Social Behavior: Bonus (plus)   Social Behavior: Correction (minus)

FIGURE 11.2   SIXTH-GRADE WEEKLY TEACHER GRADE SHEET

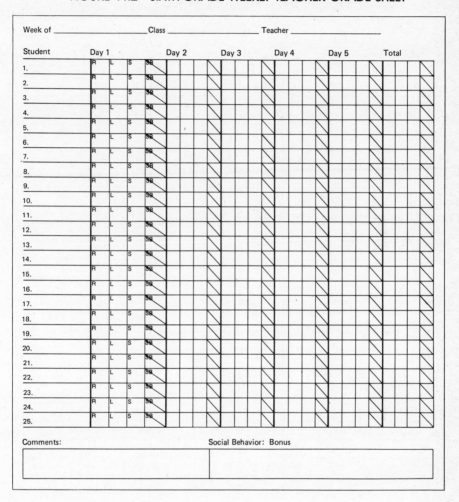

FIGURE 11.3 . ELEVENTH-GRADE SIX-WEEK TEACHER GRADING SHEET

_____ PART A _____

WORKSHEET/SOCIAL BEHAVIOR GRADES

STUDENT NAME		Week of___ M T W T F	Week of___ M T W T F	Week of___ M T W T F	Week of___ M T W T F	Week of___ M T W T F	Week of___ M T W T F	Total Score
1.	WS SB							
2.	WS SB							
3.	WS SB							
4.	WS SB							
5.	WS SB							
6.	WS SB							
7.	WS SB							
8.	WS SB							
9.	WS SB							
10.	WS SB							
11.	WS SB							
12.	WS SB							
13.	WS SB							
14.	WS SB							
15.	WS SB							
16.	WS SB							
17.	WS SB							
18.	WS SB							
19.	WS SB							
20.	WS SB							
21.	WS SB							
22.	WS SB							
23.	WS SB							
24.	WS SB							
25.	WS SB							

FIGURE 11.3 ELEVENTH-GRADE SIX-WEEK TEACHER GRADING SHEET

_____ PART B _____

LABORATORY/UNIT TEST GRADES

STUDENT NAME	Date	*LABORATORY* 1	2	3	4	5	6	7	8	9	10	Date Total	*UNIT TESTS* 1	2	3	4	Total	GRAND TOTAL
1.																		
2.																		
3.																		
4.																		
5.																		
6.																		
7.																		
8.																		
9.																		
10.																		
11.																		
12.																		
13.																		
14.																		
15.																		
16.																		
17.																		
18.																		
19.																		
20.																		
21.																		
22.																		
23.																		
24.																		
25.																		

FIGURE 11.4 SIXTH-GRADE LANGUAGE ARTS STUDENT POINT (GRADE) SHEET

NAME_____ CLASS_____ GRADING PERIOD_____

READING WORKSHEETS

	Week 1	Week 2	Week 3	Week 4	Week 5	Week 6	
Day 1	_____	_____	_____	_____	_____	_____	
2	_____	_____	_____	_____	_____	_____	
3	_____	_____	_____	_____	_____	_____	Grading Period
4	_____	_____	_____	_____	_____	_____	Total: Reading
5	_____	_____	_____	_____	_____	_____	
Total	□	□	□	□	□	□ → □	

Grade _____

LANGUAGE WORKSHEETS

	Week 1	Week 2	Week 3	Week 4	Week 5	Week 6	
Day 1	_____	_____	_____	_____	_____	_____	
2	_____	_____	_____	_____	_____	_____	
3	_____	_____	_____	_____	_____	_____	Grading Period
4	_____	_____	_____	_____	_____	_____	Total: Language
5	_____	_____	_____	_____	_____	_____	
Total	□	□	□	□	□	□ → □	

Grade _____

SPELLING WORKSHEETS

	Week 1	Week 2	Week 3	Week 4	Week 5	Week 6	
Day 1	_____	_____	_____	_____	_____	_____	
2	_____	_____	_____	_____	_____	_____	
3	_____	_____	_____	_____	_____	_____	Grading Period
4	_____	_____	_____	_____	_____	_____	Total: Spelling
5	_____	_____	_____	_____	_____	_____	
Total	□	□	□	□	□	□ → □	

_____

SOCIAL BEHAVIOR

	Week 1	Week 2	Week 3	Week 4	Week 5	Week 6	
Day 1	_____	_____	_____	_____	_____	_____	
2	_____	_____	_____	_____	_____	_____	
3	_____	_____	_____	_____	_____	_____	Grading Period
4	_____	_____	_____	_____	_____	_____	Total: Social
5	_____	_____	_____	_____	_____	_____	
Total	□	□	□	□	□	□ → □	

Grade _____

FIGURE 11.5 ELEVENTH-GRADE SCIENCE STUDENT POINT (GRADE) SHEET

NAME _____ CLASS _____ GRADING PERIOD _____

WORKSHEETS:

1	2	3	4	5	6	7	8	9	10

TOTAL

11	12	13	14	15	16	17	18	19	20

TOTAL ☐

LABORATORIES:

1	2	3	4	5	6	7	8	9	10

TOTAL ☐

UNIT EXAMS:

1	2	3	4	5	6	7	8	9	10

TOTAL ☐

GRADE ☐

SOCIAL BEHAVIOR:

1	2	3	4	5	6	7	8	9	10

11	12	13	14	15	16	17	18	19	20

TOTAL ☐

21	22	23	24	25	26	27	28	29	30

GRADE ☐

Six Week Instructional Goals

12 Worksheets (10 points each) = 120 points
8 Laboratories (35 points each) = 280 points
4 Unit Tests (100 points each) = 400 points
Total = 800 points

Grade

A = 720–800
B = 640–719
C = 560–639
D = 480–559

30 Social Behavior Days (10 points per day) = 300

A = 270–300
B = 240–269
C = 210–239

grade. The grade sheets in Figures 11.4 and 11.5 each contain boxes to mark down each set of points given out during a six-week grading period. For the sixth grade, these points are broken down into weekly totals; for the eleventh grade, they are given assignment numbers. The eleventh-grade sheet also includes a set of instructional goals and grading criteria. Both specify what the student and teacher are trying to accomplish in the six weeks. These goals and criteria could be posted with the classroom rules for the elementary student. When space is not used on the sheet because of some scheduled or unscheduled interruption, the teacher can have the students put an X through the space. The points are then adjusted for a letter grade. More is said about using this sheet in the following section.

MANAGING THE SYSTEM

Each of the fourteen steps in setting up a system contributes to the management system functions. Exactly how this is accomplished requires a description of the interrelationship of these elements in operation. There are two ways to approach such a description. The first is to describe some of the highlights of an operating system that interrelates several of the elements. The second is to describe the full system in operation. This section takes the first approach; the next section, on introducing a management system, takes the latter. Both descriptions are required for an understanding of the system and its use in the context of the classroom.

Posting and Reviewing the System   Five elements of the management system that follow need to be posted and reviewed on a regular basis:

1. The activities.
2. The classroom rules.
3. The correction procedures.
4. The academic criteria for grades and points.
5. The social criteria for grades and points.

The posting and reviewing of the first two elements (activities and rules) has been covered in Chapter 4. The rest follow those basic procedures. Correction procedures have been covered in Chapter 6. The academic criteria state the requirements for points and what they mean in terms of grades. If the number of problems is approximately equal each day for classwork and/or homework activities, the teacher can post the relation between the number of errors and a grade (to talk about the number correct is very difficult, because two extra steps are involved—subtraction and addition). In this way, students receive immediate feedback about their performance and the resulting consequences. The social criteria for grades are to follow the rules and not to lose points by performing behaviors illustrated on the list for losing points.

Recording, Totaling, and Awarding Points There is no one way to record, total, and award points. The activity structure of the class largely determines how the teacher accomplishes these events. But looking at these three aspects of the use of point systems enables the teacher to obtain a "picture" of what the use of points requires.

Recording Points. There are five times when points are recorded. The first three are almost always done during the class, and the last two are often done during nonteaching time. The five times are as follows:

1. When students exhibit inappropriate social behavior.
2. When students meet the teacher's criteria for bonus points.
3. When students provide the academic points earned during a workcheck.
4. When students have completed an activity in which social behavior points are to be given.
5. When the teacher-graded academic products have been scored.

In order to record the first four items during class, and continue with instruction and student supervision during independent work, the teacher must become efficient in the use of the chart and memorize the social and academic criteria. Also, the point chart should be placed on a clipboard or similar device to accompany the teacher, so that easy access is possible. Teachers will discover the most convenient ways to handle recording with a few days of practice. If students are extreme behavior problems, the chart will be used frequently during the class and, thus, may appear to be an impossible task to manage. But as time goes on and the contingencies the teacher has established take hold, there will be a dramatic increase in appropriate behavior and a dramatic decrease in inappropriate behavior. It must be remembered that without appropriate social behavior, students cannot engage in academic behavior.

Whenever the warning and separation correction procedures are used, they need to be immediately recorded with a symbol indicating which one was used. Such things are easily forgotten, but an accurate record offers an excellent backup for talking with administrators, parents, or the student. The ignore-reward correction procedure should be used whenever possible for the less extreme forms of social behavior (described in Chapter 6). If points are to be lost when students forget materials, this loss needs to be recorded when noticed. After a time, the students will understand what the teacher is doing (if it has not been explained) and will occasionally speak up for one another when the teacher is making a mistake and the student was engaging in appropriate behavior. The teacher need only comment with a "thank you" or "I appreciate your concern for others." When this phenomenon begins to occur, the teacher has made great progress in creating compatible contingencies.

When the students meet the criteria for bonus points, the teacher needs to record and present the points as soon as possible with an appropriate statement. Because they are rewarding a change over time, the reward statement needs to emphasize this element. At the completion of a workcheck, the student who is checking another's work needs to sign it and total the student's work. After handing the work back to the owner, the teacher calls on the students to give their points. If this is done briskly, and students have been walked through the parts they are to perform, scores from thirty students can be gotten in as little as two minutes. At the beginning of these procedures, the teacher should set conditions and reward appropriate social behavior during this period.

> "I appreciate your cooperation while I take down the points for the worksheets. You are getting much faster at giving them to me."

> "This is the first day that everyone has had their points ready to give to me the first time I asked. Can you do it again tomorrow?"

Students who have not lost points for inappropriate behavior receive all of the allotted points. The points lost are subtracted from the possible social points. This task can be performed very fast and can often be done when the academic points are being given by the students for classwork. Students can often be awarded at this time also.

Teacher-graded academic products such as homework, some tests, and papers are recorded at the time of grading. The problem here is not with recording, but determining the time and place when the students are awarded these points.

Totaling Points. Points can be totaled only when all parts of the grades are in. If all parts are in by the end of the class, the teacher can award the points; if not, the students will have to wait until the next class.

Awarding Points. Points can be awarded before the points for the whole class have been recorded. At any time in the lesson, bonus points can be awarded, as can any social or academic behavior points. For example, if worksheet points are known before the end of class, but others are not, the worksheet points can be awarded. The teacher chart and the student point chart should have a separate box if this is to be done (see the section on point charts above). If points for social or academic behavior are to be given for each activity and the activity points are known and awarded before the end of class, individual students can total their points and present them to the teacher.

One of the most important events in awarding points is the statements that accompany them. Even if all the points for a day cannot be given, at least the social ones can. If all academic work is graded by the teacher, the award of social points becomes the vehicle for statements about the academic performance of students:

> "Did anyone notice that everyone earned at least four of the five social points for the class?" (*Students reply.*) "Good, because that indicates that everyone has a shot at an A for today's work. How many think they did just as well on their academic work?" (*Students reply.*) "From what I saw, that is correct. We will see tomorrow. Remember to look at the chart when you enter tomorrow."

> "How many think they did just as well or better on their academic work?" (*Students reply.*) "I will see when I grade them. I certainly hope so."

The first example lets the students know not only how they did on social behavior but also that this behavior played a part in their gaining an A and that the same type of attention and work in the academic area will ensure another A. The second statement follows the awarding of social points and would be appropriate after the students have been shown how the elements of their social and academic behavior contributed to success.

Adjusting the System to Change Events in every class change as new activities are added or events of special importance occur. The first change requires adjustments of all of the system's elements, but the second usually can be handled with little or no modification in the elements of the system. Special classroom events such as tests, papers, and projects must be recorded, weighted, and awarded points.

Recording of special events in the point chart can be done in the space for the normal academic activity. For tests, the points are recorded in the location of the academic activity replaced. Other long-term special events such as papers and projects done at home can be recorded on the day that the projects are handed back and reviewed. But from a management perspective, the most important special school events are assemblies and similar occasions that require the students to exhibit a great degree of self-control. During these events the teacher should set the conditions by going over the appropriate behavior for the event and reminding the students that social points will be given for the event. In addition, a set of posted rules for these special activities is an effective management tool. Otherwise, the teacher can present the general activity rules, giving numerous examples and nonexamples.

The assignment of points to these events has been described in the section on weighting the importance of an activity. This time the event is simply weighted. If the event is one-fifth the academic grade, the points assigned will be one-fifth of the total possible for the grading period of the related activity. A daily score of ten in an area over a six-week grading period (thirty days of instruction) is 300 points. One-fifth of 300 is sixty points. The number of points for an A should be indicated to the students and, if possible, be proportional to the daily grade for the related activity. If a text or project is done weekly, the weight is determined in relation to the five instructional days of the week.

Awarding points for special events should be geared to the importance of the event. The students always should be clearly informed of how they performed and what it means in terms of the rest of the grade. This is not something that can be repeated only once; rather, the conditions should be set and the students prompted to study for these points when their other work is done. The statements to the students should indicate the consequences of this early practice.

Let the Students Manage the System   Teachers who can develop a system partially managed by students not only ease their own tasks (thus having more time for instruction) but also establish a set of rewards, in the form of classroom jobs, which are highly reinforcing to students. If students are checking worksheets, they are already helping the teacher manage the system. But often students can do even more, especially if they are older students who have the addition and subtraction skills required to total points. Even the teacher of younger students can obtain management help by having an older student from another class, who has met reward requirements in that class, help with the tasks in the younger students' system.

The easiest type of student-help system is one in which the points are totaled for the students after the class. In this system, the student assistant can add the daily or weekly points for the teacher and, if necessary, put them on the individual student point sheets. With this technique, the day begins with the students going over the point chart, while the teacher notes important changes that have occurred over time and any consequences the scores have or are leading to. This student-help system is especially important to teachers who have five or six classes of different students each day. The greater the immediate feedback the system gives, the more difficult it is to identify how students can help manage. If the students do not have the chance to help in the management of points, they can often help in the management of rewards by setting up reward areas, making sure the reward activities are in order, and determining which students use which rewards.

Using Statements Effectively   Statements about points make it easy to give the students a perspective on their control of the past, present, and future. These statements provide the details necessary to indicate change and what is needed for change. Some examples follow:

"Last week you earned four points each day for social behavior. This week, for the first two days, you have earned five points, close to perfect days. Can you keep it up?" (*Student replies.*) "If you do, you will get an A for social behavior."

"Five points for your social behavior is an A and indicates you followed the rules throughout the class."

"Donald, if you can add just two more points per day to your score, you can make an A. Just one more in social behavior and one in your worksheet and you will do it. Do you think you can?" (*Student replies.*) "I do too. Give it a try."

The last example is especially important because it shows the student the degree to which he has to change and what changes would gain a different reward. Both condition and reward statements can be presented at this time. The first three examples that follow are reward statements; the last four are condition statements:

"Govinda, you're on your way to your class job. That reading is worth five points."

"What a group! All members get all their points for the worksheet. A first! On Friday, I hope to give you all a recognition reward. You're on your way."

"Tonja, you have followed the rules, have earned your points, and are getting high on the points chart. You're going for your A!"

"Let's read the rules." (*Students read.*) "Can all of you sit, work, be friendly, and try hard?" (*Students reply.*) "What's it worth?" (*Students reply.*) "Yes, ten points. What do ten points do for you?" (*Students reply.*) "Do you want an A?" (*Students reply.*) "I want you to have an A too. So, let's go!"

"Marty, what do you want?" (*Student replies.*) "How do you get free time?" (*Student replies.*) "That's right, earn your points each day. Can you do it?" (*Student replies.*) "Then, let's start by doing it today. OK?"

"Point time is coming up. Are you going to make it? Do you have the correct answers? Keep going, you are getting close."

"Gosh, I want to give our recognition awards and As. Do you want them?" (*Students reply.*) "Then keep following the rules and getting your answers correct."

The point-grading system gives teachers more content for their statements, and variety promotes continued student interest and excitement.

Informing the School and Parents of the System How to inform the school about classroom procedures has been covered in Chapter 6. Added to the statements about corrections should be information about rewards and the grading system. It is best to write a letter to both the school principal and the parents. The contents of each letter should be about the same. The letter to the parents should resemble the following one. Each paragraph of the letter informs the parent of some element of the system.

Dear Parents,

I would like to take this time to tell you about how I manage the classroom your son or daughter is a part of this year. Because the classroom is a group setting, it is necessary for students to work appropriately with others. If they cannot do so, the effectiveness of instruction will be lessened. In order to promote the necessary cooperation between students and myself, I have developed a management system with the following points:

First, I set out the conditions and requirements of each task as clearly as possible. This includes telling students as clearly as possible about the academic work they are to do and informing them about what form of cooperation is necessary to perform the academic tasks. For the academic work, rules of conduct have been established and are gone over daily.

Second, I try as often as possible to inform each student of the extent to which he or she has mastered the academic work and cooperated with others. Individuals and the class are told what they have done, how it has improved over time, and what consequences result from it. Also, I have an academic award time every other week, when awards are presented to those who cooperate and achieve academic success.

Third, I have established a set discipline procedure to stop classroom disruptions. If any child interrupts instruction by talking out, refusing to work, or disturbing the work of others, the student is warned. If the behavior continues, the student is asked to separate himself or herself from the group (sit in a chair at the back of the room). If a student puts others in danger by hitting or throwing things, for example, the student is immediately separated as above. After a short time, the student is given a choice to return to the class activity and behave appropriately (clearly defined by the rules) or remain separated. If the student continues to disturb others or put others in danger after separation, the student is taken to the office. On the second trip to the office or if the behavior is very extreme, the parent is called and an interview is set up between the parents and myself and/or the principal. Whenever a child is returned to class, he or she is again given a complete chance to engage in the rewarding activities of the classroom.

Each of the above elements of my management system, I think, makes it possible for me to deliver the most effective instruction possible to *all* students in the classroom. Attached you will find a short questionnaire which I would like you to sign, indicating your agreement with the above system. If you would like more information, please check the appropriate blank on the attached sheet. I look forward to your answers and desire for further information.

Sincerely,

Your child's teacher

Page 2 of letter

I would like you to comment on the points you have just read about. Please indicate at the end if you agree or don't agree with what was stated and sign where asked.

   1. Student tasks should be set out clearly.

   ___Yes   ___No   ___Don't Know

   2. Students should be given positive rules about their conduct with others.

   ___Yes   ___No   ___Don't Know

   3. Students should be informed of what they are doing correctly, both academically and socially.

   ___Yes   ___No   ___Don't Know

   4. Students should be provided with awards for working hard.

   ___Yes   ___No   ___Don't Know

   5. Students should be corrected (disciplined) when they behave inappropriately.

   ___Yes   ___No   ___Don't Know

   6. Students should be warned, separated, or sent to the office, depending on how severe or persistent their inappropriate behavior is.

   ___Yes   ___No   ___Don't Know

   ___I would like more information on the procedures you use to manage students.
   ___I am satisfied with the explanations given.

   Date_____   Parent's Signature_____

At times a teacher will have students whose parents cannot read or read very little. If this is the case, a parent conference must be scheduled and the points of the letter gone over in understandable terms. If the parents cannot be contacted, the principal should be informed.

Never Argue about Points or Grades It is important that the teacher not be distracted during instruction by students arguing about who gets what grade or how many points. The final decision is the teacher's. This does not mean that teachers should not be alert to their own mistakes in recording and awarding points. Having a standard procedure to meet later with students who feel that a mistake has been made is very helpful. Teachers who ask at the end of activities if anyone feels that his or her points are unfair, and who specify a time to meet on the matter, will be making a first step in having students believe that the system is fair and adaptive.

THE INTRODUCTION OF A SYSTEM

The following scenario gives a rough picture of how to introduce a point system. Notice how all elements are made explicit and repeated back by the students. This introduction is made after the class already has defined activities and rules (see Chapter 4).

TEACHER: Today, we are going to start using points to determine what grades and rewards you can earn for yourselves. Why are we going to use points?

STUDENTS: (*Students answer as group; if no answer, repeat statement and answer and ask question again.*)

TEACHER: Yes, for grades and awards. Here are the awards that will be made each week. (*Shows examples.*)

    1. Special report card each week.
    2. Recognition badge for outstanding social behavior.
    3. Recognition letter to parents for outstanding academic performance.
    4. The selection of classroom jobs.

How many of you would like to get one or more of these each week?

STUDENTS: (*Reply to teacher's question.*)

TEACHER: Here is what you have to do to earn the points and, thus, the above awards. First, points will be given for each activity. They are (*lists on large paper or writes on board*):

    1. Teacher presentation—up to five points for following rules.
    2. Worksheet—up to ten points for number of problems correct and following rules.
    3. Fact practice—zero or five points for doing a fact sheet and allowing others to work on their sheet when you are finished.

So, there are a total of twenty points for each day. How many?

STUDENTS: (*Reply to teacher's question.*)

TEACHER: I will keep trying throughout the activity to tell you how well you are earning points. Each time you break a rule, you should expect to lose points. Each time you break a rule, you should expect to earn fewer points. If you gain 18 or more points in a day, you know you will have an A for the day. As we go along, I will let you know if there is any change in points. Are there any questions?

I want to use the point system; it is a fair way to give grades and rewards. How many of you are ready to start?

STUDENTS: (*Reply to teacher's question.*)

TEACHER: So, let's begin our presentation! (*Teacher goes over the rules with the students.*)

Remember, five points are possible! How many?

STUDENTS: (*Reply to teacher's question.*)

TEACHER: (*Begins math presentation.*) Melba, that was correct. You are thinking sharply. And I can see the rest of you are following the rules and earning points. Let's keep it up.

(*Continues presentation and frequently uses reward and condition statements.*) Look at these two rows; everyone is looking and answering. I wonder if everyone can do it and earn many, many points and, thus, good grades and awards. (*Ends presentation activity.*)

Let me give out the points. In the first row, everyone gets five points. Thank you, Mary, Mark, Damon, Willie, and Zuella. Let's give them a hand. (*Pauses while students clap.*) In the second row, Melba, Wally, and Jim made five points. Let's give them a hand. (*Pauses while students clap.*) Thank you. Johnny and Nelda get two points. In the third row, Quendell gets five points. Let's give him a hand. (*Pauses while students clap.*) Jane, Joe, Jerry, and Julia get four points. (*Finishes rest of rows in same manner.*)

If you got three or more points, you can still get an A. The rest of you can still get a B for the day and have a chance for awards if you work for the rest of the week. Can you do it?

STUDENTS: (*Reply to teacher's questions.*)

TEACHER: I think you can. Let's start the workbook activity. The points for workbook start now. (*Notice that the transition from one activity to another is quick and the awarding of points marks the transition.*)

Remember, ten points for getting 25 of 30 problems correct on your worksheet. How many think they can do it?

STUDENTS: (*Reply to teacher's question.*)

TEACHER: (*Gives individual help as needed, making the following types of public and private statements.*)

Jerry, you have the first five correct; just keep earning those points. I want to give you an award this week.

This row is really working for an A. They are paying attention to their work. I see many correct answers. Keep working for those awards.

(*At the end of workbook activity, collects papers.*) I can't give out points for these until after I check them, so tomorrow at this time I will give out today's points for workbook. How many think they will get their ten points?

STUDENTS: (*Reply to teacher's question.*)

TEACHER: I know a lot of you will. Now let's do fact practice. (*Passes out fact sheets.*) Remember, five points. Who can earn them?

What do you need to do?

STUDENTS: (*Reply to teacher's questions.*)

TEACHER: That's it. Do the sheet and follow the rules. If you do it now, most of you can make an A for today. Let's go!

(*Continues to set conditions and reward for academic and social behavior. At the end of the activity time, teacher collects papers and awards points.*)

The following people receive five points. (*Names students and also awards points to other students.* This includes total points for each student.) How many got all their points so far?

STUDENTS: (*Reply to teacher's question.*)

TEACHER: Well, you are almost sure to get an A for today. We will find out tomorrow! It is time to line up for the bell.

The above teacher's introduction uses statements to reference the point system rewards and what is required to earn them. The relationship between behavior and rewards is continually amplified for the student (as well as the teacher).

MANAGEMENT SYSTEM ROUTINE

To build and use a management system, teachers need to follow the steps outlined in this chapter. The following routine highlights the main points.

1. When setting up a management system, remember to do the following:
   a. Determine the activities for each class.
   b. Determine the necessary social behaviors for each class.
   c. Make a set of general activity rules.
   d. Determine which activities need a list of rules.
   e. Make a set of rules for the selected activities.

    f.   Determine the pattern of activities.

    g.   Determine the number of grading areas for a class.

    h.   Determine the number of products for a grading area.

    i.   Determine the importance each product has to a grading area.

    j.   Determine the points to be given to each product of a grading area.

    k.   Determine criteria for academic success.

    l.   Determine criteria for social success.

    m.   Determine rewards for appropriate social and academic behavior.

    n.   Make point charts for teachers and students.

2. When managing a management system, consider the following requirements:

    a.   Posting and reviewing the system.

    b.   Recording, totaling, and awarding points.

    c.   Adjusting the system to change.

    d.   Letting the students manage the system.

    e.   Using statements effectively.

    f.   Informing the school and parents of the system.

    g.   Never arguing about points.

3. When introducing the system, remember to:

    a.   Make the introduction as short as possible.

    b.   Describe the system enough so that students know what to do.

    c.   Introduce points after activities and rules, if desired.

    d.   Use questions to initiate students' agreement with system.

4. When deciding on any system element, consider whether it does the following:

    a.   Facilitate the application of teacher condition and reward statements.

    b.   Provide procedures that account for and document academic achievement.

    c.   Provide procedures that account for and document social achievement.

    d.   Provide procedures to account for correction.

    e.   Provide procedures for delivering rewards.

    f.   Is adaptable within and across as many settings as possible.

Each time a teacher builds a system, the procedure becomes easier. Most of the important elements will be experienced and developed over the first three years, so that the goal of facilitating student achievement can be readily met.

PRACTICE ACTIVITIES

1. Planning a management system for an elementary classroom (p. 234)
    1.1 Design a management system.
        a. Observe an elementary (grades K–6) or secondary (grades 7–12) classroom across the school day. (Observe the same classroom as in Chapter 2, if possible.) Describe the management procedures of the classroom for activities' organization, grouping structures, grading, and rewards/points. Use the key topics in the building routine and the detailed discussion of these items in the text as a focus. Discuss your description with the classroom teacher to confirm accuracy.
        b. Starting with the classroom description and the fourteen-step building routine, plan a comprehensive management system for the classroom you observed. Use the fourteen steps in the text to address the areas of activities, group structure, grading, and rewards/points. Specify all details in the system required for use, including materials required and procedures teachers and students would follow in using them.
        c. Review the system you have designed with one or more classroom teachers to determine workability. Modify as required.
        d. Document the system in the form of a manual for teacher use.
    1.2 Design implementation procedures to support the management system.
        a. Using the management system specifications from the previous example, design the ongoing procedures that the teacher would follow during the implementation of the management system. Target the following:
            (1) Posting and reviewing rewards
            (2) Recording information
            (3) Adjusting the management system
            (4) Using student managers
            (5) Statements for use with students
            (6) Informing school and parents
        Include in the design the procedures that teachers, students, and others would follow; an implementation schedule for each; and an example illustrating each.
        b. Review the implementation procedures with one or more teachers, school principals, and parents to determine workability.
        c. Document the procedures in the form of a manual for teacher use.
    1.3 Design start-up procedures for implementing the system. (p. 264)
        a. Referencing the examples in the text, design procedures teachers would follow in introducing the management system to students, including the explanation of point systems to be used. As appropriate, schedule the introduction over one or more days.
        b. Review the system you have designed with one or more classroom teachers to determine workability.

    c. Document the system in terms of a scripted presentation for teacher use.

1.4 Compare management system designs for older and younger students.

    a. Observe a new elementary or secondary classroom to complement the level of classroom in exercises 1.1 and 1.2. (If an elementary classroom was observed, now observe a new secondary classroom; if a secondary classroom was observed, now observe a new elementary classroom.) Compare the operational features of the observed elementary and secondary classrooms in the areas of activity organization, group structuring, grading, and rewards/points.

    b. Adapt the management system you designed in exercises 1.1 and 1.2 for use in the new elementary or secondary classroom:
        (1) Management system elements
        (2) Supporting implementation procedures
        (3) Start-up procedures

    c. Review the new systems you have designed with one or more teachers, as appropriate. Modify the systems as required.

    d. Document the systems for use in the form of a manual for teacher use.

2. Implementing a comprehensive classroom management system (p. 266)

    a. Arrange with a classroom teacher to implement the management system you have designed at either the elementary or secondary level. The implementation could consist of the entire classroom for a period of 4–6 weeks, a classroom time segment of 1–2 hours daily, or a specific content area, as appropriate. Each of the following areas in your design should be used:
        (1) Management system elements
        (2) Supporting implementation procedures
        (3) Start-up procedures

    b. Before beginning the implementation, be certain to "walk through" all essential procedures in the plan, including whatever materials are required (e.g., posters, recording forms). Carefully rehearse the initial introduction for students. Begin the implementation under the following conditions, if possible:
        (1) One person should assist the teacher as an aide.
        (2) One or more persons should observe and critique the implementation for the first two to three weeks.

    c. Make any necessary changes in the system, being sure to change the documentation for use in a parallel fashion.

    d. After the system is working smoothly, have one or more school principals observe the classroom and critique the system's operation.

REFERENCES

The terms "token economy" and "point system" have been used almost interchangeably in the research literature. Both terms present some "thing" during the interval between the task and the presentation of consequences. The efforts by Ted Ayllon and Nathan Azrin in the early 1960s provided the basic foundation for the research that followed. Not long after their work with hospital patients, classroom token economies began to appear. The success of token or point systems has been documented in hundreds of studies and classrooms across the country. The review by Alen Kazdin gives an extensive picture of this research, covering both its problems and successes. Many of the other references point out some history or embellish what Kazdin covers. The classroom research of Tom McLaughlin and J. E. Malaby, and Engelmann and Becker's point procedures in the *Corrective Reading Program,* provided critical background and perspective for this chapter.

Ayllon, T., & Azrin, N. H. *The Token Economy: A Motivational System for Therapy and Rehabilitation.* New York: Appleton-Century-Crofts, 1968.

Breyer, N. L., & Allen, G. J. Effects of implementing a token economy on teacher attending behavior. *Journal of Applied Behavior Analysis,* 1975, *8,* 373–380.

Engelmann, S., & Becker, W. C. *The Corrective Reading Program.* Chicago: Science Research Associates, 1978.

Frederiksen, L. W., & Frederiksen, C. B. Teacher-determined and self-determined token reinforcement in a special education classroom. *Behavior Therapy,* 1975, *6,* 310–314.

Gates, J. J. Overspending (stealing) in a token economy. *Behavior Therapy,* 1972, *3,* 152–153.

Hensen, M. Token economies in institutional settings: Historical, political, deprivation, ethical, and generalization issues. *Journal of Nervous and Mental Disease,* 1976, *162,* 206–211.

Kazdin, A. E. *The Token Economy.* New York: Plenum Press, 1977.

Koch, L., & Breyer, N. L. A token economy for the teacher. *Psychology in the Schools,* 1974, *11,* 195–200.

Kuypers, D. S., Becker, W. C., & O'Leary, K. D. How to make a token system fail. *Exceptional Children,* 1968, *11,* 101–108.

McLaughlin, T. F. The applicability of token reinforcement systems in the public school systems. *Psychology in the Schools,* 1975, *12,* 84–89.

McLaughlin, T. F., & Malaby, J. E. Intrinsic reinforcers in a classroom token economy. *Journal of Applied Behavior Analysis,* 1972, *5,* 263–270.

McLaughlin, T. F., & Malaby, J. E. Reducing and measuring inappropriate verbalizations in a token classroom. *Journal of Applied Behavior Analysis,* 1972, *5,* 329–333.

McLaughlin, T. F., & Malaby, J. E. Increasing and maintaining assignment completion with teacher and pupil controlled individual contingency programs: Three case studies. *Psychology,* 1974, *11,* 1–7.

McLaughlin, T. F., & Malaby, J. E. Partial component analysis of an inexpensive token system across two classrooms. *Psychological Reports,* 1975, *37,* 362.

O'Leary, K. D., & Becker, W. C. Behavior modification of an adjustment class: A token reinforcement program. *Exceptional Children,* 1967, *9,* 637–642.

CHAPTER TWELVE

ADAPTING TO PROBLEMS

T he preceding chapters have focused on teacher skills for establishing conditions and consequences in managing the entire classroom. Verbal condition and reward statements arranged with correction consequences and supplementary rewards in a contingency delivery system provide teachers with the tools for management. Their consistent and persistent use fosters appropriate student academic and social behavior.

Even when a generally effective level of classroom management has been reached, some special problems may arise or persist. For example, in an otherwise well-managed classroom, a single student may disrupt the class or sit passively during instruction. This final chapter focuses on adjusting classroom management procedures to solve troublesome behavior problems. In some cases, teachers will find that established conditions and consequences are adequate, when properly amplified for problem students. But on other occasions, conditions and/or consequences must be augmented to deal effectively with management problems.

The following procedures represent a general strategy for solving both inappropriate social behavior and academic behavior rate and duration problems (see Chapter 9). In applying this problem-solving strategy to specific classroom problems, teachers must work through all steps before attempting to implement a potential solution. If the steps are not followed, the likelihood of developing an effective solution is reduced, and the implementation of the solutions may even cause additional problems. The strategy is designed to give teachers a complete "picture" of a given classroom behavior problem in relation to existing contingencies. Determining and implementing a solution becomes comparatively easy once key problem elements have been clearly specified. Four procedures will be discussed: analyzing the behavior, analyzing the present delivery system, adapting the delivery system to solve problems, and implementing solution components.

ANALYZING THE BEHAVIOR

The problem-solving process begins by examining student behavior. Procedures for checking behavior provide teachers with questions that facilitate seeing a problem behavior from several perspectives.

1. *What classes of social behavior are appropriate for conditions?* Appropriate social behaviors are necessary for successful academic performance. Without specifying appropriate social behaviors, solving a management problem systematically is impossible. In listing these behaviors, teachers should follow the procedures (outlined in Chapter 2 and detailed in Chapter 4) for defining social behaviors.

2. *What class of inappropriate social behavior is being exhibited?* Inappropriate social behaviors are incompatible with desired academic behavior. When inappropriate social behavior is exhibited, appropriate academic behavior cannot occur. Therefore, the former are problem behaviors from a classroom management perspective. Teachers should identify these problem behaviors in observable terms (see Chapter 2).

3. *What classes of academic behavior are appropriate for conditions?* In question 3, the teacher must consider the academic behaviors that are being asked of the student during the activity or conditions when the problem exists. In specifying appropriate academic behaviors, the teacher should clearly define the quantitative and qualitative elements of the behaviors (see Chapter 2), so that the students know what they should be performing. For example, during a math activity students might be asked to do a certain number of fractions, subtraction, or word problems within a specified period; during reading, to read orally, answer comprehension questions, or follow written directions with some degree of accuracy. Making a comprehensive list of desired appropriate academic behaviors requires careful consideration of both instruction activities and objectives (see Chapters 2 and 7).

4. *What class of inappropriate academic behavior is being exhibited?* The preceding question required a comprehensive definition of the appropriate academic behaviors, but the inappropriate academic behavior class in question 4 can often be specified solely in terms of behavior quantity or quality when the problem is one of rate or duration, not of instructional development (i.e., the student cannot perform the behavior at any time). In such cases, the general classes of inappropriate and appropriate behavior are the same; but the subclasses vary in one or more significant quantities or qualities. For example, a student may work independently for five minutes, but not for the full length of the study period.

The first four questions can be summarized in a two-by-two matrix, as shown in Table 12.1. Viewing the answers to the four questions in their respective cells helps teachers ask four more important questions about behavior. Answering the following questions gives the teacher a

TABLE 12.1 PROBLEM-SOLVING BEHAVIOR MATRIX		
	Appropriate Behavior	Inappropriate Behavior
Social Behavior	Question 1	Question 2
Academic Behavior	Question 3	Question 4

fairly complete picture of the problem behavior and its relationship to other behaviors.

5. *Is the student performing both the appropriate academic behavior and the inappropriate social behavior?* The answer to question 5 indicates whether classroom instructional practices need adjustment. The academically appropriate but socially inappropriate student may need to be given more challenging tasks. Teachers can provide instruction in more advanced areas or allow the student to engage in alternative classroom activities as a reward consequence for appropriate social behavior. Advanced instruction requires establishing supplementary instructional systems and is beyond the scope of this text. To achieve the latter solution, the teacher should follow the procedures for using reward statements (Chapter 3) and exercising reward power (Chapter 10).

6. *Can the student perform the appropriate social behavior?* Question 6 can be answered yes if the student has at times performed the behavior. In regular classrooms, students typically are able to perform appropriate social behaviors for at least short periods.

7. *Can the student perform the appropriate academic behavior?* Question 7 can also be answered yes if the student has at any time performed the behavior. But this question is usually more difficult to answer for academic behaviors, because they change with continuing instruction. The behavior of the students is always in transition: Students may progress from addition with two numbers to addition with three; or from subtraction without regrouping to subtraction with regrouping. In effect, this question asks whether the problem solution requires instructional or management behavior change procedures.

8. *Has the student's inappropriate social and/or academic behavior existed for some time?* Question 8 addresses the degree to which the behavior is really a problem. If a student's inappropriate behavior has existed for some time because it has been rewarded, changes in classroom procedures are necessary. But if the behavior has occurred for only a few days, teachers may elect to wait and see whether it represents just a "bad day or two" on the student's part. In other words, teachers should stay calm at the first sign of trouble and deliberate before they change estab-

lished classroom conditions and consequences. Teachers should first reflect on what is working well and the amount of successful learning taking place in the classroom.

The answers to the above eight questions provide a full perspective on virtually all classroom behavior problems. Problem behavior and what is to be done about it are always considered in relation to the total domain of behavior in the classroom. In this sense, the procedures presented help the teacher determine (1) if the problem is real (question 8), (2) what behavior to reward (questions 1 and 3), (3) what behavior to correct (questions 2 and 4), and (4) if the behavior is a management or an instructional problem (questions 5, 6, and 7). But before any steps are taken to change the existing delivery system, it must be analyzed.

ANALYZING THE EXISTING DELIVERY SYSTEM

Once a perspective on problem behaviors has been developed, any errors in existing conditions and consequences which influence inappropriate classroom behaviors can be eliminated. In doing so, the following five questions are asked:

1. *Has the inappropriate behavior been corrected?* Question 1 asks teachers if they have corrected the inappropriate behavior when it occurred (contingent) over a period of time (persistent)? If the answer to either part of this question is no, then teachers have identified an error in implementing a classroom management procedure. To obtain accurate answers, teachers must think back over the time in which the student problem behavior has occurred.

2. *Has the inappropriate behavior been rewarded?* Question 2 asks teachers if they have committed reward errors that have strengthened the inappropriate behavior. Such behavior can be inadvertently rewarded even by infrequent errors, such as giving a special privilege to the class after an individual's inappropriate behavior.

Rewards for inappropriate behaviors can come from many sources, including teachers as well as other students. In fact, a great deal of inappropriate student behavior is rewarded by other students. Students typically smile at, look at, laugh at, and join other students' inappropriate behavior. Procedures for changing behavior deal with how to weaken these peer influences (Chapter 10). In such cases, teachers must be contingent, persistent, and consistent in their efforts to prevent other students from "countercontrolling" their efforts to eliminate inappropriate classroom behavior. Together, questions 1 and 2 ask, "Have the teacher and other students corrected the inappropriate behavior (contingent) over a period of time (persistent), and not rewarded it on any occurrence (consistent)?"

3. *Has the appropriate behavior been rewarded?* Question 3 asks,

"Have teachers rewarded the desired behavior when it occurred (contingent) over a period of time (persistent)?" If the answer to either part of question 3 is no, teachers must apply the reward procedures presented in this text. If teachers are unable to recall numerous instances of presenting rewards, then the desired behaviors probably have not been rewarded adequately.

4. *Has the appropriate behavior been corrected?* Question 4 asks, "Have teachers erroneously corrected, rather than rewarded, the appropriate behavior?" Even a teacher's turning away and ignoring an appropriate behavior or presenting a statement such as "That was *pretty* good," with the wrong tone of voice can function as a correction. A correction consequence would decrease the frequency of appropriate behavior.

The erroneous correction of appropriate behavior also can be done by other students in the classroom. This occurs when other students find another student's appropriate behavior nonrewarding. The procedures in Chapter 10 for establishing compatible contingencies are again applicable. Thus, teachers must strive to establish contingencies for appropriate behaviors that all the students find rewarding.

Together, questions 3 and 4 ask whether teachers and students reward the appropriate behavior when it occurs (contingent) over a period of time (persistent), and do not erroneously correct it on any occurrence (consistent). In answering these questions, teachers should remember that how much reward is needed to strengthen a specific behavior cannot be exactly determined—and only contingent, persistent, and consistent reward is necessary for changing behavior.

5. *Have complete conditions been established?* Question 5 asks, "Have teachers reviewed the rules (Chapter 4) using examples of appropriate and inappropriate behaviors, outlined the rewarding (Chapters 3 and 8) and correcting consequences (Chapter 6), and established conditions (Chapters 5 and 8) for students?" Another way to consider this question is to ask, "Are students *aware* of appropriate and inappropriate social and academic behaviors and the consequences of their performance?" If the answer to any part of question 5 is no, teachers must remedy these deficient management practices.

The five questions of this second procedure help teachers determine whether conditions and consequences have been contingent, persistent, and consistent with respect to appropriate and inappropriate student behaviors. By checking both the behavior and the delivery system, teachers identify the specific desired and undesired behaviors, along with relevant errors in implementing classroom contingencies which influence those behaviors.

ADAPTING THE DELIVERY SYSTEM

When the two procedures above have been followed and inappropriate student behavior still is troublesome, teachers need to initiate adaptive solutions to alter existing classroom contingencies. Only two aspects of contingencies can be changed: conditions and consequences. And each of these can only be changed through acceleration and/or expansion. Thus, teachers may adapt contingencies by accelerating conditions, expanding conditions, accelerating consequences, and expanding consequences.

Accelerating Conditions Conditions are accelerated by increasing the rate at which the teacher presents condition statements and reviews rules with the student (Chapters 4 and 5). Teachers should keep the condition statement positive and make eye contact with the problem student, even though many statements are directed toward a group or the class. Close proximity to problem students also helps set the occasion for appropriate, reinforceable behavior. Thus, teacher behavior would not change, but occur more often to make the student aware of what to do and not to do.

Expanding Conditions The requirements to expand conditions depend upon the answers to the preceding questions for checking behavior and the delivery system. These answers help teachers determine the extent to which classroom condition statements must be changed. Because appropriate and inappropriate social and academic behaviors have been identified, rule expansion can include a variety of examples and nonexamples related to these behaviors. Chapters 4, 5, and 8 provide the details for constructing and using condition statements.

Expanding the condition component (see Chapters 4, 5, and 8) provides teachers with additional alternatives: requests, challenges, games, and surprises. Each alternative contains elements reflecting potential student accomplishment, responsibility, cooperation, and competition. Their role in adaptive problem solving is explained later.

Accelerating Consequences Like accelerating conditions, accelerating consequences increases the rate or frequency at which consequences are delivered. Teachers do not change existing procedures by using extra activities, physical contact, or recognition as rewards; rather, teachers present these rewards at a higher frequency and offer verbal reward statements that refer to these rewards more often. Such statements also magnify the effectiveness of the different types of reward consequences available to teachers in the classroom setting (see Chapters 3, 8, and 10).

Expanding Consequences To expand consequences, teachers add to and amplify the consequences used. At times, expansion may require additional corrective consequences constructed according to the guidelines in Chapter 6. In general, additional correction procedures for social behavior are not needed, only the consistent and persistent use of those available. The addition of supplementary reward consequences (see Chapter 10) is of greater value. For the effective amplification and addition of reward statements, teachers should present them convincingly to the student (e.g., eye contact, physical proximity, and/or contact). Often private comments also are of great help. Ideally, the presentation of any reward consequence should communicate that students have accomplished something important and are entering a more advanced level of social responsibility (see Chapters 3, 8, and 10).

In adding to rewards presently available (e.g., grades and awards), the procedures for requests, challenges, games, and surprises used in expanding conditions can help focus on important classes of consequences. Teachers should ask themselves, "What are some of the consequences a student receives for following a request, meeting a challenge, winning a game, or deserving a surprise?" All of the consequences in our culture generate positive changes in the performer's emotional state; and, many of these consequences come from others who see the performer's behavior as favorable. When such consequences occur within a group, they establish compatible contingencies. The behaviors associated with these activities and rewarded are elements of the larger, socially important classes of accomplishment, responsibility, concentration, cooperation, and/or competition (against a criterion, preferably not another student). Thus, teacher consequence statements should also stress these behaviors, as do the following examples:

> "John, you kept a cool head and concentrated on meeting the challenge. That is an important accomplishment. I hope you can keep it up."

> "Everyone's cooperation was needed to win the game; each of you accepted your responsibility of turning in your homework each day this week. You should take extreme pride in such an accomplishment."

> "I established a very competitive criterion for an A, but each of you met the challenge through diligent study and clear writing. Your facts were correct and your organization excellent. Details are given on each of your papers. Thank you."

These are forms of the advanced statements covered in Chapter 8.

IMPLEMENTING SOLUTION COMPONENTS

Once teachers have (1) identified the appropriate and inappropriate behaviors; (2) decided that the problem is real; (3) determined how to reward the critically important behaviors; (4) constructed condition, reward, and combination statements; and (5) found other consequences to use, the adapted conditions and consequences that make up the potential solution must be implemented. To do so, teachers directly insert the adaptations into their existing management practices. However, teachers can also "package" these adaptations, at least part of the time, as a request, challenge, game, or surprise procedure that contains built-in rewards and variety. These four packaged adaptations are also vehicles that help teachers think of new conditions and consequences by providing a novel context in which to develop other alternative solutions.

None of these four alternative methods differs drastically from the others, and parts of each can be added to another. Except for the surprise, they have much in common with, and expand on, the motivational component of condition statements (see Chapter 5). They are useful because they foster compatible contingencies (see Chapter 10). The following discussion illustrates how each method may be applied.

The Request In the request method, teachers directly ask students for a desired behavior and then contingently present extra rewards previously identified through an examination of the problem. In the following example of a math workbook activity, a student, Garnella, does only a few problems each day on her worksheet. Garnella does not bother others, but just does not work. So the teacher has a problem dealing with the rate at which Garnella does math problems. Garnella has averaged only five problems per day, with a high of eight and a low of three:

TEACHER: (*To the class.*) How many think they can do all their problems correctly or more than they did yesterday?

STUDENTS: (*Reply to teacher's question.*)

TEACHER: OK. I have a list of how many each of you did yesterday. As I move around the room, I will tell you how many you have to do. So let's get started. If everyone does more than yesterday before the end of workbook time, we will spend the extra time playing Fact Quiz.

STUDENTS: (*Work.*)

TEACHER: (*After one or two students, gets to Garnella.*) You did five problems correctly yesterday. I sure hope you can do more. I see that you already have two problems done correctly. Just keep working fast. (*As often as possible, gets back to Garnella and gives her the same type of statements.*)

STUDENTS: (*Keep working.*)

TEACHER: I knew you could do these problems fast, Garnella. You already have five done correctly and one-half of the activity time is left! Keep plugging and you will do a record number.

TEACHER: (*Continues to give instruction and reward statements to others.*)

TEACHER: (*Just about the time that everyone has done more than the previous day, returns to Garnella.*) You know the most you have ever done was eight, and today you did seven in much less time. You certainly deserve to play Fact Quiz. Let's see what you can do tomorrow.

STUDENTS: *(Finish doing their required number of problems in order to play Fact Quiz.)*

TEACHER: Would everyone please stop and quickly pass in your worksheet by the procedure. *(Pause.)* I like the way the second and third rows are collecting and passing in their work.

STUDENTS: *(Finish passing in their worksheets.)*

TEACHER: Guess what! Everyone has already done one or more problems than yesterday. Fantastic! You must feel great. I do. How many feel satisfied with their work?

STUDENTS: *(Reply to teacher's question.)*

TEACHER: So, get out your paper for Fact Quiz.

In the first statement notice how the teacher simply and directly asks the students for the behavior and sets up a group contingency (see Chapter 10) with a few minutes of Fact Quiz as a reward consequence. The group contingency does not focus on Garnella, but the number of reward and combination statements given to her is high. Like the other implementation procedures, the request focuses on individual problems while allowing the teacher to manage the entire class. Thus, the academic behavior of the entire class also improves in this example, with all students completing more problems than usual in less time. In a group contingency, the direct request provides the teacher with a powerful management tool. Second, the example does not show how to incorporate the procedure for rewarding rate problems (discussed in Chapter 9). This procedure requires the teacher to intermittently reward the desired behavior at a high frequency. Third, at the end of the activity, the teacher asks the students to pass in their work before saying anything about their accomplishment. If this statement were given before they finished the task, the students might begin to get excited and fail to complete the last part of the activity because of conflicting social behaviors. With older students and students who have extensive social repertoires and self-control, this concern is less important. The biggest caution in using the request procedure is that mentioned for group contingencies: The students must be able to perform the behavior.

The Challenge The challenge can be used with most behaviors, academic or social. The challenge is a comparison of what the students have done (e.g., their number correct from a previous day, their time following a classroom rule) or what another group has done (e.g., the first-hour class had everyone doing more than yesterday; can this second-hour class do the same?). The challenge example below repeats the above situation with Garnella:

TEACHER: *(To the class.)* I feel great today. How do you feel?

STUDENTS: *(Reply to teacher's question.)*

TEACHER: Good, but I bet not everyone will do more problems correctly than yesterday. In fact, I will bet you five minutes of Thumbs-Up that not everyone will do one more problem correctly than yesterday. And I have yesterday's scores on this sheet. Can you meet my challenge?

STUDENTS: (*Reply to teacher's question.*)

TEACHER: OK, let's go.

STUDENTS: (*Work.*)

TEACHER: (*To Garnella.*) You have to get six correct to meet my challenge. Can you do it?

STUDENT: (*Garnella replies.*)

TEACHER: I hope you can and you have a good start, these two are correct. (*Tries to return to Garnella periodically.*)

TEACHER: (*To class.*) Thus far, I see that everyone is meeting my challenge. You are showing the maturity necessary. You're making my day go even better because of the smiles your hard work is giving you. Keep the solutions coming!

STUDENTS: (*Continue to work as teacher gives out challenge-related statements.*)

TEACHER: (*Returns to Garnella.*) You are meeting the challenge and gaining my respect. You are so close, don't stop now.

STUDENTS: (*All meet the challenge.*)

TEACHER: Please stop working and pass in your papers. You know the procedure. (*Pause.*) I notice everyone is smiling as you pass in your papers. That must be a clue! (*When all papers are in.*) You did it! You met the challenge of doing more today than yesterday, and you did it in much less time. What math workers! Let's get ready for Thumbs-Up.

The challenge is similar to the request, but facilitates the teacher's referencing important behavioral classes which give students a broader perspective on improved social behavior (see Chapter 8). In telling students that they are mature, responsible, and diligent, the teacher is presenting powerful verbal reward consequences.

The Game The game method requires that the class be divided into at least two groups. If possible, each group should contain equal numbers of students who are performing the appropriate behaviors and equal numbers who are not. This helps match the groups to the degree that they can achieve the behavior of interest. If this is not possible, the teacher should give the weakest group additional support by her increased proximity and greater numbers of reward and combination statements (see Chapters 3 and 8).

The following example involves several students who continue to bother others during the teacher presentation of new language arts material. The appropriate behavior, attending to the teacher, is a duration behavior (see Chapter 9).

TEACHER: How many think they can pay attention to the whole presentation today?

STUDENTS: (*Reply to teacher's question.*)

TEACHER: Let's play a game to see. For each *row,* I will put a box on the board. (*Draws on board.*)

Row 1	Row 2	Row 3	Row 4
☐	☐	☐	☐

During the presentation I will look at each row many times. Each time I do and the *whole* row is paying attention, I will give the row a check. I will make at least ten looks, and to be a winner a group must have eight checks. All rows can be winners if they try hard. All winners will get the Attention Check Award designed, typed, and xeroxed by your teacher. (*Shows award to students.*) Can you do it?

TEACHER: Let's start.

STUDENTS: (*Paying attention for about thirty seconds.*)

TEACHER: (*Visually sweeps each row.*) I just looked hard and everyone was working; every row gets a check. See, you can do it. Look at Garnella paying attention and answering the questions. This is fun.

TEACHER: (*Later.*) Another check for rows 1, 2, and 4. Just look at Marvin, Marilyn, Jane, and everyone else in these rows. Row 2, can you do it for the rest of the checks? How about it, Garnella, John, Mark, David, Erwin?

STUDENTS: (*Reply to teacher's question.*)

TEACHER: (*Later, as students continues to work, gives individual comments such as the following to problem students when they are attending.*) Joseph, thank you for attending to the presentation; your hand is up, so what is your answer to the question?

STUDENT: (*Replies to teacher's question.*)

TEACHER: (*Continues to reward and check the students. Ends presentation.*) Let's look at the marks. Row 1 has nine; row 2 has eight; row 3 has nine; and row 4 has ten. What a demonstration of self-control and cooperation. I am proud that all rows have won. Let's give ourselves a hand! (*Names several stu-*

dents, including those with the attention problem.) Everyone, let's applaud Garnella, Joseph, John, Mary, Zelda, and Tim! Here are the awards which you so much deserve. (*A few notes of music help the presentation.*)

During a teacher presentation it is much harder to reward individuals than during independent work. In the example above, one of the problem students raises his hand to answer a question and the teacher's reward statement relates to the academic behavior and the problem behavior as well. It is helpful for teachers to contrast instances of the problem behavior with the desired appropriate behavior for students.

The Surprise The surprise technique involves not telling the students the behavioral criterion for reward. The teacher identifies a large behavioral class for the students, but does not state the requirement for an undefined surprise. This allows the teacher to observe the problem and appropriate behaviors students exhibit and make moment-to-moment or day-to-day adjustments in the criterion. For example, if the student normally does about one-half of the class worksheet, the teacher starts from that rate of behavior and gives the surprise when the student has exceeded the rate. The awarding of the surprise mentions an amount just below what the student has performed. In the future, the teacher may ask for this amount of behavior daily because the student has performed it in the past. In one sense the student sets the future criterion. This helps to increase appropriate student behavior as fast as possible.

The example below is an independent reading activity in which the students read a passage and answer questions. The problem is one student's failure to finish more than three or four of the twelve daily comprehension questions. The objective is to increase this student's rate of questions answered and reduce the inappropriate daydreaming behavior. The problem student in the example is Sterling:

TEACHER: Everyone, today is surprise day. If you do as many as or more questions correctly on your worksheet than I have thought of, you will get a surprise. So let's begin and really do it right.

STUDENTS: (*Work.*)

TEACHER: (*Privately.*) Sterling, I like the way you are starting to work on these questions. It is important to keep working. This first one is correct. (*Makes random contingent comments to class and to other individuals.*)

STUDENTS: (*Work.*)

TEACHER: (*Later and privately to Sterling.*) You are certainly doing the problems fast today. You're working hard. That is important. Don't stop; ten questions done, not many left.

STUDENTS: (*Keep working.*)

TEACHER: (*End of worksheet. Sterling has finished eleven questions.*) How many of you have completed eleven or more problems? I see Sterling's hand, John's, Mary's, Mark's, Zendella's. For those with more than eleven, you get a chance to play a surprise game of Seven-Up. Let's give ourselves a hand. (*Pauses while students clap.*) Your hard work has shown that you are responsible workers!

The strength of the surprise method is flexibility in the adjustments teachers make in the reward criterion. This allows the teacher greater assurance that all of the students will make the criterion and achieve reward consequences while encouraging maximum improvement. The weakness of the surprise is its dependence upon the teacher's skill in remembering the extent that the behavior has changed from previous occasions during the ongoing class. If the teacher cannot accurately recall what the students have done in the past, then the surprise method will fail to improve their behavior.

FAILING TO MEET THE CRITERION

One important question has been avoided: What is done when a student, group, or class fails to meet the criterion related to the request, challenge, game, or surprise during "reward time"? A simple answer is for teachers to give these students alternate work when the others are involved in reward activities. For the request or challenge, the class or activity group fails as a whole, so academic activities would continue. For the game, any or all groups could fail, so that the failing groups would have to continue academic activities. For the surprise, any number of individuals could fail, but if the criterion has been adjusted, conditions set, and consequence statements delivered at a high rate, then failure is unlikely.

But other events are as important as having an alternate activity available in case of failure. Suppose a teacher has adjusted the criterion as much as possible, but sees that failure is about to occur. First, the teacher should start to deliver individual reward statements to the students who are working hard and meeting the criterion:

"Hilda, you are doing your part to meet the challenge. I am sorry that others are not. I hope you keep up the work and find it enjoyable."

"James, you must like to do this math; you are meeting the request and doing what you can to get some extra free time. I wish that all others would put in the effort you do. Thank you very much."

"I like how you work for games, Mabel. You have already done your part; I am sad that your group has not worked as hard as you. I hope you keep it up."

The "doing your part" and "meeting the challenge" elements refer to behavior specified at the start of the procedure, so an exact description of behavior does not need to be stated. These statements are designed to function as alternate individual rewards when the contingencies are not strong enough for full class success.

Second, the teacher should present statements for the class or group that requires a great deal more description and directness:

"I would like to thank everyone who did more problems than yesterday. You know that you did your part and I appreciate it and will remember it whenever a little extra time comes up. Maybe next time you can again try hard and set another example."

This statement is a positive reward for those who achieved through hard work and describes the desired behavior to those who failed to make the criterion because of inappropriate social behavior. If everyone had tried hard, but the time ran out, the statement would be phrased differently:

"I would like to thank everyone for trying hard. We were very close to making it, just a little bit away. I know we will do it next time because practice helps. Let's take a moment to relax before we move to our next activity. How many will make it next time?" (*Students reply.*)

This statement is intended to function as an alternate reward, as does the opportunity to relax. It provides a total positive perspective on the students' behavior and looks to their future chances for reward and accomplishment.

In another situation, the class or group might meet the criterion, but have no time left for the extra reward activity. Here, alternate statements that promote student acceptance of a delay in receiving rewards are important:

"Each of us should feel a sense of accomplishment: The criterion has been met. You finished the required problems just at the end of the activity. I am sorry that there is not time for the extra award activity. But we can still take time to congratulate each other on the job well done. Shake your neighbor's hand and say thanks for the cooperation."

Because such complex statements may become long, students should be involved when possible:

"Each of you should feel a sense of accomplishment. How many do? Let me see your hands. (*Students reply.*) You finished the required problems just in the nick of time. We have a few mintues, but not enough to have a little biology fact quiz. Can I save these few mintues for next time? (*Students reply.*) Great, I appreciate your maturity. Let's take a moment to congratulate each other on a job well done. Shake hands with your neighbors and say thanks for their cooperation." (*Students reply.*)

In this complex statement, students are involved three times. This student participation technique should be used whenever a statement becomes too long, for example, more than 15 or 20 seconds without student participation. Adding an extra point to the grade for the activity can often be an alternate reward; this takes almost no time.

From the above discussion, three important questions arise concerning the use of the four methods for implementing solutions:

1. What are some alternate, quick rewards that can be used when the group criterion is not met by one or all, but everyone tried hard?
2. What kind of individual or group statements can be constructed for when the individual or the group fails the response criterion?
3. What kind of alternate academic activities are appropriate for those who do not make the criterion?

Once these questions have been answered, teachers are prepared to use the techniques presented in this section. Also, teachers should be certain that they have followed all steps in the problem-solving procedure and, if desired, the four implementation techniques. Teachers who first plan and then implement will have a much better chance of effectively changing inappropriate behavior and, at the same time, increasing appropriate behavior.

SOME ALTERNATIVES FOR OLDER STUDENTS

The four techniques for implementation of solutions are fine for older students; most of the wording in the statements and examples will suffice. But because the older student has more independent work behaviors, teachers can adjust the operation of the four methods so that students who meet a criterion can immediately start an alternate reward activity. The rewards used for individual students may include any preferred activity that does not disturb other working students (e.g., reading a book or working on a special project).

Introducing these procedures to older students also is different. The teacher informs the students as indicated, but states that when they have met their requirements, they can have their work checked and then do the reward activity. An introductory statement for a challenge follows:

> "I feel that a challenge is in store for today. How does that sound?" (*Students reply.*) "Good. I bet each of you can't do one or more problems correct than yesterday. If you can, you will be given the rest of the period to work on your personal projects for the science fair. I have your number from yesterday here and will give it to you as you are working. Can you do it? (*Students reply.*) "OK, let's see if you are as smart as you think you are."

If the thirty or forty seconds to set this introduction up are positive and rewarding, the teacher will see an hour of fast, hard work. But the teacher also has to monitor, give statements along the way, and deliver additional instruction as needed.

THE PROBLEM-SOLVING ROUTINE

With the identification of a possible problem, the use of the following routine will lead to the remediation of the problem. The routine also provides a summary of Chapter 12.

1. Check the behavior by asking the following:
   a. What classes of social behavior are appropriate for conditions?
   b. What class of inappropriate social behavior is being exhibited?
   c. What classes of academic behavior are appropriate for conditions?
   d. What class of inappropriate academic behavior is being exhibited?
   e. Is the student performing both the appropriate academic behavior and the inappropriate social behavior?
   f. Can the student perform the appropriate social behavior?
   g. Can the student perform the appropriate academic behavior?
   h. Has the student's inappropriate social and/or academic behavior existed for some time?
2. Check the delivery system by asking the following:
   a. Has the inappropriate behavior been corrected?
   b. Has the inappropriate behavior been rewarded?
   c. Has the appropriate behavior been rewarded?

    d. Has the appropriate behavior been corrected?

    e. Have complete conditions been established?

3. Adapt to the problem by using any of the following:

    a. Accelerating conditions

    b. Expanding conditions

    c. Accelerating consequences

    d. Expanding consequences

4. If desired, use one of the following techniques for implementation:

    a. The request

    b. The challenge

    c. The game

    d. The surprise

5. If the techniques from 4 are used, consider the following:

    a. What alternate, quick rewards are available when the group criterion is not met by all?

    b. What kinds of individual and group statements need to be constructed when the individual or group fails to meet the criterion?

    c. What alternate academic activities can be used for those who do not meet the criterion?

    d. What modifications need to be made if you are dealing with students who have independent work behaviors?

The first few times teachers attempt to solve problems, they must follow this routine with the help of information from other chapters. Afterwards, the use of the routine in this chapter will likely be sufficient. *The routine should always be used;* it helps teachers to look at problems analytically and relieves them of the emotional involvement they may have when confronted with new classroom problems.

LIMITS ON SOLVING PROBLEMS

Teachers' means to solve or adapt to problems are limited. This is true of all problem solvers and always will be. Teachers have only so much control over conditions and consequences; they can be just so contingent, persistent, and consistent, and can accelerate and expand conditions and consequences just so much. The classroom environment, scientific principles of behavior, and teachers' knowledge are all limiting factors. Therefore, some problems may not be fully solvable. However, what has been learned throughout this text and in this chapter should help teachers adapt to virtually all regular classroom problems. In addition, these skills offer at least three ways to help maintain a problem-solving equilibrium: First, teachers can talk accurately to other expert professionals about problems and, in doing so, may discover solutions. Second, they can problem-solve well enough to alleviate a problem's intensity. And, third, they can examine their own behavior, rewarding themselves for problems they have solved and encouraging themselves to "keep trying." Anchored in such a fashion, teachers are better able to maintain a productive perspective on their classroom management and problem-solving skills.

P R A C T I C E   A C T I V I T I E S

1. Rehearsing the problem-solving procedure
   1.1 Examine the behavior. (p. 273)
      a. Practice rehearsing the eight analysis questions in the text for examining behavior until you can say them aloud at a rate of five seconds per question.
      b. Have a classmate prepare answers to each of the questions for a "behavior problem in a classroom setting." Then ask the analysis questions in order, with the classmate responding. Summarize the student behavior problem in terms of the answers to the analysis questions and obtain feedback from the classmate on the accuracy of your summary. Repeat this exercise with a series of questions for a new behavior problem until you can summarize the answers accurately in a relaxed manner.
   1.2 Analyze the delivery system. (p. 275)
      a. Practice rehearsing the five analysis questions in the text for examining the delivery system. Note that each question focuses upon a different form of contingency error that could contribute to behavior problems. For each example, specify how a teacher could eliminate each form of error.
      b. Use your prior classroom observations and experience to list five examples illustrating each form of error targeted by the analysis questions.
   1.3 Adapt the delivery system. (p. 276) List five examples illustrating the procedure you would follow in implementing the following:
      (1) Accelerating conditions
      (2) Expanding conditions
      (3) Accelerating rewards
      (4) Expanding rewards

2. Solving classroom management problems (p. 287)
   2.1 Identify a classroom with an unspecified management problem. Observe the classroom and identify one specific "problem" student or group of students.
      a. Analyze the student problem behavior and the classroom delivery system.
      b. Decide on one or more adjustments to the classroom management system using one or more of the following as appropriate:
         (1) Accelerating conditions
         (2) Expanding conditions
         (3) Accelerating rewards
         (4) Expanding rewards
   2.2 Specify a plan for implementing the techniques selected in 2.1, including the steps to carry them out and the predicted change in student behavior across time.
      a. Implement the techniques either by arranging to work directly with students or by working with the classroom teacher. Monitor

the implementation of the procedures over a period of five to ten
days. Adjust the plan as necessary. Record the change in student
behavior.

b. Repeat the above activity as a cooperative group project in two
to five different classrooms.

REFERENCES

The procedures in Chapter 12 serve as a framework for using the teacher skills
developed throughout this text to diagnose and solve classroom management
problems. The references present complementary perspectives of classroom problem solving. Shavelson and Stern review and interpret current research on the
teacher's pedagogical decision making. Romiszowski's survey of systems analysis
methodology and Zifferblatt's discussion of classroom behavior systems help expand the problem-solving strategies. Some broad surveys of classroom management research provide teachers with alternate views of many of the concepts
presented in this textbook in a manner that helps facilitate the classroom problem-solving process. This category includes Duke's survey of topics in classroom
management, Emmer and Evertson's short synthesis of classroom management
research, and Brophy's anaylsis of teachers' classroom statements.

Brophy, J. Teacher praise: A functional analysis. *Review of Educational Research*, 1981, *51, * 5–32.

Duke, D. L. (Ed.) *Helping Teachers Manage Classrooms*. Alexandria, Va.: Association for Supervision and Curriculum Development, 1982.

Emmer, E. T., & Evertson, C. M. Synthesis of research on classroom management. *Educational Leadership*, 1981, *38, * 342–347.

Romiszowski, A. J. *Design of Instructional Systems*. New York: Nichols Publishing Company, 1981.

Shavelson, R. J., & Stern, P. Research on teacher's pedagogical thoughts, judgements, decisions, and behavior. *Review of Educational Research*, 1981, *51, * 455–498.

Zifferblatt, S. M. Behavior systems. In C. E. Thoresen (Ed.), *Behavior Modification in Education*. Chicago: National Society for the Study of Education, 1973.

Index